DESIGNWHYS

DESIGNING WEB SITES THAT SELL

FOR GRAPHIC DESIGNERS | **SHAYNE BOWMAN & CHRIS WILLIS**

First published in the English language in 2002 by
Peachpit Press
1249 Eighth Street
Berkeley, CA 94710
Phone: (510) 524-2178
Fax: (510) 524-2221
www.peachpit.com

Library of Congress cataloging-in-publication data
are available

ISBN 0-201-79304-0

10 9 8 7 6 5 4 3 2 1

Design: Elisabeth Gerber
Layout and Production: *tabula rasa* graphic design
Series Editor: Cynthia Baron

Printed in China

BNA 2005   9-1-04

CONTENTS

Introduction
DON'T GET IT PRETTY— get it right.

As designers, we have been told throughout our careers to "make it look pretty" or "exciting" or "classy." But that's not the true value of design. What we really do is persuade people to act—to read a story, to buy a product, to see a movie, to vote for a presidential candidate.

Take this book, for example. What compelled you to pick up this one when there are thousands of others available? Perhaps it was the color, or the title, or maybe it was the smooth texture of the cover. Did you look at the typefaces and layouts and make judgments about the quality of the authors and their advice?

Many of today's Web designers cut their teeth in the print world. We study the theory of color, typography, and layout. We pour over type specimen books to find just the right cut of Bodoni. When we create something, like a book, we can hold it and show it to others.

But no one would be absurd enough to ask us how to use a book. You open it up, start at the first page, and turn pages until there are no more left. Contents, indexes, chapter titles—they all work the same in every book.

On the Web, it's not that simple. In fact, when you tackle a commerce site, you will face the most complex Web-design challenge of all. You will be expected to find the right mix of aesthetics, brand identity, and interactivity, and then you'll be expected to fit that into a technical tangle of databases, customer service, and fulfillment systems.

To succeed, you need to master the Web's hallmark: interactivity. This requires you to become intimate with a customer's motivations, goals, and tasks. In a sense, the Web site is a conduit for the conversation between the business and the consumer. A site's survival depends on customers being able to browse, build desire, make a decision and hand over a credit card. And it has to be as easy as—and more convenient than—shopping at your local store.

Businesses, too, have motivations, goals, and tasks. Their commerce sites, naturally, are about making money—not brand awareness, or "stickiness." Mistakes on a commerce site don't show up as a drop in page views, they show up as inventory stacked to the ceiling in a dusty warehouse.

This begs the question, are well-designed commerce sites more successful? The onslaught of usability pundits seems bent on criticizing slick sites in favor of more rudimentary ones. But as a designer, you have witnessed how imagery, color, and words can affect emotion. We believe great design is a key element in a site's usability, thereby proving its worth to the business. It can also be an intimidating signal to competitors.

Successful projects thrive by respecting a process, and commerce design requires a healthy dose. In this book, we will describe your responsibilities, give you the right questions to ask of others on your team, and guide you through a site launch. We will put your tasks into perspective within the site-development process.

This book includes:

Chapter 1: Design Process and Project Management defines your role in the process of building a commerce site. It also explains the unique challenge of Web-commerce design.

Chapter 2: Five Principles of Good Commerce Design highlights critical elements such as speed, usability, personalization, brand identity, and consistency.

Chapter 3: Information Design for Commerce will help you understand the customer, the content, and the technology.

Chapter 4: Interaction Design for Commerce focuses on how a designer can learn to think like a site visitor.

Chapter 5: Presentation Design for Commerce discusses choosing a visual style to suit the brand. It also explains how to build a site that will be easy to update.

Chapter 6: Site Launch and Maintenance helps you get a handle on proper techniques of testing and revising the site.

Chapter 7: Real-World Examples gives you an in-depth look at great commerce-design sites.

Also, the appendix (beginning on page 236) explores the challenges of designing for emerging technologies.

Designing Web Sites That Sell is the result of our team's fifteen-plus years of experience in Web strategy, project management, and design. We've had the luxury of making mistakes and learning from them. Still, there is much more to explore. We are all pioneers, yourself included, in this young, ever-changing medium. We hope that you can use this book to get a head start on creating a winning Web-commerce solution.

chapter 1

DESIGN PROCESS AND PROJECT MANAGEMENT
Defining commerce and your role in it

Designers are accustomed to creating within a comfort zone. We usually work alone or in small teams. We expect to have supreme control over the type, color, and layout of the products we produce. And within reason, we can expect reliable results throughout the production process.

But imagine what design would be like if every brochure we produced looked different every time a new person opened it. This is the challenge of Web design, where we no longer have ultimate control. Web design must adapt to individual idiosyncrasies, including a customer's Internet connection speed, browser, operating system, and monitor resolution. These can lead to sloppy results—from different typefaces and sizes to broken graphics and bizarre colors—a design far from your original intent.

Web-commerce design magnifies the challenge, because it adds a complex interactivity to the experience. The site must direct a visitor through a wide range of pages and levels of interaction—immediate purchase of products and services, information about the company, discussion forums, e-mail site feedback. The deeper they go into the experience, the greater the danger that visitors will lose interest.

To keep the customer engaged, you'll need to design an experience that is simultaneously appealing and informative. Ideally, this interactive design should bring about a call and response—a conversation—between your Web site and the consumer. You have to anticipate what the customer will request and how your site will respond to it.

Before you sketch the first navigation button, you'll also need a thorough understanding of business goals, brand experience, target audience needs and available technology. These valuable criteria, which direct your design, can only be learned by collaborating with specialists in your company or your client's. Commerce design cannot be generated by any one individual, however talented.

Web guru Jeffrey Zeldman likens the site-development process to making a film.

"Movies are created by teams of specialists.... Good movies always feel like they are created by a single storyteller even though dozens or hundreds of people worked on them."[1]

Likewise, great commerce sites feel like they come from a single intelligence, though they are created through a collaboration of many teams. These teams succeed, in large part, because they follow a clear path of development. This is a rigorous process, but the payoff is substantial. The adage "hours of thinking can save weeks of programming" is true. It's much easier to scrap a paper prototype than to spend thousands of dollars recoding a Web site.

In this chapter, we will orient you to the unique environment you'll experience as you approach the design of a commerce Web site. We will identify the types of commerce you may have to face; outline what it takes to build one of these sites; show you where you fit in the development process and who you will work with along the way.

The Role of a Web Site in Business

Today's companies use the Web primarily for marketing and commerce.

Marketing

Companies such as Pepsi use their site to extend brand experience to a global Web audience. That's a fancy way of saying their Web sites are big, interactive advertisements. On Pepsi.com, you can buy Pepsi clothes, play games featuring Pepsi personalities such as Britney Spears, watch commercials, participate in contests, learn about the history of their products, or submit a resume to Pepsi Co.

Every commerce site has elements that are marketing driven. Among them: product or service descriptions, the voice of the copy, access to customer service, the history of the company, and even the online logo treatment.

	Consumer wants	Business offers
Inform	To know more about the products or service that they might purchase.	• Product information • Product comparisons • E-mail alerts, newsletters
Communicate	To communicate directly or indirectly with the company or with other buyers and sellers. Communication can occur before, during, or after the transaction.	• Customer service • Technical support, guidance • Customer reviews, ratings • Forums • Affinity program
Transact	To exchange money, products, or personal information for products, services, or access to information.	• Auctions, exchanges • Merchants, malls • Registration • Download product demo

FIGURE 1.1
Enabling marketplace conversation.

Commerce

Simply put, the role of the commerce site is to enable a business transaction to occur. This transaction can take different forms and meet different goals. For some businesses, a Web site is another vehicle to serve the customer, much like retail stores or catalogs. These companies are likely to adopt a Web design that will make a transaction more convenient, easier, and less time consuming. Others use Web commerce to procure goods and services for operations or product production. They'll adopt a Web design that makes the business more efficient, or that boosts the bottom line.

Whether buying a pair of sneakers or 50 metric tons of acetone, just about every customer has one of three goals when they visit a commerce site. Each of these goals—inform, communicate, and transact (See Fig. 1.1)—is a critical component of commerce.[2]

Almost half of all consumers trying to purchase online during the Christmas 2000 period left Web sites without placing an order, according to a Creative Good report.

Customer experience is Job 1

Because so much is riding on every trans-action being completed successfully, the customer experience is the most significant factor of success in commerce. Noncommerce sites can do a few things poorly and survive, as long as they do others exceptionally well. A person might not like the blinking banner advertisement, but they'll put up with it to get the free e-mail account on their favorite portal. No purchasing agent of office sup-plies will put up with an awkward registra-tion process or out-of-date inventory for an instant. They'll just click over to one of your competitors who has a site that better understands their needs.

Your challenge is to understand that the customer experience goes well beyond the sharp logo or navigation scheme. While those play an important role in usability and consistency, they are not the only contribu-tors to experience.

Effective designers understand their client's business model and how it defines the simple or complex transactions they will construct. The size of audience, the ever-changing inventory, issues of privacy and security—these are all elements that will concern you.

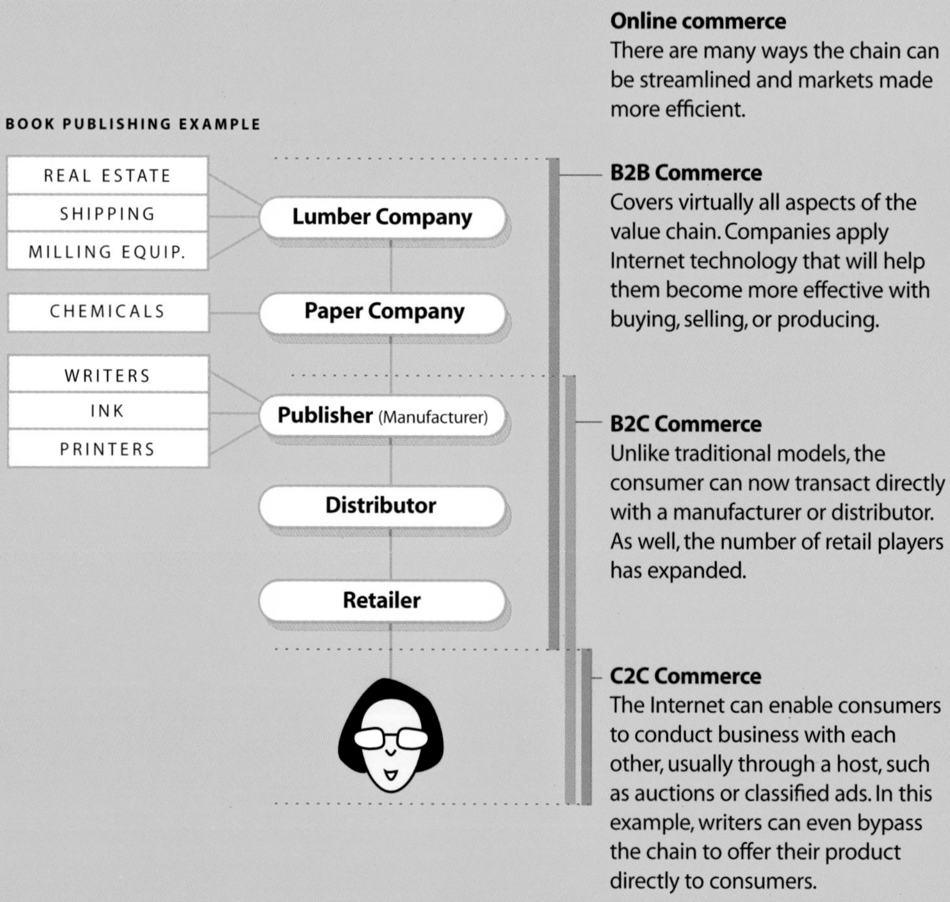

BOOK PUBLISHING EXAMPLE

| REAL ESTATE |
| SHIPPING |
| MILLING EQUIP. |

Lumber Company

| CHEMICALS |

Paper Company

| WRITERS |
| INK |
| PRINTERS |

Publisher (Manufacturer)

Distributor

Retailer

Online commerce
There are many ways the chain can be streamlined and markets made more efficient.

B2B Commerce
Covers virtually all aspects of the value chain. Companies apply Internet technology that will help them become more effective with buying, selling, or producing.

B2C Commerce
Unlike traditional models, the consumer can now transact directly with a manufacturer or distributor. As well, the number of retail players has expanded.

C2C Commerce
The Internet can enable consumers to conduct business with each other, usually through a host, such as auctions or classified ads. In this example, writers can even bypass the chain to offer their product directly to consumers.

FIGURE 1.2: TRADITIONAL VALUE CHAIN
Business models are defined by a company's position in the value chain. Only one segment of the chain, usually the end point, interacts with the customer.

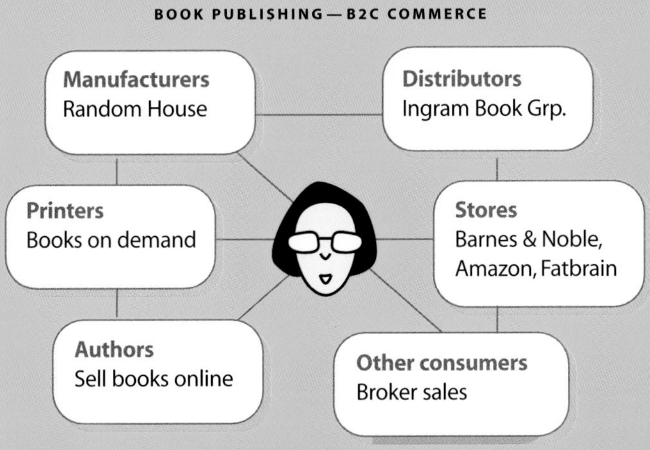

BOOK PUBLISHING—B2C COMMERCE

FIGURE 1.3: VALUE WEB
The customer is now at the center, with many segments having direct contact.

Know your business model

In its basic form, a business model describes how a company makes money by specifying where it is positioned in the value chain—the series of activities that begins with processing raw materials and ends with a finished product in the customer's hands. A company's core competency—the things it does best in creating value for customers—defines its place on the value chain. This is also called a "value proposition" (See Fig. 1.2).

Some models are simple—a company manufactures a product or service, then distributes it to retailers who sell it to customers.

Other models, such as exchanges, are much more intricately woven. Business models can be implemented in a variety of ways. Any given company may combine different models as part of its Web strategy. A merchant model, for example, may be blended with a subscription model to yield an overall strategy that is profitable.

Barnes & Noble is a classic business-to-consumer (B2C) example of the merchant business model, in which wholesalers and retailers offer goods and services through mail order or store. The same business model holds true for their online version. But now, sales can be made based on list

prices or through auction. In some cases, the goods and services may be unique to the Web and not have a traditional "bricks-and-mortar" storefront. Some goods may be delivered only in digital form, such as e-books, MP3 music files, or computer software.

As you can see, online commerce transforms traditional models and gives birth to new ones. The value chain has turned into what some call a "value Web" (See Fig. 1.3). The Internet has enabled companies to leverage their core competencies and bypass other segments of the chain. For example, Random House can offer books in digital form on a Web site directly to customers worldwide, bypassing the need for paper mills, printing presses, shipping, and retail stores.

The Internet has allowed more players to have direct contact with the customer. As a result, the customer has become more powerful by raising expectations for how companies should deliver their goods or services, as well as for how they are treated in the selling process. The designer can control a site's speed, navigation, organization, ease of use, and personality—all crucial factors in meeting a customer's expectations.

	Auction	Exchange/barter	Aggregator	Merchant
Transaction	Price based on offer by highest bid. Seller handles payment and fulfillment.	Value set by seller or marketplace in exchange for money or items of similar value.	Transaction handled by seller but fee or portion of sale may be paid to aggregator.	Price is usually fixed and transaction is handled by site.
Characteristics	• Highly dynamic • Time-critical sales • Many different items • Many sellers • Many different prices	• Dynamic information • Time-critical sales • Many different items • Many sellers	• Dynamic information • Similar items • Several sellers	• Less dynamic information • Similar items • One seller

More complex ⟵――――――――――――――――――⟶ **Less complex**

FIGURE 1.4

Types of commerce sites based on transactions.

Once you understand your company's value proposition (how it will make money), you need to understand the kind of transactions that will take place. The type of transaction sets the scope of your project's complexity (See Fig. 1.4).

The depth of the inventory will also factor into the scope of your project (See Fig. 1.5). On eBay, for example, there are millions of items up for auction across thousands of categories on any given day. Managing eBay's vast, ever-changing inventory requires a sophisticated database system. On the other hand, Sotheby's online auction inventory is much smaller. It has only a few hundred categories whose content changes several times per week. Thus, the technology and design for Sotheby's is not nearly as complex to build.

Make it known to your client that understanding the business model can inform your design. The strategy or business development team should explain the company's business model and value proposition to you, as a thorough understanding of these parameters is the first step in the process of creating effective commerce sites.

FIGURE 1.5

Commerce sites categorized by inventory and complexity.

Planning phase
Ideas are evaluated and turned into projects.

Design phase
Project requirements guide the conceptual and technical development.

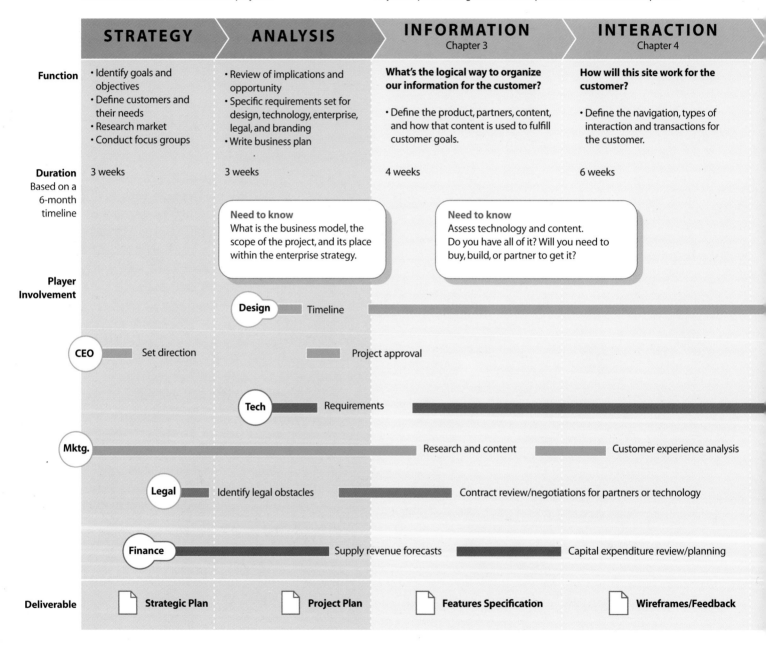

	STRATEGY	ANALYSIS	INFORMATION Chapter 3	INTERACTION Chapter 4
Function	• Identify goals and objectives • Define customers and their needs • Research market • Conduct focus groups	• Review of implications and opportunity • Specific requirements set for design, technology, enterprise, legal, and branding • Write business plan	**What's the logical way to organize our information for the customer?** • Define the product, partners, content, and how that content is used to fulfill customer goals.	**How will this site work for the customer?** • Define the navigation, types of interaction and transactions for the customer.
Duration Based on a 6-month timeline	3 weeks	3 weeks	4 weeks	6 weeks

Need to know
What is the business model, the scope of the project, and its place within the enterprise strategy.

Need to know
Assess technology and content.
Do you have all of it? Will you need to buy, build, or partner to get it?

Player Involvement

Design — Timeline

CEO — Set direction / Project approval

Tech — Requirements

Mktg. — Research and content / Customer experience analysis

Legal — Identify legal obstacles / Contract review/negotiations for partners or technology

Finance — Supply revenue forecasts / Capital expenditure review/planning

| **Deliverable** | Strategic Plan | Project Plan | Features Specification | Wireframes/Feedback |

Implementation phase

The site is built and modified based on testing and feedback.

PRESENTATION	BUILD	TEST	MAINTAIN
Chapter 5	Chapter 6	Chapter 6	Chapter 6

How will this site look to the customer?

- Define the style and organization of visual elements like buttons and forms.
- Begin usability testing with simple paper prototypes, then refine.

4 weeks

Need to know
How to balance between what's eye-catching but not slow and what's useful but not complex.

- Design templates and test on browsers.
- Tie back-end systems, such as databases, to interfaces.

4 weeks

- Usability tests
- Stress tests
- Quality assurance
- Beta tests

4 weeks

Need to know
What are the results of the tests?
Can performance or usability be improved by your design team alone?

- Collect feedback
- Analyze server logs and visitor behavior
- Prioritize revisions
- Continue to test

Ongoing

Design/Build   Modify   Revise

Prototype approval   Site approval   Revise

Design/Build

Review of branding on site

Rights, privacy, and disclaimers

Revise forecasts   Revise forecasts

Prototypes   The site   Revisions based on feedback

FIGURE 1.6: THE PROCESS
Companies that follow a standard Web-development process can ensure that all parts of the organization contribute to the creation of a seamless, interactive experience that meets customer expectations. This figure is an overview of all functions in this process, when they take place, who the key players are, when they are involved in the process, and what roles they play. A design team usually becomes involved after the initial strategy and analysis is complete. The design team focuses on three key areas: information design, interaction design, and presentation design. These phases of development help designers put the customer before the cart.

What's their stake in the process?

	Their stake in the process	Effect on the process
Executive management President, CEO, Board of Directors, division heads	Maintain enterprise strategy, meet financial expectations	Approve project. Can encourage or mandate collaboration.
Business development Directors, strategists, analysts	Expand the business into new areas to remain competitive.	Provide initial market research and financial forecasts. Usually oversee technology and content partnerships.
Marketing Directors, researchers, copywriters	Build and defend the company's brand.	Provide customer research, competitive market analysis. May provide content and graphics.
Technology Chief, database administrators, programmers, specialists	Make sure appropriate technology is in place, integrated, and reliable.	Provide the technical resources to build and operate the site.
Customer service Directors, customer relationship managers	Provide better solutions and speedy customer response.	Provide feedback and greater understanding about the customer.
Sales & Financial Directors, account managers	Sell more products, goods, or services, and meet financial goals.	Can force radical redesigns if revenue does not meet expectations.
Project manager	Keep the project on time, on task, and on budget. Communication between development team and departments.	Skilled PMs can articulate and sell your design. They try to shield the team from department interference.

When will you meet?	When you meet them …	Be prepared to …
Seldom	Listen closely. When answering questions, keep focused on the positive impact of the site to customers and the enterprise.	Defend your design decisions in a clear and informed manner. Be prepared to explain how customer loyalty will benefit.
Early in process	Don't be afraid to ask questions. They have intimate knowledge of customer wants, needs, and business goals.	Understand how your design will provide a competitive advantage in the marketplace.
Often	Pick their brains about the target customer and the customer's specific needs. Get understanding of ideal brand experience.	Explain how your design will provide positive experience to customers and bolster the brand.
Most often	Know they will have the greatest effect on the realization of your design. Be specific — you'll be more likely to get what you need.	Clearly outline feature specifications of your design in concrete terms. We'll talk more about this in Ch. 3, 4, and 5.
Occasionally	Expect an earful of stories. Customer service is called when problems occur. Ask for specific suggestions to improve the site.	Explain why your designs or clever functionality will not light up the phones. Be flexible and open to their ideas.
Seldom	Listen to what's selling, what's not, and why that might be.	Decipher product sales issues from usabilty and design issues.
Most often	Ask how you can better help the team or provide better information to help the PM sell your ideas to the other departments.	Explain how your work will fit well with other parts of the project. Meet all your deadlines.

FIGURE 1.7: THE PLAYERS
The development process is an organization-wide effort that will bring you in contact with many different departments. It's important to remember that each department will view the project from a position of self-interest. As a result, each has the potential to be an advocate for or adversary against your good work. This figure shows the departments, how they affect the process, and their concerns.

A Designer's Role

You'll notice that the last player mentioned in Fig. 1.7 is the project manager (PM). This person is the liaison between the development team and the rest of the organization. As such, the project manager must be able to juggle competing interests, track various subprojects, and mediate disputes that arise. In some cases, you could be tapped to take the project manager role. If so, be aware that design will become secondary to keeping the project on track.

Fig. 1.8 shows a typical Web-development team and your potential roles. The responsibilities you will have depend on several factors: The size of the company, their level of Web experience, the complexity of the commerce transactions, and, of course, your skills.

It is possible for one person to assume several roles on this chart. The larger the team, the more likely you are to have a more specialized design role. Regardless, you will be expected to move freely between disciplines, collaborating or assuming the roles of:

Your role in the process

At medium to larger companies, the development of a commerce Web site will be assigned to a project manager and team leaders. This person will direct workers from other areas of the organization dedicated to this project.

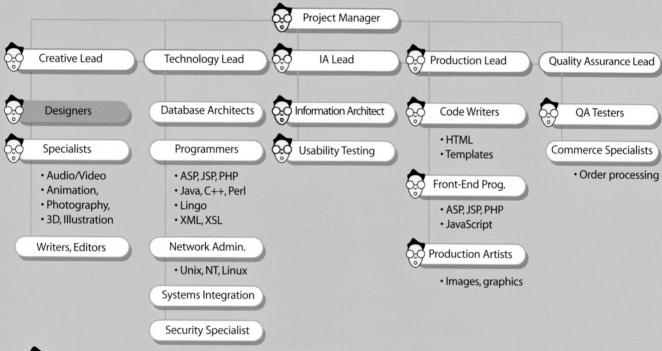

 = Possible design role. What you take on will depend on three factors: Your talent and skill level, size of the company, and complexity of the project.

SMALL INC.	MEDIUM INC.	LARGE INC.
You will do it all, including project management, programming, coding, testing, and research.	Focus on interaction and presentation design. Light programming and testing.	Design team leader or part of that team; focus on presentation design only.

Less specialized ⟵――――――――――――――⟶ More specialized

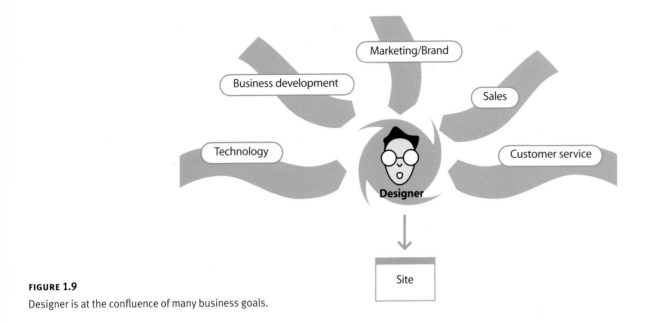

FIGURE 1.9

Designer is at the confluence of many business goals.

Creative: Responsible for the creative concept of the site. Designers transform the information and interaction design into a visual style. This team is also responsible for creating illustrations, graphics, and other multimedia elements.

Technology: The technical team takes the information and interaction requirements and builds databases, servers, and scripts to support them. They are also responsible for integrating online commerce with existing business systems. Rarely is the designer asked to perform these tasks. A working knowledge of the technology involved is required.

Information Architecture: Responsible for site maps, interface, navigation, and interaction design. This person's skills may overlap with the designer. While information architects can be influential in many aspects of the design phase, their main concern is to define the customers goals that can be met within the general site specifications. In other words, they define the playing field but not all the rules or the colors of the players' uniforms. On small teams, the designer is also the information architect.

Production: Translate the visual design into code. Prepares content such as photos, graphics, video, and audio for the Web. On small teams, the designer is heavily involved in production.

Testing: Make sure that what's been built works as planned. This covers everything from appearance to technology and order processing. On small teams, the designer is usually asked to test production values.

Regardless of the organization or team size, designers often find themselves in the turbulent confluence where an organization's competing internal goals collide. It's an unenviable place to be. In spite of the countless meetings you attend or the storyboards you draw, you will realize that chaos is part of site development. Seldom does a home page go up without a few battles breaking out.

To be a hero, you will have to find some way to make all of these competing interests and requirements come together in a seamless experience for the customer.

But, it's usually not necessary for you to be a Lone Ranger. Anticipate trouble and prepare a strategy. Look to the project manager to divert conflicts or erase indecision early in development. With your hands full of design responsibilities, you won't want to break away from the deadline crunch to referee a difference of opinion between marketing and customer service.

Now you have an understanding of the different types of commerce; the process of building a commerce site; and what your role is in the development process, large or small. In Chapter 2, we examine the hallmarks of good commerce design that will guide you through creating desirable customer experiences.

---

[1] Interview with Jeffrey Zeldman on Adobe.com (http://www.adobe.com/web/features/zeldman20010702/main.html). Zeldman's book *Taking Your Talent to the Web* is an excellent resource for understanding the differences between print and Web design. Learn more at http://www.zeldman.com/

[2] Saffo, Paul. "Consumers and Interactive New Media: A Hierarchy of Desires." http://www.saffo.org/consumers.html

chapter 2

SIX PRINCIPLES OF GOOD COMMERCE DESIGN
Guidelines to keep in mind throughout the process

Web-design books are usually more focused on style than design. Design focuses on understanding your subject or content and devising a useful way for it to serve its audience. Style is a necessary component of design but one that is narrowly concerned with visual presentation.

The distinction is important and often overlooked. As Web designer Jeffrey Zeldman says, when the distinction between style and design is lost, "we get meaningless eye candy that gives beauty a bad name."[1]

In the best designs, style takes a back seat to the appropriate solution. On the Web, issues of speed, organization, clarity, and consistency drive your solution.

During the site-building process, you will be frequently challenged and sometimes confused about the right design choices to make. In Chapters 3, 4, and especially 5, we provide concrete ways to design a total commerce experience for your customers. This chapter focuses on putting customer experience first and the customer's low tolerance for poor performance and service. Keeping the following principles in mind will make it easier to do the right thing.

Principle 1: Speed Is the First Priority

Most designers do not think of speed as a design issue. But the Web is an interactive experience, not purely a visual one. Interactive experiences put the user in control of the pace. When a user has to wait, they have lost control and the experience is diminished.

Customers don't care why they have to wait—a poor dial-up connection, Internet congestion, or problems with your server. They want what's on your site now, and not a second later. Site visitors who have to wait too long for your page to display will go elsewhere, no matter how useful or relevant your site is.

Much research has focused on the time it takes to for a Web page to load in a browser and what effect that has on purchasing.

Studies have revealed the significant impact of poor download time. Consumers believe that the Internet provides service on demand. Asking them to defer their requests results in loss of customers.[2] An estimated $25 billion in revenue is lost annually due to Web performance issues.[3]

Zona Research found that one Web site had a home page abandonment rate of 30 percent. That means that about 1 out of every 3 site visitors left after requesting the home page. By reducing the load time of this page by approximately 1 second, the site was able to lower this rate to 6–8 percent.

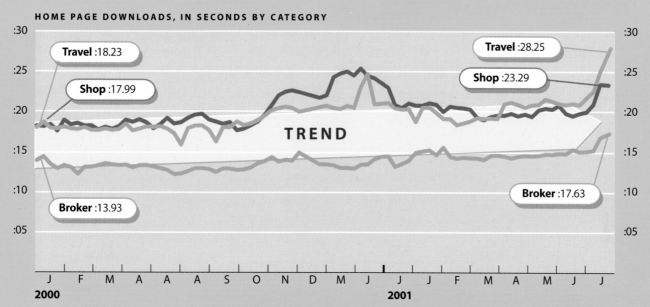

HOME PAGE DOWNLOADS, IN SECONDS BY CATEGORY

Travel :18.23

Shop :17.99

Broker :13.93

TREND

Travel :28.25

Shop :23.29

Broker :17.63

J F M A A A S O N D M J J J F M A M J J
2000   **2001**

Source: Keynote Consumer 40 Internet Performance Index

FIGURE 2.1: HOME PAGE PERFORMANCE SLOWING DOWN

Data suggests that the trend in commerce sites is for slower-, not faster-, loading home pages, despite research that shows site visitors respond negatively. The addition of more advertising and the prevalence of dynamically generated pages have contributed to the sluggish performance. This chart shows average response times (access and download) on 56-Kbps connections to popular travel, shopping, and stock brokerage sites.

It seems as though there is little attention paid to the issue of speed. Fig. 2.1 shows that the home page of commerce Web sites are getting increasingly slow, despite complaints from users. This is largely because companies focus solely on content quality as the key to constructing a meaningful experience. But, as research shows, customers regard a sluggish site as unusable (See Fig. 2.2). Therefore, meeting acceptable download times is a top priority in designing a usable commerce site. As a designer, you can play a significant role in meeting this need.

The realities of the network

The Internet is a complex, distributed network that supports an ever-increasing amount of data and users. It was born as a service to connect academic, government, and military institutions and was never designed to handle billions of dollars of international commerce. As a consequence, it has limitations. The most noticeable is called latency, or lag. As packets of data travel from one computer to another, delays are bound to happen. Latency is the time that elapses between the request and response for information between computers.

During the past few years, a large portion of Web content, like that served by many commerce sites, has become dynamic. Assembling content in real-time (dynamic) rather than delivering static pages requires not just adequate bandwidth but highly responsive Web servers and applications. Any delays caused by information processing will only add to the network delays. Much of the responsiveness of your site depends on a complex interplay of networking technology, software, and hardware.

A prerequisite to designing for maximized speed is understanding how a page gets from your server to the customer and where the potential slowdowns can occur along the way (See Fig. 2.3).

Many commerce sites use specialized content delivery services such as Akamai and Digital Island. These companies have devised sophisticated systems that intelligently remove much of the latency in the network.

The blame game

Although so much can go wrong with the networking process, most of these factors are invisible to the casual user. If the page loads slowly with gaping blank rectangles where images should be, teams call the designer first, because your work is supremely visible. Plus, it's easier for the team to ask you to shave another kilobyte off your pages than to debug a logjam in the application server.

You can be valuable to your design team by being prepared to handle such situations. Having a copy of Fig. 2.3 is a good start. It will help you understand what you can fine-tune in your design and suggest other places for your team to search for the problem when your fine-tuning isn't enough.

If you get blamed for slow downloading pages, gather ammunition. Begin with any pertinent performance data. Log the sizes of your pages complete with HTML and images. Some HTML editing software programs, such as Macromedia's Dreamweaver, will calculate this for you. Set a page size limit and make sure none of the pages exceed it. Get a contract with a company like Keynote Systems[4] that can measure the download times and latency of your site continuously. The speed of your site should be a priority for frequent testing. We cover the testing process in Chapter 6.

FIGURE 2.2: DON'T LET SLOW DOWNLOADS TEST PATIENCE OR HAMPER USABILITY

With the majority of the world still using low-bandwidth connections, try to keep as few elements on your page as possible. For example, if you are using graphics for navigation, group them together as one graphic instead of separate ones.

This site has chosen to break up their navigation into ten separate elements. The browser will need to query the server for each element. You end up with an erratic display, as each request is fulfilled. If the server is overloaded, some pieces may never load.

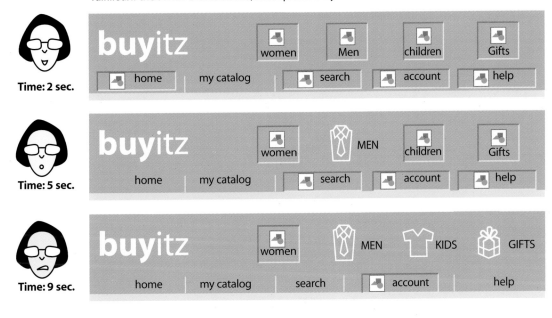

Now, the site is only sending two requests to the server, and it's delivered in less time.

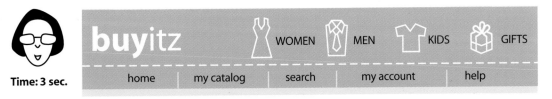

FIGURE 2.3: SPEEDING UP THE PROCESS

Before you design a fast site, you must understand how a Web page gets from your servers to the customer. This is a complex, and mostly invisible, process that is loaded with potential potholes.

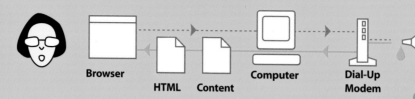

1 Customer types in URL: http://www.buyit.com

2 Computer directs modem to send the request

Browser
HTML   Content
Computer
Dial-Up Modem

3 Modem sends request to a bank of modems connected to a router, which forwards the request to the local Internet Service Provider (ISP).

Router

How a designer can improve download speed
Focus on reducing on the number page elements and the total size of the page. Using fewer separate graphics will help too. When possible, reuse graphics to take advantage of the browser's cache. Clean up your HTML code and always have HEIGHT and WIDTH tags defined in tables.

4 The ISP lets the DNS convert the URL into an IP address, i.e., www.buyit.com becomes 255.15.9.12

6 The Internet is made up of millions of other routers that pass along the request the quickest way possible.

5 With the IP address, the request can now be sent to the Internet.

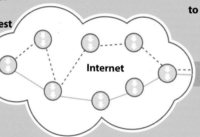
Internet

Router

Local ISP

Domain Name Server (DNS)

7 The request is routed to the site and a connection is established, much like making a phone call.

Router

Get content closer to your customer
Add more servers in regions where most of your customers are, or hire companies like Akamai to reroute your content faster.

9 The Public Server looks for the right page—home.htm—and calls upon other servers to provide any other content or processing.

8 With the connection open, the HTTP request can be answered. HTML can be sent.

1001110101110 1000

Firewall

Public server

Secure server

Application server

Tune your servers and network
In the early days of the Net, mostly static pages were sent. Their speed was mainly dependent on the size of available bandwidth. Now, many commerce sites are dynamic, with pages being generated on the fly. Adding more servers (a cluster), optimizing databases, and tuning the application servers, which do the heavy processing, will speed up dynamic page generation considerably.

10 The appropriate HTML and other content are sent back to the customer's computer and assembled by the browser.

Percent of total Internet audience

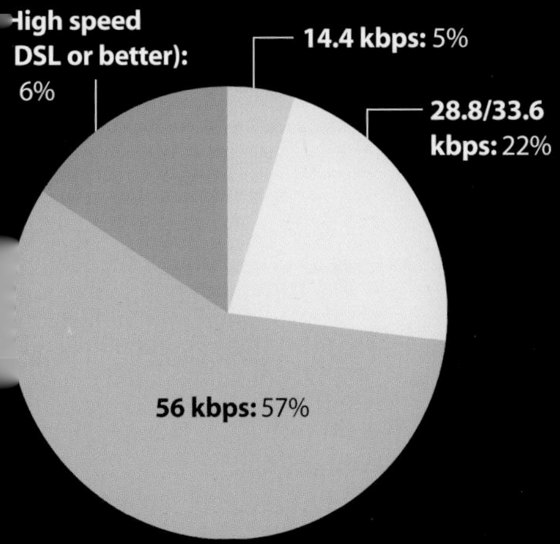

High speed
(DSL or better):
6%

14.4 kbps: 5%

28.8/33.6 kbps: 22%

56 kbps: 57%

Source: Zona Research, "The Need for Speed II" April, 2001

FIGURE 2.5: CONSIDER BANDWIDTH

This chart is useful to estimate how long a given page will take to download on an optimal network. However, remember that latencies in the network will add delays.

Connection Speed			
28.8 kb	**33.6 kb**	**56.6 kb**	**ISDN 128**
10k	00:02	00:02	00:01	00:00
20k	00:05	00:04	00:02	00:01
30k	00:08	00:07	00:04	00:01
40k	00:11	00:09	00:05	00:02
50k	00:14	00:12	00:07	00:03
60k	00:17	00:14	00:08	00:03
70k	00:19	00:17	00:10	00:04
80k	00:22	00:19	00:11	00:05
90k	00:25	00:21	00:13	00:05
100k	00:28	00:24	00:14	00:06
110k	00:31	00:26	00:15	00:07
120k	00:34	00:29	00:17	00:07
130k	00:36	00:31	00:18	00:08
140k	00:39	00:34	00:20	00:08
150k	00:42	00:36	00:21	00:09

Tolerable   Exceeds average tolerance

Source: Intel Download Calculator
http://www.intel.com/home/tech-center/calculate_download/

The bottom line

While a growing percentage of users are adopting faster access connections, knowing that the bulk of the online audience is still using dial-up access is crucial (See Fig. 2.4). Testing shows visitors' download tolerance levels range from 2 to 10 seconds. Since all evidence shows that faster is indeed better, shoot for a target of 4–5 seconds per page (See Fig. 2.5). Meeting this mark could mean the difference of hundreds of thousands of dollars to your bottom line.

With a clear idea of historical performance and an inventory of page sizes, you'll be able to refocus the team on other culprits. More important, you can become the user advocate on speed issues and make it the primary criteria for delivering a good user experience.

Imagine that someone from the sales department walks in and says "We need two more ad positions on this page." You should be able to respond, "Adding these positions will also add an average of 28KB per page to the download time. That slowdown will affect sales negatively. Are you willing to make that tradeoff?" Granted, it won't always be that simple to explain, but by connecting requests to reality you'll be able to educate all parties involved on this issue.

Speed is a design issue, but it's not the only area in which you can make a difference. As a designer, you can do more than crunch JPEGs or clean up HTML. If you design your site to be easier to use, your customers will perceive your site as being fast, even if its actual download times remain the same.

Principle 2: Make It Easy to Use

Making your site easy to use is, well, easier said than done. According to usability expert Jakob Nielsen, visitors trying to find or buy something on a commerce site are only successful about 56 percent of the time.[5] Your company might have invested in blazingly fast servers and ruthlessly squeezed extra bits out of your graphics, but if every other customer can't use the search engine or find the shopping cart, what hope do you have of delivering a valuable user experience?

Be familiar

"Make the interface intuitive!" is the battle cry voiced by CEOs and designers alike. We all say this because we've been told hundreds of times that an intuitive interface will win us friends and customers. Unfortunately, there is no such thing as an inherently intuitive interface.

In his book *The Humane Interface,* Jef Raskin explains: "When users say that an interface is intuitive, they mean that it operates just like some other software or method with which they are familiar."

Yes, it's true. You don't have to explore the depths of your customers' collective unconscious to design an interface. A successful interface incorporates many familiar elements already established on popular sites. If it's familiar, then there is nothing new to for the site visitor to learn. The more your site follows standards and design conventions, the better chance it will be easier to use.

Learning from convention does not necessarily mean that you must sacrifice the appearance of your Web site. Rather, your site's interaction and response should be predictable. Imagine how awful it would be if the dial pad of every phone worked as differently, as so many sites' interfaces do. The number of phone calls would certainly plummet.

Designers sometimes wrestle with conventions. Developing something fresh and new is part of our job. However, there are some things that shouldn't be messed with. A classic example is the shopping cart (See Fig. 2.6). For years, companies have tried to use other metaphors for the cart and failed miserably. One clever outdoor products company tried a shopping sled. No one understood it. They converted to the cart and revenues took off.

Vincent Flanders calls this rollover icon design "mystery meat navigation." As he says on his site, Webpagesthatsuck.com, "Web design is not about art, it's about making money (or disseminating information). To make money, you don't want to design a site that might confuse someone."

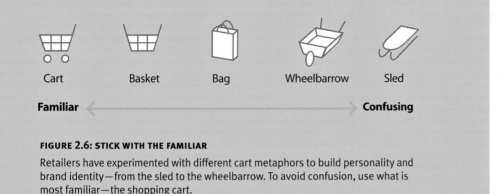

FIGURE 2.6: STICK WITH THE FAMILIAR
Retailers have experimented with different cart metaphors to build personality and brand identity—from the sled to the wheelbarrow. To avoid confusion, use what is most familiar—the shopping cart.

Organize in a logical way

Your site's success will also depend upon your ability to organize information. But organization requires understanding your customer's goals.

In a Blockbuster store, you'll find your favorite Jackie Chan movies under the aisle labeled Action. However, if a brand new Chan film comes out, it can only be found under New Releases. Stores deal with physical products, so a copy of Jackie Chan's latest movie can't be in two departments at once.

Because of this limitation, Blockbuster minimizes the number of categories for the customer and reduces the risk of ambiguity. Ambiguity in the store arises when something can be categorized in more than one way, but can only exist in one location (i.e., "It's action-packed and funny but it also has a heart.") A customer looking for a Chan film might first think to look under the Action section. If they couldn't find there, Comedy would be a next likely choice.

Online, you're not limited by the physical constraints. Categorization can be broader, but still effective. Ambiguity is averted by placing the Jackie Chan film in many likely areas: Action, Comedy, Martial Arts, Foreign Film, New Release, and Popular.

Some designers of commerce sites make the assumption that they can apply an off-line organizational scheme to their Web site. Unfortunately, the two situations are not equivalent. First, your Web customers might not be familiar with the nomenclature or departments of your "bricks-and-mortar" store. For example, the store might have a department called "Relaxing," which has recliners, massagers, TVs, stereos, and soothing CDs. Online, the products are more likely to be discovered in literal categories: Furniture, Electronics, Music.

Navigating your way through a retail store is different than searching for something online. In a store, because a customer can scan in a large amount of visual information quickly, it's easy to browse through thousands of items in minutes. Online, that would be tedious and unnecessary because you can present the customer with a categorization scheme that best fits what they want to do.

For example, you own a Mac and want to buy some learning software for your child. In a store, you might go to the Mac section, and be presented with ten titles. However, in the Windows section, there are another fifty titles labeled For Windows and Mac. You probably didn't think to look in that section. Online, you could be presented with all sixty at once and even be given the option to sort this list further.

There are several useful schemes for categorization:

• **Alphabetical:** The most logical organization scheme for a dictionary or phone book. It is typically used to provide order within other schemes. For example, Blockbuster organizes by movie genre then alphabetically by title.

- **Chronological:** Organizing by date is useful for subjects like automobiles, antiques, and wines.

- **Geographical:** Organizing information based on place is useful for gardening, real estate, and travel. It's also valuable when location is relevant to buying, i.e., shipping costs or physical store locations.

- **Task oriented:** Requires that content be organized as an outline of a process. For example: Select a home, find an agent, choose a mortgage. The organization reinforces the steps a customer needs to take.

- **Topical:** More challenging than the first four options, designing topical schemes requires defining limits to the breadth of content. Do you want to cover every topic like the *Encyclopedia Britannica* or a focused few like the Discovery Channel?

- **Visitor specific:** You might wish to design your information to fit into neat categories for different types of visitors, based on psychographic or demographic traits. For example, an apparel site might have site content arranged differently for women than men.

In some instances, you might need to use a hybrid of schemes. Figure 2.7 shows how a national retailer could take advantage of a mix of topical and alphabetical groupings.

What information does your customer need and how they might be guided to a decision? Organize around a customer task so you can understand your visitors' goals.

"Chunking" is an important principle for organizing site information. In 1956, a Harvard psychologist named George A. Miller published a groundbreaking article titled "The Magical Number Seven, Plus or Minus Two."[6] In this article, he reveals that people are adept at recalling small chunks of information as long as there are no more than nine pieces, with seven being an optimal number. Breaking information into appropriately sized chunks improves comprehension and our ability to find and retrieve information.

Be clear, stay simple

Knowing that people need information to be presented in easily digestible chunks means our designs and navigation must be simple and direct.

This might seem obvious to you, but it seems to have been forgotten by legions of other designers. As an example, take the phenomenon that can still be found on many sites, which we call "concentration navigation."

Concentration navigation is one of the cardinal sins of interface design. A rollover button forces visitors to mouse over an icon

to identify it and then remember it for future use. The problem is exacerbated the more icons there are to identify. A few years ago, a global soft drink manufacturer used a navigation bar similar to the first example in Fig 2.8. The fifteen icons are almost twice as many as Miller's "chunking limit." In an information-overloaded society, the last thing you want to do is force your customers to memorize your navigation—because they won't.

Another complication when designing a navigation structure is that your site does not exist in its own consistent world. It's an interface within an interface within an interface—your site, within a browser, within an operating system—each with its own look and feel. The combination can be the source of endless frustration. For example, if your site disables the browser back button or scroll bars, you are killing something that customers are already familiar with. This unexpected change will make visitors impatient and confused.

Designing in a nested environment such as this calls for simplicity. Once customers have found your site, don't scare them off with an overwhelming flood of animated graphics, intricate backgrounds and strange buttons. Your most important job is to engage them to buy, not to marvel at your design acumen.

1 Unorganized/Random	**2** Alphabetical	**3** Topic + Alpha
GIFTS	BABY	**ENTERTAINMENT**
SCHOOL TIME	BED + BATH	Books, Movies, Music
BED + BATH	CLEARANCE	Sports
HOME FURNISHINGS	CLOTHES	**FASHION + STYLE**
HOME OFFICE	ELECTRONICS	Accessories, Jewelry
KITCHEN	GIFTS	Beauty, Health
BABY	HEALTH + BEAUTY	Clothes
CLOTHES	HOME FURNISHINGS	Luggage
JEWELRY + ACCESSORIES	HOME OFFICE	**HOME**
HEALTH + BEAUTY	JEWELRY + ACCESSORIES	Bed + Bath
ELECTRONICS	KITCHEN	Electronics
MUSIC / MOVIES / BOOKS	MUSIC / MOVIES / BOOKS	Furnishings
SPORTS + LUGGAGE	SCHOOL TIME	Kitchen
TOYS	SPORTS + LUGGAGE	Office
CLEARANCE	TOYS	**KIDS**
		Baby
		School Time
		Toys
		GIFTS
		CLEARANCE

FIGURE 2.7: RATIONAL ORGANIZATION

A navigation list needs some measure of order if it is going to be quickly parsed by the site visitor. Example 1 has no discernable logic and is not useful. Grouping and alphabetizing make a list easy to use.

Try it

With each list, try to locate Kitchen or Baby products. Then wait about 30 seconds and come back and try again. Notice how the lack of organization in example 1 makes you reread the entire list each time.

---

1 Icons with no clear organization

The icons fail to be clear about what they represent. Can you pick which icon represents the Music section? The visitor has to roll their cursor over each icon just to figure out what it represents. This navigation feels more like a game than a useful tool for finding information on the site.

2 Unorganized with text labels

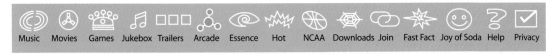

| Music | Movies | Games | Jukebox | Trailers | Arcade | Essence | Hot | NCAA | Downloads | Join | Fast Fact | Joy of Soda | Help | Privacy |

Adding labels to the icons begins to clear up confusion over what the icons represent but not necessarily what they mean. They are also seemingly redundant. What's the difference between Music and Jukebox or Arcade and Games? Aren't these the same? And what exactly is Essence? This still feels like a game, not navigation.

3 Organized with text navigation

| Download | Games | Movies | Music | Sports | Soda Facts | Help | Join | Privacy |

The best solution is to replace icons with larger type and rethink the number of navigation choices. This example is much more direct. We have reduced fifteen choices down to nine understandable areas of the site—an approach called "chunking."

FIGURE 2.8: CONCENTRATION NAVIGATION

Typically, using icons as the sole means for navigation does more harm than good. Here's an example of pitfalls found on a menu bar of a large soft drink manufacturer site and some possible solutions.

Principle 3: Keep It Consistent

Newspaper designers have long understood the importance of consistency in their work. Look at the front page of any paper. Although the news may be very different day to day, the page's navigational elements stay in the same place. The newspaper's logo stays at the top. The index is usually fixed in a corner. No designer at a newspaper wastes time worrying if the headlines should run horizontally or vertically. As a result, people feel comfortable with a newspaper and designers don't have to reinvent it every day.

Jakob Nielsen has said, "Consistency is one of the most powerful usability principles: when things always behave the same, users don't have to worry about what will happen. Instead, they know what will happen based on earlier experience."[7]

For your visitors to benefit, your site will need to follow consistency in both design and interaction. Design consistency includes grid, navigation, link colors, button styles, font usage, control elements and metaphors. Use templates, cascading style sheets, and style guidelines to help manage this task (See Fig. 2.9).

Interaction deals with the behavior of your site, which should be understandable, predictable and persistent. People don't like to learn things unless they feel they can apply that knowledge in many places. Strive to reduce what a user needs to learn to complete a desired task.

"A foolish consistency is the hobgoblin of little minds."
—Emerson

FIGURE 2.9

BE CONSISTENT

Consistency makes things easier to design. A Web designer doesn't have to rethink the navigation or how the page should fit with the overall design. Use templates, cascading style sheets, and style guidelines to help in manage this task.

GUIDE AND DIRECT

Navigation and search stay in the same place because customers depend on these elements for finding what they want. Maintaining consistency will build confidence as the customer continues deeper into the site.

ACT THE SAME

The grid structure and color palette are important elements of creating consistency. Notice that all action buttons are designed the same, and placed in relative proximity to the task.

Of course, consistency doesn't guarantee a usable site. Poor visual and interaction design used consistently is still consistently bad design. Consistency has several benefits to your Web site:

• Consistency reinforces a sense of place, helping users to know where they are on the site and what to expect next.

• Consistency makes things easier to use. Every successful task performed reinforces familiarity.

• Consistency makes things easier to design. A Web designer doesn't have to rethink the navigation, the location of content elements on a page, or how the page should fit with the overall design.

• Consistency protects design from passing fads by keeping navigation simple and direct.

• Consistency reinforces branding.

Principle 4: Have a Personality

Our traditional notions of branding have given way to a much deeper focus on understanding the customer experience. Brand has become more than a sharp logo. Brand identity is equal to the sum of all the impressions an organization makes on its customers.

For those designing commerce sites, this is a significant shift in thinking. The Web is a highly public, visual, and interactive medium. Therefore, it has the power to build or erode an established experience quickly.

It is critical to understand how an organization defines its brand before beginning a project, since your job is to successfully interpret this brand idea into an interactive experience. A designer must always be asking, "Does the final site properly represent the company?"

Companies are now in the experience business, and brand identity equals experience. Walk into an Apple store and you will be immediately aware of how true that is. Apple's stores use refined architecture, lively signage, and interactive displays to direct the consumer towards a consistent, coherent and unique experience (See Fig. 2.10).

Apple's marketing message on its Web site promotes the computer as something that will unleash your creative power. The physical store reinforces that message by allowing you to flex that power with unlimited verve. For example, walk up to the display called "And the award for Best Director goes to… you!" You are presented with several video cameras tied to Macs running iMovie. Right there, you can practice your skills.

Smart approaches to branding result in designs that are appropriate and responsible to the original intent of the brand; consistent and coherent identity; and a memorable experience that distinguishes the company from its competition.

A hands-on experience at the Apple store in Plano, Texas.

Photo by Shayne Bowman/Hypergene.net.

ADVERTISING	WEB SITE	STORE
Using images of Alfred Hitchcock, Albert Einstein, Miles Davis, and Jim Henson, Apple aims to associate the customer with undisputable creative geniuses.	Tutorials, testimonials, forums, and case studies portray Apple products as enablers of creative expression. Some functionality, such as iTools, allow easy Web creation.	Predominance of hands-on displays invites you to get a taste of creative energy. Every device in the store is ready for you. The signage is always a call to action: "Rip. Mix. Burn."

MESSAGE

Apple computers unleash your creative power.

FIGURE 2.10: TRUE TO THE MESSAGE

Branding defines the total customer experience. Personality is a subset of branding that deals with the distinctive face you put on that experience.

The designer's challenge is to extend the offline message into a complementary online experience.

Every choice a designer makes in a traditional medium—from typeface to the packaging—takes into consideration the consumer's experience. Will the type be too hard to read? Will the package style be appropriate to the brand?

Personality is vital because it paints a unique and distinguished portrait of the brand experience for the consumer. Your visitors interact with many kinds of sites from the familiar to the strange. If handled skillfully, your site's personality will separate it from the mass of competitors and make it more memorable.

Personality manifests itself in every element of your site, from the colors you choose to the writing style to the photography and the grid. Your site's personality should reflect its purpose. How thoughtfully you combine elements such as words, image, video, animation, sound, color, and interactivity on a page will either reinforce or corrode what you've established. Some thoughts to consider:

Words: While you may not be responsible for the writing, be sure that the copy you are given is consistent and authentic in tone and voice. According to Jakob Nielsen, the best writing style is concise, scanable, and objective, free of marketing lingo and hyperbole.

Bad

LL Bean's World Famous Lined Field Coat: No trip out into the woods would be complete without this sturdy, workaday cotton canvas coat. One of our most popular products sports the legendary 3M™ Scotchlite™ Reflective Material back patch. Of course, it comes with the quintessential button-out Bean pile lining. Comes in four fashionable colors that never go out of style: Soft Olive, Saddle Brown, Cardinal and Hunter. Imported from Peru, featuring 100 years of family craftsmanship.

Good

Bean's Lined Field Coat

- Button-out pile lining in a polyester/ acrylic blend.
- Prewashed, heavyweight 10 oz. cotton canvas.
- 3M™ Scotchlite™ Reflective Material back patch.
- Imported.
- Machine wash and dry.
- 4 colors: Olive, Brown, Red, Green

Photography: The quality and style of the photography is an important factor in establishing personality. Images should be chosen with an eye not only for style, but for how useful they are to the customer in making a purchase decision.

Animation & Video: Video is good for showing features of products that can't be demonstrated with text and images, such as a QTVR of a home. Video and animation are also good for high-end, stylized advertisements. But be wary of using this type of content. It requires special talent, skill, and technology to pull off properly. It also requires that your customer have a good enough connection to experience it. Cheesy animations and choppy, low-quality video are death to personality. Allow site visitors to request video. Do not force them to view it before getting to what they want.

Sound: Use sparingly, because it adds significantly to download time. Allow site visitors to request sound. Do not force it on them. If the sound is only used as background, make it easy for site visitors to turn it on or off.

> *Your site's brand identity and personality are as important as the information it contains and the technology it uses.*

Personality manifests itself in every element of your site, from the colors and language to the photos and grid. The personality should reflect the site's purpose, as well as match offline identity.

HIP

Many sites that want to attract a hipper clientele put style before substance. Notice that the text accompanying the product and in the navigation is not instructional but more about mood and emotion. The color palette on sites like these tend to be brighter, and bolder. Many elements of design are decorative, and do not operate in conventional ways. This approach may be entirely appropriate to your brand, but it has usability pitfalls.

URBANE

Clientele for sites like these are equally image conscious, but in a different way. Notice that the language in the navigation is direct. But the language with the product contains a little touch of personality. The color palette tends to be more restrained. Many elements of design are also decorative, but operate in conventional ways. This approach may be appropriate to your brand as well.

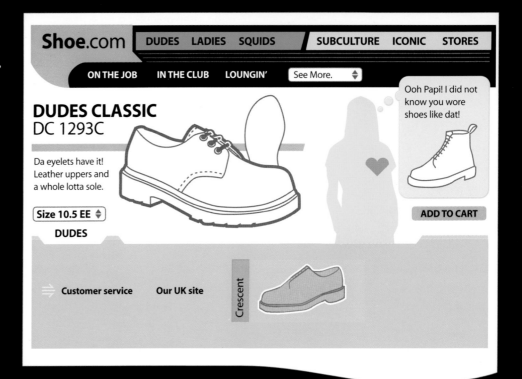

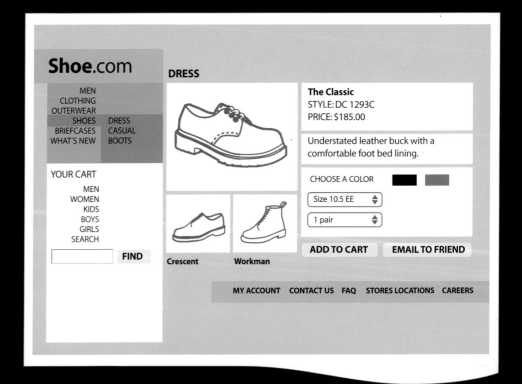

Color: A key indicator of personality. Pick a color palette that differentiates you from competitors. Don't be too loud with colors because too many active colors can become distracting (see first example in Fig. 2.11). Color is excellent for providing direction. For example, you could use a unique color to signal action buttons like Find or Add to Cart or Checkout (See Fig. 2.12).

Interactivity: Your social interactions define your personality. The same is true of your site's interactions. Think of interactions as a form of conversation. The site says something and the user says something back. So what are some of the qualities of good social interaction? Ask for permission first. Say please and thank you. Invite a friend along. Play nice with others. (You get the idea.) A site that makes users sign in before they do anything, has the potential to project different personalities, depending on how it's presented and handled. It may say "We care about your privacy," or it may say, "Members only. Stay out."

All of these elements should add up to a single personality. Is your company witty? Reserved? Irreverent? Dependable? Nerdy? Cool? In Figure 2.11, we show two approaches to site personality.

In the rush to be hip or sophisticated or clever, some designers take personality too far. Remember the cart example in Figure 2.6, where a garden store used a wheelbarrow for the cart? That's not personality, it's a cheap gimmick on the face of something meaningful. Likewise, having a bat fly across your screen might sound neat for Halloween but would jeopardize the trustworthiness of a brokerage site like Charles Schwab or the sophistication of a retailer like Williams-Sonoma.

The ultimate job of brand identity is to create a company personality that customers can identify and want to associate themselves with. If they can customize or personalize that association in any way, the relationship will deepen and become longer lasting.

eNormicom.com is one of the smartest send ups of the dot-commoditization of Web brand identity. Satire by 37 Signals, a smart Web-design firm out of Chicago.

Principle 5:
Enable Meaningful Personalization

Of all the jargon Web builders must decipher, personalization is among the most baffling. For the sake of our discussion, we define personalization as the functionality that allows your customer to tailor or modify their experience on your Web site.

Personalization typically requires an investment of the customer's time. It also requires the customer to entrust the business with their personal information, such as credit card numbers, address, and income. They need to be able to trust the business. So your site must have a credible privacy policy if you hope to persuade customers to adopt personalization. Likewise, personalization is costly and difficult to implement, and the payoff is sometimes elusive.

Web designers are confronted by three fundamental questions: Is personalization necessary? What should be customizable? How should personalization be accomplished?

Web designers should recognize that site visitors have tastes and needs that are uniquely related to their personal goals. For example, most mobile phones allow customers to choose custom ring tones. Not just a gee-whiz option, this personalization is meaningful. It helps distinguish your phone calls from others in a room.

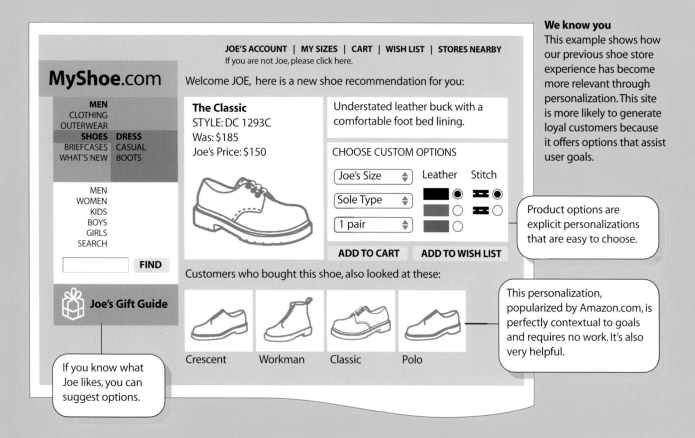

We know you
This example shows how our previous shoe store experience has become more relevant through personalization. This site is more likely to generate loyal customers because it offers options that assist user goals.

Product options are explicit personalizations that are easy to choose.

This personalization, popularized by Amazon.com, is perfectly contextual to goals and requires no work. It's also very helpful.

If you know what Joe likes, you can suggest options.

FIGURE 2.12: RELEVANT PERSONALIZATION

Consider the customer experience when choosing which personalization options to offer. Options that are simple and context-sensitive will have the greatest impact.

Designers should allow customers to personalize elements that will be meaningful to their purchasing or selling goals. Personalization that is simple and context-sensitive will help customers be more effective when they revisit a site (See Fig. 2.12). Consider these examples of relevant commerce personalization:

• **Save my buying & shipping preferences** — Good for frequent customers.

• **Save my buying history** — Good for all customers.

• **Watch lists** — Good for customers monitoring varying prices, such as stocks, commodities, or auctions.

• **Product recommendations** — Good for generating awareness of products related to the customer's interest.

• **Sort list by price, category, or alpha** — Good for search results.

Customers need to be given a certain amount of personal freedom and control in order to feel secure with a Web site. If a site is too restrictive, your customers may be frustrated and find reaching their goals nearly impossible.

Principle 6: Avoid Fads

Web design has evolved from simple text to advanced multimedia and is poised for a wealth of new possibilities. As with anything concerning aesthetics or style, what's "hot" today will become tomorrow's "tacky." Unfortunately, some Web designers tend to grab onto the hottest new trend, despite its relevance or need.

Why does this happen? The answer is ego. Many design firms do not design for the customer. They design for themselves and their competitors, to say "look what we can do."

A great example of fad is the loathsome animated Flash home page introduction. Very few customers come to a site to watch these ridiculous commercials. They come for information or to conduct a transaction. A Flash intro falls directly in conflict with their goals.

If anything, the leaner years of the dot-com era are forcing companies to do more with less. Simple fixes to navigation can make a big impact on business. As Web-design expert, Jakob Nielsen, reminds us: "The opportunity cost is high from focusing attention on a fad instead of spending the time, money, and management bandwidth on improving basic customer service and usability."[8]

Appropriate graphic design

Graphic design works best when it is appropriate to the customer's goals. In this chapter we have described the elements that add up to an appropriate commerce experience: speed, ease of use, personalization, branding, and consistency. But these parameters merely begin to define the level of graphic depth that is appropriate to the experience.

Mark Hurst, founder and president of Creative Good, is widely credited for popularizing the term "customer experience" and the methodology around it.

Hurst says that it is the experience itself that defines the level of graphic design: "At a banking site, for example, what customer wants to be slowed down by flashy graphics, no matter how 'compelling'? Sites at which customers want to conduct bland transactions as quickly as

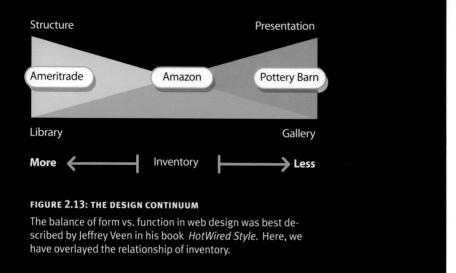

Structure   Presentation

Ameritrade   Amazon   Pottery Barn

Library   Gallery

More ⟵   Inventory   ⟶ **Less**

FIGURE 2.13: THE DESIGN CONTINUUM
The balance of form vs. function in web design was best described by Jeffrey Veen in his book *HotWired Style*. Here, we have overlayed the relationship of inventory.

possible will naturally become visually bland and fast and easy! And sites where customers want a more visual experience should and will become more visually compelling."[9]

The balance of form versus function in Web design was best described by Jeffrey Veen in his 1997 book *HotWired Style: Principles of Building Smart Web Sites*. Veen makes the point that all Web sites fall somewhere on a spectrum, with structure on one end and presentation on the other (See Fig. 2.13). Highly structured sites focus on pure functionality and information. Sites concerned with presentation focus on style and appearance.

The same holds true for commerce. Banking sites, like Ameritrade or Schwab, are on one end. Catalog sites, like Pottery Barn or JCrew, are on the other. Most fall in between, like Amazon. In Fig. 2.13, we have overlaid the impact of commerce inventory on Veen's spectrum. It's more difficult to have a graphic-intensive design if you have 100,000 products. But if you have only a hundred products, the level of graphic intensity can be high.

Keeping your design appropriate to your visitor's needs is an excellent jumping off point for entering the first phase of building a commerce Web site: information design. During the information-design phase, you will develop a thorough understanding of your customer, their product inventory and the technology that will be used to build the site.

[1] Zeldman, Jeffrey. "Style vs. Design" Adobe.com. (Aug. 2001), http://www.adobe.com:80/web/features/zeldman20000821/main.html

[2] Bhatti, Bouch, Kuchinsky. "Integrating User-Perceived Quality into Web Server Design" http://www9.org/w9cdrom/92/92.html

[3] Bhatti, Bouch, Kuchinsky. "Integrating User-Perceived Quality into Web Server Design" http://www9.org/w9cdrom/92/92.html

[4] Keynote Systems can be found online at http://www.keynote.com/

[5] Nielsen, Jakob, "Did Poor Usability Kill E-Commerce?" Alertbox, Aug. 19, 2001 http://www.useit.com

[6] Miller, George A. "The Magical Number Seven, Plus or Minus Two." The Psychological Review, 1956, vol. 63, pp. 81–97.

[7] Jakob Nielsen. Alertbox, May 30, 1999: "Top 10 New Mistakes of Web Design" http://www.useit.com/alertbox/990530.html

[8] Jakob Nielsen. Useit.com Alertbox May 30, 1999, http://www.useit.com/alertbox/990530.html

[9] Hurst, Mark. "The Web's Identity Crisis." GoodExperience.com, January 21, 2000, http://www.goodexperience.com/columns/012100identity.html

chapter 3

INFORMATION DESIGN FOR COMMERCE
Building a foundation for the user experience

In this book, we stress the importance of process. Naturally, there are moments in the process that are more critical to the project's success than others, because they will have an impact on decisions made later on.

Information design is one such juncture. You establish awareness of your company's goals and your customer's goals. Once you have this understanding, your Web team can choose appropriate technology and information to achieve those goals, inter-action designers can create navigation, and presentation designers can combine navigation and content. The information-design stage is not unlike building the foundation of your home. If it's not level, you are destined to a life where your coffee slides off the kitchen table every morning and you roll out of bed each night.

In their insightful book, *Interactivity by Design,* designers Ray Kristof and Amy Satran show that there is no perfect formula for designing such interactive products as a commerce Web site. "There is no interactive product," they wrote, "that cannot benefit from clearly expressed goals, a well-defined audience, and a focused design plan."[1]

To design something both useful and visually appealing, your team will have to brainstorm, explore, and test many concepts. Add the competing political interests of any organization and the vagaries of constantly evolving technologies, and it will be easy to lose sight of the problem you set out to solve. To keep the development team in sync with the organization, you must come together and articulate a set of goals.

Even if you're on a team with a separate information designer, you should be involved or be explicitly made aware of all information design decisions. Many information design tasks may seem more like project management and less like traditional design to you. But in truth, this is design at its core—defining the problem, and devising a solution.

Know Thyself

The first step for a Web-development team is to make sure that everyone, including executive management, understands and agrees on the project's goals (See Fig. 3.1). You must have answers to these important questions:

• **What is the company's mission statement?**

This usually exists somewhere in an annual report. If not, just ask for it. It will help you understand what business the company is in, and how they view their role in society. A mission statement might read something like this: "Make money by marketing and selling inexpensive, casual clothing to teenagers and young adults in the Pacific Northwest."

• **How does the Web site support that mission?**

The purpose of the Web site may be to help market the clothes, sell the clothes, or both. Or, the goal of the Web site may be to strengthen relationships with existing customers.

Corporate Vision/Strategy

Web Site Goals

Question: How will the Web site help our business achieve its goals? How will we measure the site's success?

User Profile

Question: Who is the target customer and what are their goals when coming to the site?

Content Inventory

Question: What content will customers need to achieve their goals?

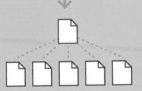

Information Organization

Question: What is the best way to organize the content so that customers can achieve their goals?

- **What are the short-term and long-term goals for the Web site?**

Is the short-term goal to sell the company's top products and test the waters? Then, in the long-term, incrementally expand the Web site to include the rest of the product line and go after a national customer base?

- **How will the company measure success?**

Usually there is a revenue goal involved here, laid out by executive management, such as: "We need to make at least $400,000 in revenue in our first year." Or it could be combined with a customer relationship goal: "We want to get 35,000 registered customers in our database by the fourth quarter, and make an additional 15 percent in revenue."

Understanding a company's vision, business plan, culture, and resources is part of defining goals. Goal statements usually come from a strategy team or Web commerce executive leadership. Your job is to simply have these goals spelled out for you and the development team.

If no one has already done so, take it upon yourself to write a Web site goal statement and present it to management and the rest of the development team. It's imperative that everyone be on the same page.

A Web site goal statement is not unlike a company's mission statement. "Company X needs to create a commerce Web site" is not a goal statement. A more appropriate goal statement would be: "We will provide incentives for customers to purchase our products online, rather than offline, because it is more cost-effective for our company." A Web site's goal statement is most useful when it includes a little more detail. Consider this example for a regional clothing retailer:

- Reinforce the image of our products as well-made, cost-efficient, and smart (short-term goal).

- Make incremental revenue by allowing customers to buy our clothes directly over the Internet using credit cards (short-term goal; supports company mission statement).

- Provide an online catalog of our products to reduce production and distribution costs of the current printed catalog (short-term goal).

- Extend the reach of the business to national or global audience (long-term goal).

These goals will define the intended result and give you a barometer with which to measure progress. Goals will also guide every decision: Does this solution move us closer to our goals? If not, then the company is unlikely to support the decision and you will have to devise a better solution. Conversely, you will have ask yourself if a design decision moves you closer to meeting user expectations? A good design effectively balances both considerations.

FIGURE 3.2
STARTING TO UNDERSTAND YOUR CUSTOMER

Most customer research focuses on identifying the demographic, psychographic, and geographic characteristics of a particular audience. This information can greatly assist you in developing a profile of your target customer.

Demographic
Tangible and specific characteristics:
• Age
• Gender
• Income
• Job
• Education
• Ethnic group
• Stage of life (college student, married, retired)

Psychographic
Less tangible traits, dealing with attitudes, beliefs, needs and desires:
• Lifestyle
• Adventurous/ Cautious
• Frugal/ Spendthrift
• Socially conscious/ Self-centered
• Active/Couch potato

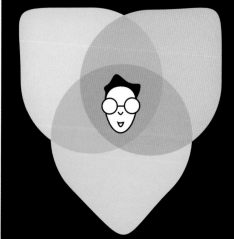

Geographic
Based on the location of your target customer:
• Home/Work
• City/Town/State
• Country
• Climate

Know Thy Customer

If there were Ten Commandments for the online business world, "know thy customer" would be at the top of the tablet. Yet, it's clear that many commerce sites need guidance to the path of righteousness. Forrester Research graded thirty business-to-business Web sites and found that each one failed basic tests of value, ease of use, and reliability.

According to the report, "Web sites ignore customer goals and fail to meet the basic require-ments of a good user experience."[2] No wonder so many sites end up redesigned or elimi-nated when the economy tightens.

During the information-design phase, the Web team should have been given voluminous binders of research about your site's target audience. Research reports are bursting with tables and charts of psychographic and demographic characteristics, which tell you where your customers live, what they shop for, how old they are, what they like and what they don't (See Fig 3.2).

FIGURE 3.3
PROFILES PROVIDE FOCUS

Extensive customer research, on its own, fails to provide a precise portrait of a site visitor. Broad interpretations won't be enough to effectively direct the design process.

SEEING TOO MANY CUSTOMER SEGMENTATIONS

We want to be hip to attract the teen crowd. Our site has to have a lot of flashy animation and thumpin' background music.

We're going after males in 18–34 demo. We gotta have a sports component. Can we do something with NASCAR?

It says here that 52% of our target demographic has kids. Should we make a section with games for kids?

We've got 13% of our target audience who are power users with broadband access. We should have streaming video.

USING A CUSTOMER PROFILE

Our profile, Dave, is 25. He wants to learn about the features of our product quickly. He's not interested in flashy graphics.

Dave is a loyal Red Wings fan. Maybe we can add some related hockey merchandise to his personal shopping page.

Dave cares more about getting the best price than finding the name brand. We should offer product comparisons.

Dave is most likely to access our site from home. He has a 56Kbps modem. We should make sure our pages download fast.

But what do you do with all this material? The marketing manager might be able to boil it down to a target segment for you: "We are going after women, 25 to 35, with household income of $75,000+, college graduates, like to travel, shop online, with 2.17 kids."

This faceless audience description gets a designer into the ballpark, but it's not going to help you to hit a home run. High-level market segmentations don't provide the insight needed to drive an effective user experience (See Fig 3.3). No one is a mother of 2.17 children. To design a valuable experience, you need a precise tool to guide your decisions during the development process.

Designing for One

Your tool will be a profile—a hypothetical, but detailed, person. The profile concept was pioneered by interaction design expert Alan Cooper. In his book *The Inmates Are Running the Asylum,* he presents this powerful, but simple, concept: Develop a precise description of your visitor and what he or she wants to accomplish. Success will follow because you created a "goal-directed" solution for one rather than a compromise for many.[3] (See Fig. 3.4).

The unassuming roll-aboard suitcase is a potent example of how a profile drives a successful design (See Fig. 3.5). This small suitcase with wheels and a retractable handle revolutionized the luggage industry. Walk through any airline terminal and you'll see plenty of people rolling their luggage close behind.

However, that luggage was never intended to be used by the average traveler. The roll-aboard suitcase was originally designed for commercial airline crews. The precision of the crew profiles made it easy for the luggage designers to see the scope of the problem. As a result, they created luggage that maneuvered well through aisles and stowed easily in overhead compartments. Success came when someone realized that this design solved a problem for the general traveler, not just airline personnel.

Traditional approach

To attract the largest audience, sites add many features and services. The problem with this approach is that it will compromise one customer's experience or another's. As a result, most leave with an unsatisfactory experience.

Profile approach

Focusing on a great solution for one person increases the likelihood that you will have created a better solution for many others. Of course, you'll never please them all.

FIGURE 3.5: ROLL-ABOARD SUITCASE

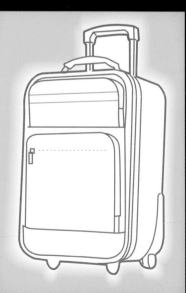

Profiles provide many benefits. They reveal the specific needs of target customers. It costs less to develop a site that meets your target profiles' goals, rather than a site with every possible function and feature for every possible customer. The end result is feature creep—a Web site that is jack of all trades, but master of none. Customers are overwhelmed with the choices, and end up only using core features.

Profiles aid in communication and decision-making during the site-development process. A team brainstorming session might reveal a hundred useful Web site functions, but you have the resources to create only ten. How do you choose between

adding 3D-product photography versus a feature that enables customers to post product reviews? You can say, "Our target profile, Shelley, has a 56k dial-up connection. She wouldn't wait for a 500KB download, but she definitely would want read what other users have to say."

A profile is not meant to exclude a secondary audience but to guarantee that your primary target customer is completely satisfied. You can have up to three target profiles, each requiring unique solutions. If you need more, you probably need to rethink the scope of the site.

A profile is a hypothetical person, not to be confused with the precise description of any one customer. The problem with picking one real person is that they have idiosyncrasies that are not found across the population. For example, you might not like to type and only use the mouse. To design a site that requires only input with the mouse would clearly be unacceptable to many others.

Market research
From this research you will get the initial parameters of your intended target. For example, if you are targeting 18- to 24-year-old males, then your profile should be of that age and gender.

Informal research
Some of the best information can come from interviews with friends and co-workers or by holding informal lunches with people who are similar to your target audience. Ask them questions that might provide insight into their daily behavior. "Why do you shop online, if there's a mall next to your home?"

In the designer's mind
Take all of this information and create a profile that seems believable but not overly representative of any one person.

Shelley Cruise
Age: 42
Occupation: Psychologist
Height: 5'4"
Weight: 135 lb.
Right-handed
Personal: Shelley is in good health and just gave birth to her son Kellen. She has been married to Koz for six years and does most of her shopping online at home on her Dell 800Mhz Pentium, because it's more convenient than going to the mall.

Building a Profile

According to Cooper, the profile should be described in explicit detail, until the customer becomes real in your mind. Average customers are too elastic, they can be stretched in your mind to fit any scenario. Profiles are clear and specific and will respond to a specific solution.

The information to build a profile comes from a variety of sources (See Fig 3.6). A profile has a name (like Shelley), a profession (psychologist), a place of residence (1234 Canyon Road, Irving, TX), maybe a pet (a three-year-old German shepherd). Before you create a profile, keep in mind:

• **Your profile must be precise but not necessarily perfect:** In the suitcase example, it was more important to describe the target profile as an airline captain rather than a generic pilot. If the profile was a student pilot, their luggage needs would have been much different. A student pilot trains in small airplanes that don't have aisles.

• **You are not the target profile:** You must separate your habits and skills from that of your customer. You are probably a power user, with a broadband Internet connection and a powerful computer. Your experience and familiarity with interactive environments is likely more advanced than your target profile.

- **Stay away from stereotypes:** Stereotypes are one-dimensional. Profiles are idealized but real. Thinking that "Bubba" drives a truck, hunts, and has kids isn't helpful when designing a Web site. But, knowing that Bubba is a big Aggies fan, drives a red Dodge Ram pickup thirty minutes to his Dallas office, and enjoys finding antique carpentry tools on eBay *is* useful.

Everyone on your Web-development team needs to have a copy of the profile to ensure that when they create or debate a solution, they do so with the profile in mind. Profile awareness is especially useful for the technology members of your team, who are often too far removed from intimate customer details. Without it, the tech team might make decisions that will prevent designers from creating a good customer experience.

Customer goals

A good Web site design team understands and exploits customer motivation—the universal and transcendent psychological conditions that provoke us to act (See Fig. 3.7). These wants, desires, or needs drive us to create goals. Understanding customer goals helps you to identify, prioritize, and structure information in a way that helps customers achieve these goals as easily as possible.

En route to a goal, a person performs tasks that have unique objectives that are in service to the ultimate goal. These tasks can be singular (perform a search for something) or describe an entire process (find the cheapest plane fare). We will build further on this concept in Chapter 4.

FIGURE 3.7: DEFINING EXPERIENCE
Experience is the sum of tasks and objectives carried out on a site. Motivation fuels the desire to complete these steps to reach the ultimate goal.

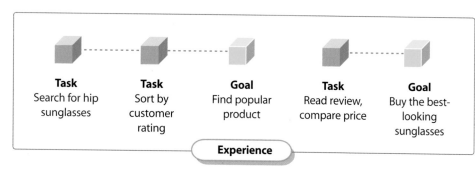

Motivation
"To be liked."

Task
Search for hip sunglasses

Task
Sort by customer rating

Goal
Find popular product

Task
Read review, compare price

Goal
Buy the best-looking sunglasses

Experience

Ultimate Goal
"To look more attractive."

Techno, Ergo Sum

World-renowned media theorist Marshall McLuhan described a vision of technological determinism by saying that we shape our tools and, in turn, our tools shape us.[4]

This vision will be true for your commerce site, because technology is often the tail that wags the dog. It's not uncommon for technologists and designers alike to become enamored with the latest whiz-bang tool—whether it's a new version of Shockwave or a Solaris server. But it's not smart to deploy a technology of fad and fancy on the Web site of a Fortune 500 business.

A popular concept in tech circles is the goal of being "technology agnostic." If you are technology agnostic, you judge tools on their merits and don't allow yourself to become inflexibly or blindly committed to one solution. However, this philosophy is seldom applied in practice. People are biased toward familiar tools and seek comfort in technology that has worked before, even when that technology may not be appropriate for a different task.

It's easy to allow personal comfort—your own and that of others—to affect your technology choices without considering the end results. But remember that, as the designer, it is your mission to speak for the customer. While others on your team might be blinded by their own comfort or their desire to strut their technical expertise in the newest technologies, you need to take a firm stand to guard the customer's key goals.

For example, say you have begun outlining a commerce site and the tech team recommends using Active Server Pages on a Windows NT server with a Microsoft Access Database. Is that the best combination of tools to run your site, or just the most familiar one? You might not have the expertise to know, but you should not hesitate to ask questions from the customer's viewpoint, as well as your own (See Fig. 3.8).

1. Will this technology limit our audience?

2. Will it prevent us from meeting our profile's needs?

3. Will it contribute to a fast site? How fast can we deliver search results?

4. Will it handle a large amount of simultaneous traffic (i.e., will it scale)?

5. Will it force the design team to compromise usability?

6. What flexibility in template design does our system provide?

7. How frequently and easily can we make changes to the design?

8. Does the technology place any other constraints on the designer?

9. Will I need to learn any programming or special code to implement this technology?

10. What can the design team do to help?

Much of the technology your site will use works behind the scenes. Unlike the world of print design, where you could see, hear, and touch the printing press, the mechanisms that publish your site are usually hidden away in some bunkerlike room. Because they're invisible, it's easy to convince yourself that they don't exist, or at least don't have anything to do with your work as a designer.

On the contrary, it is important to understand the technologies your site will use. Greater background knowledge will help you:

- Translate user goals and content into a structured technical concept.

- Uncover possibilities and limitations of the chosen technology for your design.

- Effectively participate on the Web-development team.

- Modify or write basic code as needed without having to rely upon the tech team.

- Better understand the problems and frustrations inherent in the technical-development process.

The biggest obstacle to achieving a solid understanding of technology is a lack of clear or agreed-upon nomenclature. When you talk about technology, you are talking about ideas and concepts instead of physical objects—terms like business logic, platform, content repository, middleware. These ideas are brought to life as lines of code. Their abstract nature can cause confusion when you communicate with others on your team.

Even well-known terms can be interpreted differently. For example, look at these definitions of the term "portal":

- "A term, generally synonymous with gateway, for a World Wide Web site that is or proposes to be a major starting site for users when they get connected to the Web or that users tend to visit as an anchor site." —*whatis.com*

- "Web site or service that offers a broad array of resources and services, such as e-mail, forums, search engines, and on-line shopping malls."

  —*Webopedia.Internet.com*

- "Major visiting center for Internet users." —*www.harvardcomputing.com/eGlossary*

If someone tells you "we want you design a portal," based on these definitions, would you create something rich with features like e-mail, shopping malls, and forums? Or would creating a wildly popular site, regardless of features, fit the bill? To add to the confusion, two of the definitions don't specify that a portal has to be a Web site at all.

The chance for misunderstanding rises substantially when you're handed technical diagrams of oil cans, gears, and Lego blocks, or when conversations turn to the verbal alphabet soup of today's Web technology: JSP, XML, XSL, PERL, and so on (See Fig. 3.9).

Terminology is not a trivial point. Poor communication and understanding can threaten the success of a Web project. If someone on the tech team says, "The Oracle database has search capabilities built-in. With that, we could build a search engine in a few days, at very little cost." Don't say, "Great!" and walk away, thinking the problem has been solved. It's now your turn to ask exactly what kind of results that search will yield, how quickly it produces results, and will it scale to the demand of 10,000 simultaneous searches. This conversation should proceed until both parties feel that they have a collective understanding of what's expected.

If you find yourself walking out of technology meetings with your head spinning, there are two things you need to do. First, realize that you don't need to know everything about technology. Racing out to buy the latest Java book might throw you into a deep despair. Don't sweat it. You just need to learn enough to be dangerous—to be able to see the big picture and possible red flags for usability.

Next, try to find someone on the tech team who is willing and able to translate "geek-speak" into something that's understandable. Make them your ally. Take that person out to lunch and pick their brain on the most basic of concepts. You can't hope to tackle the larger issues unless you can grasp the simple stuff like the difference between HTML and XML. Figure 3.10 is a good place to start learning the basics.

Let's cover some general concepts you'll need to recognize when developing a Web site.

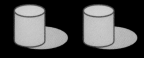

FIGURE 3.9
A DATABASE IS NOT AN OIL CAN

The database icon seen on most presentations looks like an oil drum.

This icon is a visual vestige of an era when computers filled rooms and information was stored on rotating magnetic drums. Today's disk drives are actually very simple databases. They store items in known places for future use.

The modern day database (or relational database) was invented by E. F. Codd at IBM in 1970. Today, the Internet's most powerful sites depend on the flexibility and power of the organization that it provides.

FIGURE 3.10: MARKUP LANGUAGES

These are the most likely technologies with which a designer will have to become intimately familiar.

	Description	Example	Features	Drawbacks
HTML	Hypertext Markup Language: Tags that describe how a browser should display words and images in a Web browser.	`<H1>` `<font color="blue">` **Howdy** `</font></H1>`	• Easy to learn • Saved as text file • Easy to edit • Ignores mistyped tags	• Poor design control • Not rendered by all browsers the same way
DHTML	Dynamic Hypertext Markup Language. HTML with added tags and options.	`<div align="center">` **Howdy**`</div>`	• Enables Web items on a Web page to change their look in response to a customer's actions	• Not interpreted or supported by all browsers
CSS	Cascading Style Sheets: A simple way to control the style of a Web document's visual elements (fonts, colors, tables, margins, etc).	H1 { font-size: 36pt; font-color: blue; font-face: Georgia, Times }	• Gives designer greater control over typography • Can reduce page sizes • Easy to change style without rewriting HTML	• Inconsistent browser support
XHTML	Extensible Hypertext Markup Language: The latest version of HTML that adheres to XML standards.	`<font color="blue">` **Howdy**`</font> `	• Same as HTML but allows you to create your own custom tags	• Same problems as HTML • Tags can seem confusing
XML	Extensible Markup Language. Unlike HTML, XML describes something about the data, not how it should look.	`<greeting>`**Howdy** `</greeting>`	• Can create custom tags • Describes data, not page layout • Saved as text • Easy to exchange data with other sites	• Tags can seem confusing and get verbose
XSL	Extensible Stylesheet Language. Describes how a XML file should be presented to the user.	`<xsl:value-of select="greeting" />` ` `	• Set styles for XML data without affecting it — for example, make all movie titles black and any cast member gray	• Programming logic adds to complexity

What is a server?

A server is a computer program that provides files, data, or other content in response to a request from another computer. The program might use one computer, or several computers linked together to handle more visitor traffic. Such a setup is called a "cluster."

There are several types of servers. Some handle simple local networks so groups of people can share files or printer resources. Others, like application or mail servers, are highly specialized, while Web servers orchestrate other servers and complex tasks. For a list of common server types, see Fig. 3.11.

Client-server architecture

The Web is based on client-server architecture, a means of consolidating computing resources at one point in the network. One server (or cluster of servers) can serve many clients, such as Web browsers. HTTP (Hypertext Transfer Protocol) provides the rules for communicating between the two. The advantage of this approach is a network that responds quickly and with little cost to the client because the user's computer and Web browser draw on the server's capabilities.

The front-end of this site architecture (aka the client-side) is the most visible part of the site, and the one designers should know best. It includes the most familiar components of a Web page—HTML, images (GIF, JPEG) and various other types of content (QuickTime, MP3). The front-end also

FIGURE 3.11: DIFFERENT SERVERS USED ON COMMERCE SITES

Commerce sites are highly dynamic, handle large amounts of changing information, and must adeptly handle e-mail and credit transactions securely. Given those requirements, commerce sites must distribute the labor to specialized servers so that overall performance and functionality of the site will remain robust for the visitor.

	What it does
Application Server	Used for complex transaction-based sites, application servers handle the requests between the visitor's browser and databases on the site's back-end. Application servers also improve performance and provide additional server security. **Examples:** BEA WebLogic, ColdFusion, Oracle, Orion, Netscape, WebObjects, WebSphere
Transaction Server	Processes and maintains integrity of check and credit card transactions with banking computers using encrypted transmissions. **Examples:** IBM CICS Transaction Server, Microsoft Transaction Server
List Server	Distributes e-mail to customer lists and handles subscriptions, newsletters, and other scheduled mailings. Not to be confused with a mail server, which handles e-mail for individual Internet users. **Examples:** LISTSERV, Majordomo
Web Server	A program that serves HTML content to browsers over the Internet using HTTP. **Examples:** Apache, iPlanet, Microsoft IIS

FIGURE 3.12
KNOWING YOUR BACK FROM YOUR FRONT

Designers should be somewhat knowledgeable about the technical architecture of their commerce system, from the client to the back-end. This behind-the-scenes knowledge will make you better qualified to participate in decisions about technology. It will give you greater appreciation for how specific technical choices will affect the customer experience.

Front-end

Customer directly interacts with technology here

Customer

Browser

Computer

Presentation layer

The front-end (or browser-side) encompasses the technologies that the customer comes into direct contact with, like HTML or Flash. Designers spend most of their time dealing with scripts and creating graphics.

HTML

Back-end

The customer doesn't directly interact with these technologies

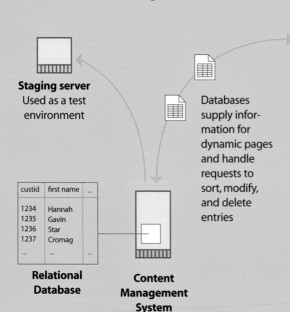

Staging server
Used as a test environment

Databases supply information for dynamic pages and handle requests to sort, modify, and delete entries

custid	first name	...
1234	Hannah	
1235	Gavin	
1236	Star	
1237	Cromag	
...	...	...

Relational Database

Content Management System

Public Web servers
Deliver HTML from templates, static files with images, content

Secure server
Used for transactions

Application server
Routes request, passes information between servers and the database

LDAP server
Used to identify customers

Business layer

The glue that holds the front and back-ends together. Requests are received and processed. For example, the server takes a search word for a product and turns it into a question for the database. The resulting data is inserted into the appropriate search page template. The processing component of this layer is sometimes referred to as "business logic," which is a bit misleading because most of this processing has nothing to do with business.

Database layer

Relational databases are the backbone of dynamic commerce sites. Relational databases let you organize, sort, and link information.

FIGURE 3.13
WHAT IS A RELATIONAL DATABASE?

A relational database stores information in tables. Tables are made up of rows and columns not unlike an address book or spreadsheet. The key difference is that database tables must have one column with a unique identifier. This identifier or primary key enables the database to link or relate different tables.

It is this unique ability to relate different databases that allows the same information (products, reviews, customers) to be manipulated and presented in a way that is most useful for the visitor.

Example of a table:

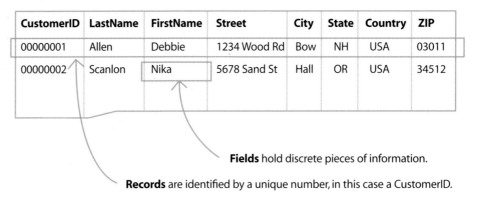

CustomerID	LastName	FirstName	Street	City	State	Country	ZIP
00000001	Allen	Debbie	1234 Wood Rd	Bow	NH	USA	03011
00000002	Scanlon	Nika	5678 Sand St	Hall	OR	USA	34512

Fields hold discrete pieces of information.

Records are identified by a unique number, in this case a CustomerID.

Example of related tables:

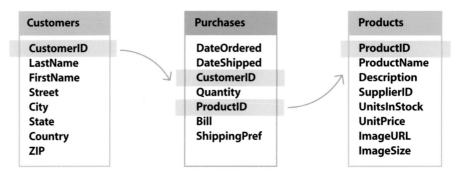

Customers
- **CustomerID**
- LastName
- FirstName
- Street
- City
- State
- Country
- ZIP

Purchases
- DateOrdered
- DateShipped
- **CustomerID**
- Quantity
- **ProductID**
- Bill
- ShippingPref

Products
- **ProductID**
- ProductName
- Description
- SupplierID
- UnitsInStock
- UnitPrice
- ImageURL
- ImageSize

How information is retrieved

Relational databases let applications access and modify them using a standard set of commands called Structured Query Language (SQL). SQL queries return data in the form of a "result set." The result set is like a small custom-built database that can be tailored to the customer's request.

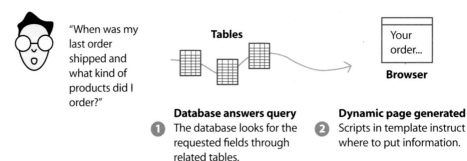

"When was my last order shipped and what kind of products did I order?"

Tables

Your order...

Browser

Database answers query
1 The database looks for the requested fields through related tables.

Dynamic page generated
2 Scripts in template instruct where to put information.

includes some programming (aka scripting) that allows Web pages to exchange information with the servers.

The back-end of this system includes components of the Web site that support, but do not come in direct contact with, the visitor. Databases, mail servers, and transaction servers are common examples. For the typical designer, the back-end can be an intimidating place. But don't be overwhelmed, because no one on your team will expect you to worry about these details. They are fully the responsibility of your technology-development team. Figure 3.12 shows an overview of how this architecture works.

Databases

Databases reside in the back-end of a Web-production system and are the backbone of any commerce site. When someone on your team refers to a database, they are usually talking about a "relational" database. Figure 3.13 explains what a relational database is and how it works. Amazon.com is a great example of database magic in action. Type in a book title and Amazon returns a wealth of information from the bare-bones (author, price, page count) to the obsessive (a look inside, similar books, reader reviews and rankings).

Publishing systems

Publishing systems, also known as content management systems (CMS), are applications that make it easy for different people to simultaneously contribute to producing a site. The division of labor is enabled by sophisticated programs, which coordinate the exchange of information between databases, template designs, and input from editors or other content producers. Figure 3.14 outlines how a publishing system makes these updates possible. Companies such as Vignette and Broadvision are the leading vendors of these systems.

Architecture issues that affect design

Workflow isn't the only seemingly technical issue that can have a significant effect on how you design and how successfully your work is implemented. Several other seemingly obscure tech-talk issues are important to you as well.

Network transparency

Transparency refers to the illusion that the server is acting only for the person accessing it. When the server doesn't respond quickly, sends back the wrong data, or lets someone else buy the last DVD in stock even though another customer ordered it first, transparency is lost. When transparency is lost, the business is probably losing customers.

Server modification

Many factors can affect a server's ability to respond to a visitor's request. When discussion turns to modifying the server, a designer should ask how the server's performance or its ability to handle traffic would be affected.

Session management

Session management requires that the server follow and remember a series of requests by a customer and then process all of them at once. For example, you wouldn't want the server to open your bank account, add a deposit and then forget to update your balance. Session management programs affect usability. The programs figure out when a shopping cart has been abandoned or keeps track of an order while the customer jumps around the site (See Fig. 3.15).

FIGURE 3.14: HOW A CONTENT MANAGEMENT SYSTEM WORKS

It's likely that your commerce site will use some type of content management system. Each system operates in the same basic way. A large database is connected to group of applications, which in turn generates pages based on your design templates. Understanding the workflow in such a system will help the designer become aware of how it might affect design.

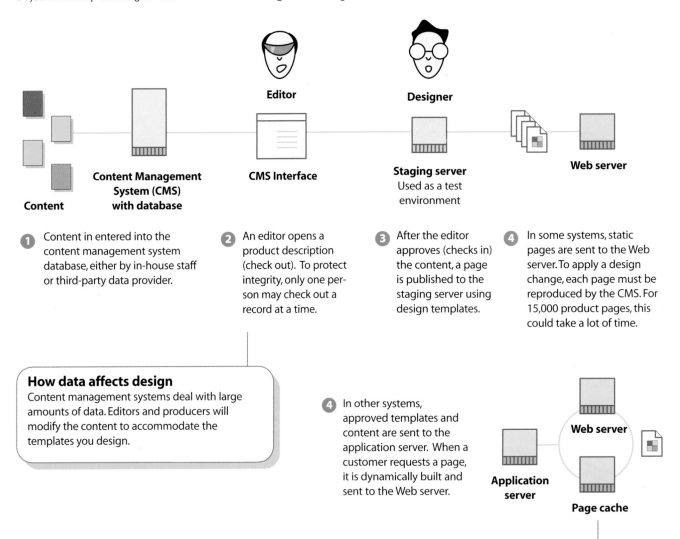

Editor

Designer

Content

Content Management System (CMS) with database

CMS Interface

Staging server
Used as a test environment

Web server

① Content in entered into the content management system database, either by in-house staff or third-party data provider.

② An editor opens a product description (check out). To protect integrity, only one person may check out a record at a time.

③ After the editor approves (checks in) the content, a page is published to the staging server using design templates.

④ In some systems, static pages are sent to the Web server. To apply a design change, each page must be reproduced by the CMS. For 15,000 product pages, this could take a lot of time.

How data affects design

Content management systems deal with large amounts of data. Editors and producers will modify the content to accommodate the templates you design.

④ In other systems, approved templates and content are sent to the application server. When a customer requests a page, it is dynamically built and sent to the Web server.

Web server

Application server

Page cache

What is caching?

To help speed the delivery of dynamic pages, many pages, such as search results, may be stored and reused for the next site visitor. This is called "caching." When a change has been made to a piece of content like a photo, or a template has been revised, the CMS must clear the cache in order for the customer to see this change reflected on the site.

FIGURE 3.15: HOW SESSION MANAGEMENT WORKS

Session management is how a Web server tracks who a visitor is, where they go, what they put in their cart, and various other information. It is a critical component of any commerce site and can affect usability, for example, by making a visitor register on your site before buying.

Without session management

"Show me the product page."
"Get me search results for shoes."
"Add this to my shopping cart."
"Go to checkout."
"Add this to my shopping cart."
"Go to checkout."

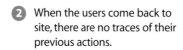

1 Without session management, the server doesn't connect each visitor to their requests.

2 When the users come back to site, there are no traces of their previous actions.

With session management

"Show me the product page."
"Get me search results for shoes."
"Add this to my shopping cart."
"Go to checkout."
"Add this to my shopping cart."
"Go to checkout."

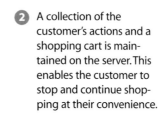

1 The server sets a cookie in the customer's browser. The cookie holds a unique ID that the server uses to track the customer and what they've bought.

2 A collection of the customer's actions and a shopping cart is maintained on the server. This enables the customer to stop and continue shopping at their convenience.

Need to know

Session management can be complicated. Ask the tech team how you can keep session management invisible to the customer. For example, a smart session management system should work even if the visitor's browser does not accept cookies.

FIGURE 3.16: STATIC VS. DYNAMIC

Web pages that are assembled when requested by the site visitor are called dynamic. Most pages on the Web are considered "static," meaning they are HTML files whose content does not change. Static pages are also referred to as "flat files."

Static page

① Visitor clicks on Movies

Server
② Server looks for file movies.html

Send HTML
③ movies.html is sent back to the visitor.

Need to know
Dynamic pages are not always entirely built on the fly. Only a small piece of information can be dynamic, such as date or time. Some systems save assembled pages as static pages to keep the workload on the server low.

Dynamic page

① Visitor clicks on Movies

Server
② Server looks for file movies.jsp

Find template page
③ movies.jsp is found and the server looks for any scripts in the file.

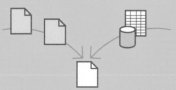

Assemble page
④ Server interprets scripts and adds HTML code and information from the database.

Send HTML
⑤ Server sends HTML to visitor.

Dynamic vs. static pages

Web pages fall into one of two categories: static or dynamic. Designers used to painstakingly produce pages by hand, coding in every graphic, text element, and line of HTML. These static pages were a nightmare to update and maintain because every small change required personal attention. Over time, site designers realized that maintaining these pages was a drain on staff resources.

Thankfully, the front-end has become a much more exciting place for designers because most pages are produced dynamically. Dynamic pages are built on the fly as a direct response to a visitor's requests. Commerce sites could not survive without them. Figure 3.16 shows the difference between these two page types.

For the designer, there are some important benefits to dynamic pages:

• Fewer pages (templates) to maintain.

• More opportunity for meaningful interaction design.

• Allows content to be updated frequently.

• Easy to implement site changes.

Dynamic pages let the designer focus more on the design than on cutting and pasting HTML. But working in this realm does require some basic scripting skills. Dynamic sites use templates, which are HTML pages filled with special instructions that you insert. These instructions are part of a scripting language like Java Server Pages, Active Server Pages or PHP (See Fig. 3.17).

When a visitor requests a dynamic page, the server reads the scripts and fills in the rest of the page with the proper information—usually from a database. JSP is a popular scripting language based on Java. For example, this code, inserted into an HTML file, thanks a first time customer:

```
<html>
<body>
<!-- Get the top navigation -->
<%@ include file = "topnavbar.html" %>
<% if (userorders = 1) {
out.println ("Thank you for your first order!")
  } %>
</body>
</html>
```

Dynamic pages and the supporting scripting languages might sound intimidating. But they provide powerful tools for the enterprising designer. This technology gives a designer the ability to create pages that transform based on the changing nature of the content and the way the content has been used. An auction that is about to

Some good technology books for your library: JSP: *A Beginner's Guide by Gary Bollinger;* Learning XML *by Erik T. Ray,* PHP and MySQL Development *by Luke Welling;* Designing Active Server Pages *by Scott Mitchell.*

	Description	Example	Features	Drawbacks
ASP	Active Server Page: An HTML page with embedded VBScript, which is processed by a Microsoft server when the visitor hits the page	The time is <%=Now()%>	• Uses popular scripting language VBScript • Lots of learning resources on the Web and in books • Generally easier and faster to code than more structured programming languages	• Only works on Microsoft server platforms • Scripts slow and reinterpreted each time they are requested
CGI	Common Gateway Interface: Protocol allows HTML to be dynamically created based on data passed to it	Not language specific	• CGI lets the Web server communicate with a program written in any language — most commonly Perl or C	• Each page request relies on a new program being launched, which slows server performance
JavaScript	A scripting language that's interpreted by the Web browser	**document.write ("Howdy");**	• Useful for adding interactive elements like rollovers • Can validate and respond to customer's input before sending it to the server	• Can be slow • May not work the same on all browsers
PHP	A popular, freely shared scripting language. Originally named Personal Home Page Tool	<?echo ("Howdy");?>	• Designed purely for Web-page development • Code more succinct than VBScript or JSP • Works on many platforms	• Helps to have some modest programming experience
JSP	Java Server Page: Similar to ASP. Based on Sun Microsystem's Java language. Lets you add powerful scripts to HTML pages	The time is <%= **new java.util.Date() %>**	• Works on many platforms • JSP page is cached after the first request, which reduces work done by server • Faster than ASP • Can make pages more dynamic with little effort • Uses Java for scripting	• Java is complex • Java not originally designed to serve Web pages • Difficult to debug
VBScript	Scripting language designed for Web servers. A subset of Microsoft's Visual Basic programming language	The time is <%=Now()%>	• Lots of learning resources on the Web and in books • Generally easier and faster to code than more structured programming languages	• Only works on Microsoft server platforms • Scripts slow and reinterpreted each time they are requested

expire, for example, might get presented at the top of a page for only its last hour of bidding. When you begin to work intensively with dynamic pages, you may discover that there is really not as great a distinction drawn between "technical" and "creative" as there is in other types of design. We'll cover this in more detail in Chapter 5.

Tools of your trade

You might not have a choice in the tools you use to design your site. Depending on whether you are part of an in-house team, a consulting design firm, or a freelancer, you may end up working with tools supplied by your client. If you are able to choose your tools, you'll want ones that are robust and sufficiently well-designed for the task that they will save you precious time.

In Fig. 3.18, we examine the types of tools you need to have and the most likely candidates in each category.

Technology is not the sole province of Webmasters, engineers, and programmers. A little knowledge and understanding of technology is a helpful thing for most designers. A deeper knowledge will help you to create powerful customer experiences.

	Tasks	Programs
WYSIWYG HTML editor	• Instant visual representation of code • Good for template design • Program writes code for you • Some can handle special code like JSP	• Adobe GoLive • Macromedia Dreamweaver • Microsoft FrontPage • HotMetal Pro
HTML Text editor	• Can assist code writing by highlighting different HTML tags with color • Good for search and replace functions	• Macromedia HomeSite • BBEdit • NotePad, WordPad
Illustration	• Excellent for prototyping pages • Design navigation bars, logos, buttons, and other graphics	• Adobe Illustrator • Macromedia FreeHand • Corel Draw • Deneba's Canvas
Image editing	• Color correct images • Touch-up image quality • Compress images for fast download • Convert image file formats	• Adobe Photoshop • Macromedia Fireworks • Corel Photo Paint • Lemke's Graphic Converter • Media Cleaner Pro
Specialty	• Web animation — Macromedia Flash & Shockwave, Adobe LiveMotion • Editing movies, video clips — Adobe Premiere, QuickTime Pro, Final Cut Pro • Optimize movies — Media Cleaner Pro • Printable documents — Adobe Acrobat	

Before you buy...
While their programs are more expensive, Adobe and Macromedia have tightly integrated their software, which might save you a lot of time in production.

FIGURE 3.18: DESIGNER'S TOOLBOX

Mining Raw Materials

Now that you have a handle on the goals of the business, your audience, and the production environment, what information does your audience need to be persuaded to buy or sell on your site?

Most companies do not believe they are in the information business. It is true that information is not a core competency of most businesses. In Blockbuster Video stores, they put boxes on the shelf and the product speaks for itself. Good packaging design attracts the eye and guides the customer through basic product information. Sometimes, salespeople in the store can fill in any lacking information and add personal insights.

However, when a company takes its business online, information becomes an integral element for success. To sell a product online, all of the packaging has to be transferred into usable chunks of digital information. This includes not only what's on the product box but also the insights of sales personnel who are trying to sell you the product. At the very least, your online customers will expect a photo of the product and the equivalent of what's on the box. But don't be certain that will close the sale. Because they can't touch the product, customers need a wealth of information to feel comfortable about making a purchase. Consider the difference between buying a piece of software online versus in a store (See Fig. 3.19).

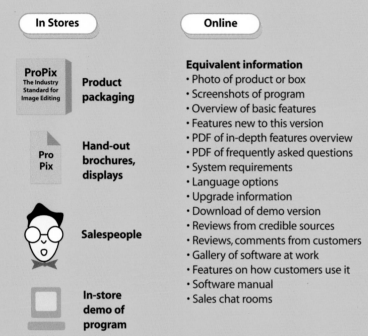

In Stores

ProPix
The Industry
Standard for
Image Editing

Product packaging

Pro Pix

Hand-out brochures, displays

Salespeople

In-store demo of program

Online

Equivalent information
• Photo of product or box
• Screenshots of program
• Overview of basic features
• Features new to this version
• PDF of in-depth features overview
• PDF of frequently asked questions
• System requirements
• Language options
• Upgrade information
• Download of demo version
• Reviews from credible sources
• Reviews, comments from customers
• Gallery of software at work
• Features on how customers use it
• Software manual
• Sales chat rooms

FIGURE 3.19
OFFLINE VS. ONLINE PRODUCT INFORMATION

In a store, the product packaging speaks for itself. When you take a product online, you will have to harvest or create equivalent product information. The question is, how much content do you need to close the online sale?

When you transfer information to an online store, understanding audience expectations becomes valuable. You must anticipate what someone needs to know before they are willing to buy. In stores, some products, like clothes or furniture, live or die on their physical attributes. A customer can feel a sweater, observe its craftsmanship, and try it on with a favorite pair of jeans. Online, that physical contact does not exist. So what type of information will your site provide as a substitute to this powerful tactile experience?

The type of business somewhat defines customer expectations of information. For example, a product manufacturer like Nikon or Sony is expected to provide in-depth product details on its site. A distributor like Best Buy or Amazon may only need to provide a limited subset of this information, but will have to offer customers the ability to compare it with other products.

The questions you must answer in this phase are:

• How much and what kind of content do you need to satisfy your audience?

• Do you have the money in the budget to create the content?

• Do you have the staff with the talent/skills needed to create the content?

• How much time will it take to produce and/or gather this content?

FIGURE 3.20
CONTENT INVENTORY LIST FOR AN AVERAGE COMMERCE WEB SITE

This list will vary widely depending on what you are selling, but it's a good indication of what you might need to consider. Don't forget ancillary content like company info, or help files. Also remember that much of this content may need to be harvested from existing catalogs, brochures and marketing collateral. That will take time, and money, so plan for it.

	Content Item	Task	Have	Need	How to Acquire
Company Information	History	Get from annual report	✓		In-House
	Investor relations	Get from annual report	✓		In-House
	CEO interview	Script, record, digitize		✗	Outsource
	Staff profiles	Shoot digital photos; copy		✗	In-House
Help, Customer Assistance	Site FAQ	Write copy		✗	In-House
	Contact information	Write copy		✗	In-House
	Product manuals	Digitize, PDF convert	✓		In-House
	Discussion forum	Hire moderators		✗	Partner
	Privacy statement	Write copy		✗	In-House
Product Information	Product photos	Digitize	✓		In-House
	Product 3D photos	Shoot, digitize		✗	Outsource
	Product description	Edit copy	✓		In-House
	Product brochure	Edit, digitize, PDF convert		✗	In-House
	Product FAQ	Write copy		✗	In-House
	Competition comparison	Write, HTML & PDF version		✗	Outsource
	Customer comments	Solicit on Web, edit		✗	In-House
	Industry reviews	Edit, acquire permissions	✓		In-House
Advertising and Promotion	Banner ads	Write, design, digitize		✗	In-House, Partner
	Contextual discount ads	Write, design, digitize		✗	In-House, Partner
	Special product photos	Scan, digitize	✓		Outsource
	Marketing copy	Write, edit	✓		In-House
Interface, Web site elements	Logo art	Digitize	✓		In-House
	Control elements	Design, optimize		✗	In-House
	Navigation elements	Design, optimize		✗	In-House
	Category headers	Design, optimize		✗	In-House
	Partner logo art	Digitize	✓		In-House

To answer these questions you create a content inventory list— often the first reality checkpoint in creating a commerce Web site. To this point, everything has been theoretical. Now the rubber meets the road for resources, budgeting and timetables.

The earlier you create this list, the better you'll be able to predict the consequences of your design decisions. This is why you shouldn't waste valuable time prototyping early in the process. We've seen too many designers walk into meetings and absolutely wow a management team, only to have the design compromised by lack of resources to follow through on the necessary content.

Creating the list

A content inventory is a list of raw materials needed for the Web site. These materials are the core building blocks of the site, but they also play a critical role in defining a site's brand identity and personality. List every text, audio, video, illustration, and photographic element in granular detail. For example, instead of just writing "Staff Profile" on your list, go one level deeper and say "250-word bio, contact info, and photograph."

In Fig. 3.20, we show an abbreviated example of a content inventory list for a commerce site. Note the content categories. While Product Information is obvious, it's easy to overlook other areas such as Help or Advertising/Promotion. Every department in the company will want some presence on the Web, so make sure that they are all represented on the list. This will help prevent having to create content at the last minute.

Begin by analyzing the content-inventory list of your major competitors. This will help you see what content you need to be on par with the competition, as well as help you define how you will differentiate from them.

Have vs. need

Good content is rarely easy to create or inexpensive to acquire. It's important to evaluate the sources and quality of your content. The following list isn't just helpful for you; it's for all the bean counters and executives who will be budgeting the site, too. Here are the potential sources for commerce content:

- **In-house:** The company or Web-development team will create the content. Assuming the right talent is available, you are most likely to get what you want and have it match the brand personality and site design.

- **Legacy content:** This content is harvested from the existing infrastructure, such as product boxes or packaging, catalogs, annual reports, and marketing collateral. Don't immediately mark "have" next to these items. The design team will need to digitize and edit many of these materials to make them appropriate for the Web.

FIGURE 3.21: EXAMINE WORKFLOW

When deciding what content to create, consider the process needed to support it.

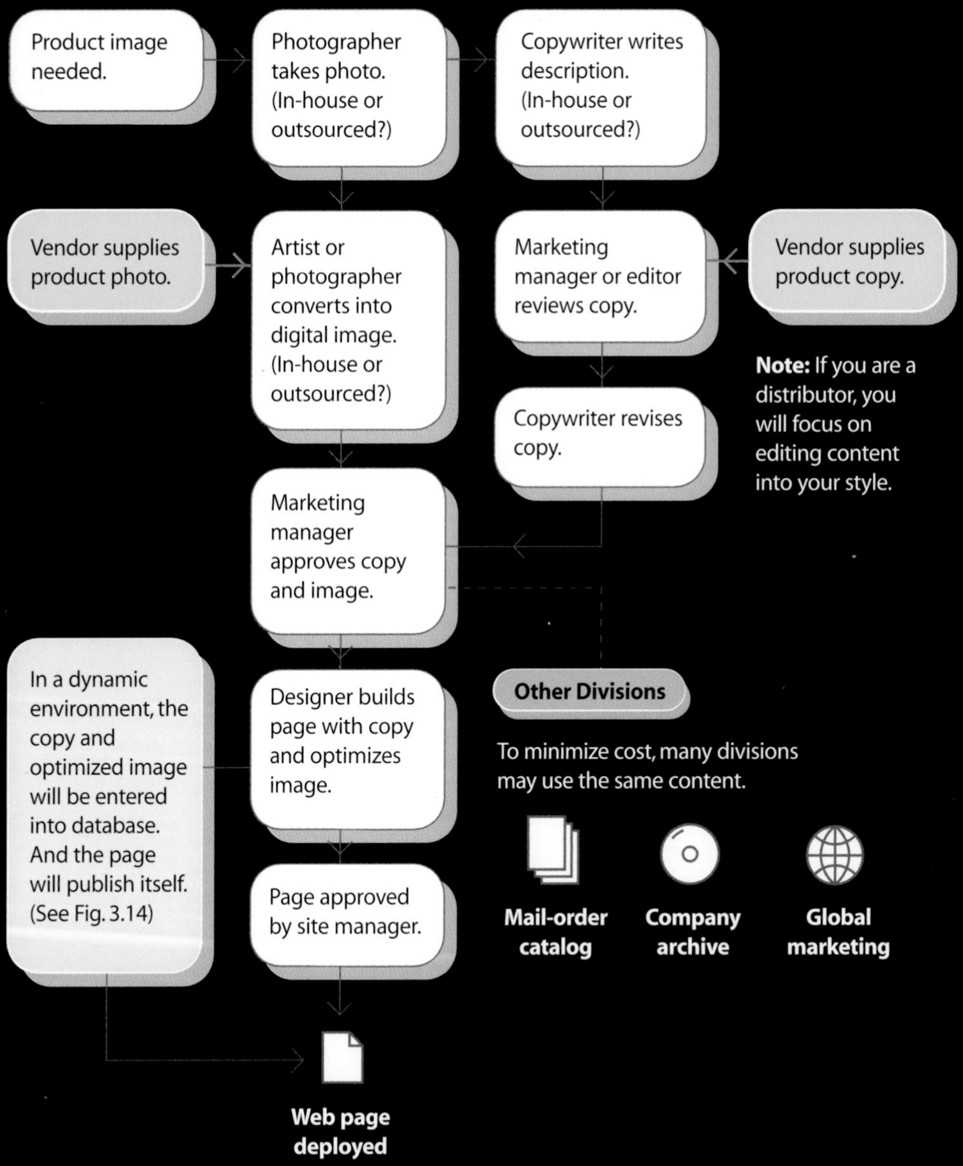

Product image needed.

Photographer takes photo. (In-house or outsourced?)

Copywriter writes description. (In-house or outsourced?)

Vendor supplies product photo.

Artist or photographer converts into digital image. (In-house or outsourced?)

Marketing manager or editor reviews copy.

Vendor supplies product copy.

Note: If you are a distributor, you will focus on editing content into your style.

Copywriter revises copy.

Marketing manager approves copy and image.

In a dynamic environment, the copy and optimized image will be entered into database. And the page will publish itself. (See Fig. 3.14)

Designer builds page with copy and optimizes image.

Other Divisions

To minimize cost, many divisions may use the same content.

Mail-order catalog

Company archive

Global marketing

Page approved by site manager.

Web page deployed

- **Outsource:** It's likely you are already using freelancers or contractors in other parts of your business. Perhaps you will extend those contracts to include materials for Web delivery. Outsourcing is also a good option for tasks that your company has never done before.

- **Manufacturer:** Content from manufacturers has the potential for brand identity conflict. If you use content from a manufacturer, expect it to be laden with marketing lingo. It can also be intentionally misleading or filled with typos. The quality of product photography provided by manufacturers varies widely. Neither the copy nor the photography is likely to match the overall tone of your site. So you may need to edit out the manufacturer's personality from the content, and so that it does not interfere with your site's personality.

- **Partners:** Content from partners brings the same risks. Are you willing to be responsible for the quality or accuracy of the data?

Even if you are using a reputable provider, it's best to clearly label the source of content—partner or manufacturer—so that the customer is not mislead.

The cost of each option is fuzzy at best. Converting existing content into digital form will cost money, but how much? There is no formula.

As well, repurposing existing content into a usable online form will require some editing. Nothing in print completely translates to the Internet. A five-hundred-word description of a product would never get read online. It would need to be broken up into a bullet list, or ten fifty-word chunks. A common goof in repurposing content is the inclusion of state-dependent references: "See more clocks on page 36" may appear in a catalog product description, but it would look ridiculous online.

Sometimes, there are other hidden costs. Online rights is major wormhole.

A company's print catalog division may have paid a photographer for one-time rights to use photos in a catalog. But did they pay for the use of those photos on the Web site? If not, they will have to pay the photographer again or expect a legal action.

The challenge of predicting the cost of producing content with an existing company can be equally vexing. When deciding what content to create in-house, consider the workflow and employees needed to support it. In Fig. 3.21, we show an example of the workflow for creating photographs for a Web site.

The primary purpose of considering workflow is to reveal exactly who is needed to create content. Who will supervise content creation? Who will edit copy, scan photos, optimize graphics? Once you have figured out all the players, you'll be able to identify how much time and effort will go into each item.

Now, multiply this process by the number of products your site, then begin to ask:

- Do we have the hardware and software to support this process?

- How much will this cost to do in-house vs. freelance?

- How long will this take?

- Can parts of the process be automated?

Looking at workflow is important because many companies chose to create content internally without realizing the long-term implications. Too many commerce Web sites have content that is out of date — a guaranteed way to lose business and project a poor brand image. When projecting the cost of content creation, make a separate note about maintenance cost. Is the company you are working with willing to make the long-term investment of hiring staff to not only create this content but maintain it? Many companies choose to outsource initial creation, then hire a small team to maintain and update the content.

FIGURE 3.22: SAMPLE BUDGET PROJECTION

For a three-week project. Note that these rates are provided for example only. Your own research and local rates should be used for your budget projections.

Task	People	Day rate	Days	Total
Project management	1	$500	15	$7,500
Research	1	$350	5	$1,750
Writing	2	$350	8	$5,600
Editing	2	$350	12	$8,400
Interface design	2	$500	10	$10,000
Graphics/Photography	2	$500	5	$5,000
Database entry	5	$250	15	$18,750
Producers	3	$250	10	$7,500
Tech support/authoring	1	$250	5	$1,250
Tech support/publishing	1	$250	5	$1,250
User testing	5	$250	1	$1,250
			Subtotal	$68,250
			+15%	$10,237
			TOTAL	$78,487

Create a budget and task plan

Once you have created the content inventory and considered workflow implications, calculate a budget projection. The simplest way to project cost is illustrated in Fig. 3.22. With this chart, you fill in the number of people, their rates and the number of days to complete the job. This should give you an estimate of what it will cost to create content for a commerce Web site.

Add at least 15 percent to this estimate, in case of unexpected costs due to overtime, poor project management, varying rates, and other unforeseen problems. Someone in the company will need to approve this cost. Anticipate that they will ask you to lower it. Be prepared to explain each item and its implication for sales.

Coping with outsourcing

"Mama don't let your boys grow up to be consultants." — Mark Russell, satirist

Assuming that your budget provides the option, you might have to hire a consulting firm to help meet a deadline or bring a technical or editorial competency that the development team is lacking. Unless you are acting as the project manager, you probably won't be directly involved with the decision to hire, although you may be asked your opinion about whether outsourcing is needed.

Regardless, keep in mind one word when dealing with consultants: Beware.

The sad truth is that consultants are not always looking out for your project's best interests. Their job is to make as much money as possible. Like lawyers, they are paid based on billable hours. An afternoon conference call between their team and yours can easily cost thousands of dollars. Your job is to find the best solution for your customers.

How do you make sure your consultants will be fiscally responsible? How can you tell that they are not recommending a solution just to showcase their latest service offering? The best way is to get multiple bids from reputable and recommended firms. Ask for references that you can interview on your own. When you contact their references, ask if their estimates and actual billable hours were in the same ballpark. And, of course, look at the work they've done before. For example, have they consistently integrated technology that made for a valuable experience?

When you've settled on one firm, don't be sheepish about questioning their recommendations. If someone says: "No problem, we can use an Enterprise Java Bean to perform a data migration to our content repository. It's an optimized solution." Ask them to explain that in English or sketch it on a wipeboard. You don't need to take an adversarial stance. Be calmly persistent and they will learn to show up to meetings with explanations prepared.

Unless you are working for a large company with a broad range of talent, you will have to outsource some aspect of technology or content creation. This will take some time to get approval from executive management, so submit requests for outsourcing as early as possible.

After the content inventory and budget have been approved, you or a project manager should immediately create a Gant chart (See Fig 3.23). This is a schedule that plots the tasks, people responsible for these tasks, and a timeline.

With the content inventory in hand, you can begin the first phase of information architecture: organization.

Task	Start	Finish	Owner	June	July
Product photography	6-01	6-14	Sally		
Image optimization	6-14	6-21	Steve		
Product descriptions	6-14	6-28	Gary		
Help documentation	7-07	7-31	Victoria		
Convert annual report	6-01	6-14	Stephan		
Digitize CEO interview	6-14	6-21	Sally		
Logo design	6-14	7-14	Sally		
Database entry	6-01	7-31	Bill, Ted		

FIGURE 3.23: SAMPLE GANT CHART
The tool of choice among project managers for creating these charts is Microsoft Project

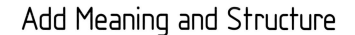

Add Meaning and Structure

"Where is the knowledge we have lost in information?"—T. S. Eliot

Do not confuse information and meaning. By giving customers 2,000 additional pieces of information, have you given them a greater understanding of what they want to buy? Information and meaning are inversely proportional—as information increases, we usually reach a point where the meaning that we are capable of deriving decreases. This state is often referred to as information overload.

By adding organization and structure to information, you can make the information digestable, understandable, and familiar. For example, imagine pages of paper scattered on a table. How many pages are there? Is this a manuscript, a screenplay, or just random pages? Who wrote it? What's the title? Not much meaning can be derived from piles of loose sheets. Add a contents page, chapter titles, section headings, subsection headings, page numbers, and an index. What was a pile of paper is now instantly familiar as a book. By organizing the information, you've added value and meaning.

Schemes manifest in different ways depending on the nature of the customer experience.

Topic + Alpha Scheme

Action & Adventure
Adult
African-American
Anime
Art House
Boxed Sets
Classics
Cult Movies
Comedy
Disney
Documentary
Drama
Family
Foreign
Gay & Lesbian
Health & Fitness
Horror
Independent
IMAX
Kids & Family
Music Video
Musicals &
Mystery & Suspense
Performing Arts
Playboy
Sci-Fi & Fantasy
Soundtracks
Special Interests
Sports
Studio Specials
Television
War
Western

Exact Scheme

Chronological — year
of theatrical release.

MyFlix.com

| DVD | Video | Players | About | Help |

| ACTION | COMEDY | DISNEY | DRAMA | FAMILY | FOREIGN | HORROR | MUSIC | SCI-FI |

BROWSE GENRE
Action/Adventure
Comedy
Documentary
Drama
Family/Kids
Foreign
Horror/Suspense
Music/Musicals
Sci-Fi/Fantasy

▶ Movies > **DVD** > **Sci-Fi/Fantasy** > **The Matrix** > **Keanu Reeves**

Navigating, browsing, and location

Once the product inventory has been organized into topics, the designer can use the scheme to give customers a way to access the main sections or subsections of a site or to enable customers to browse a list of products. Notice how these schemes also help the customer understand where they are on a site. It's not necessary for an entire scheme or all schemes to presented, in order for them to be helpful to the customer (see Browse Genre).

"Known-item" searching

Schemes help customers refine the parameters for finding a product or piece of information on the site. Schemes can also enable a customer to sort a list of products into an order that suits their goals.

SEARCH

| All Genres ▼ |

| keanu reeves | **GO** |

Advanced | Tips

| All Genres ▼ |
Action/Adventure
Anime
Comedy
Disney
Documentary
Drama
Foreign
Horror/Suspense
Kids/Family
Music/Musicals
Sci-Fi/Fantasy
Western

▶ **Search** > **DVD** > Results

We found 5 results for "Keanu Reeves" in "Sci-Fi"

Currently sorted by: **User Rating** | Re-sort results by clicking on label

Name	Year	User Rating	Price	Availability
Johnny Mnemonic Superbit Collection	1995	★★★★★	**$22.95** 25% off	**24** In stock Ships in 24 hours
The Matrix Special Edition	1999	★★★★★	**$15** 40% off	**15** In stock Ships in 24 hours
The Matrix Revisited Special Edition	1999	★★★★★	**$25** 20% off	**2** In stock Ships in 24 hours

1-3 of 5 results | Next   Show all

As we mentioned in Chapter 2, you can make your site easier to use by determining the best way to organize it to suit your customers' tasks and goals. The information architect (IA) plays a key role in site development by determining this optimum organization, which provides a unifying portrait of the collaborative end result. By doing so, the IA's work will have a profound effect on:

- Design of navigation and interaction elements

- Content creation, acquisition, level of detail, and language

- Database creation and other technical considerations

The information architect's blueprint defines the structure of the Web site and the possible ways a visitor can explore and retrieve information. The object is not to design navigation, but rather to design the foundation that will enable the navigation to be designed. Figure 3.24 provides a holistic view of how the blueprint will end up driving the user experience.

The IA thinks much deeper than the interface. More conceptual than visual, the IA is interested in developing a harmonious relationship between what customers want to do and what the Web site can provide. A good IA can make the designer's job much easier by clearly defining the playing field and rules.

If there is no information architect on your development team, appoint a designer or technologist to this role. A good information architect needs to be a generalist, keeping multiple perspectives in view at all times. A good IA also has solid interdisciplinary knowledge and can collaborate well with other team members.

Getting Organized

To illustrate the concepts of organization, we will use a fictitious retail Web site called "MyFlix.com" — a business-to-consumer seller of movies and movie players.

According to Argus Associates, pioneers in the field of information architecture, information on Web sites is organized by scheme and structure. A scheme defines the attributes and grouping of the items. A structure defines the relationship between items and groups.[5]

Schemes

There are two primary types of schemes: exact and ambiguous. In exact schemes, information can exist in one place. For example, your name can only appear in one location of an alphabetical list. Therefore, it's easy to locate. However, not all information can be classified this neatly. Some movies, for example, are both comedy and drama. Ambiguous schemes aim to alleviate uncertainty by allowing information to be categorized in multiple ways.

Exact organization schemes are usually familiar to your audience, and as a result, are extremely useful. They are most useful for "known-item" searching, as when the customer knows the name of the movie and could find it in an alphabetical list. Here are several types of exact schemes to consider:

- **Alphabetical:** From childhood you have understood and used this method of organization—A, B, C. For MyFlix.com, we might use an alphabetical scheme to organize actor names, movie names, or names of genres.

- **Chronological:** Time is universally familiar, assuming there is certainty about the time something took place. For MyFlix.com, we might organize by the year a movie was made, or the month and day the movie was issued on VHS and DVD.

- **Geographical:** Location is also easily understood by customers, but it's not always relevant to the task. In commerce, location is usually good for origin, store locations, or shipping choices. On MyFlix.com, we might consider organizing content by the country in which a film was made (USA, France, Japan, etc.).

- **Numerical:** Numbers are good for arbitrary indexing. If the company has a print catalog, like Pottery Barn or Sears, the products have a product number or ID. Your customers may be familiar with this arbitrary numerical index and want to use it to locate items on your Web site. On MyFlix.com, we could use a numerical scheme for revealing magnitude, such as how many items are in stock or how many of a particular item has been sold.

- **Continuum:** This scheme organizes according to a value scale or rank. This is an exact scheme because an item can only fall on one point in the spectrum. In the case of MyFlix.com, it would be user ranking of movies (the range between good and bad).

- **Existing standards:** There are industry standard schemes that you might need to adopt, such as UPC (Universal Product Code) or ISBN (International Standard Book Number). Standards are usually more useful to the goals of your business than your target profile. For MyFlix.com, we could consider adopting the ISBN number that all movies are assigned. MPAA ratings (G, PG, PG-13, R, NC-17) are another standard we could accommodate.

The other type of organization scheme used for Web sites is called ambiguous. Remember the Jackie Chan movie from Chapter 2? We couldn't decide if it should be described as an Action, Buddy, Comedy, or Martial Arts film. It's all of those, and perhaps others. But none of these are the exact, unique definition for the movie. Language and personal perspective create ambiguity.

Ambiguous schemes are most useful for finding items when customers may not be sure of their goal. On MyFlix.com, our customer might not know Jackie Chan's name, but might remember that he was funny and he was good at karate. So our profile might

look in a category called martial arts. Here are some ambiguous schemes to consider:

- **Topic or subject:** This is the most common in the commerce world, because it's helpful for customers that are browsing or just looking around. They need a place to start and a broad subject is helps get them started. A Sears catalog is a good example of a catalog organized on a subject scheme whose grouping and naming is somewhat arbitrary. Should dishwashers be in "home appliances" or "kitchen appliances?" Should we name the category "home appliances" or "housewares" or "the majors"? For MyFlix.com, we might use genres like Action, Drama, and Family as parts of our topic scheme. Genres are somewhat familiar, because they are already used by most movie sellers.

- **Task or series:** Good for organizing information that supports a process or for a unique sequence of customer actions. You often find this type of categorization on business-to-business (B2B) exchanges or auction sites. For MyFlix.com, we might use "Browse, Compare, Buy, Sell, Track, Collect, Discuss" for organization.

- **Audience:** Some groups of customers have explicit purchasing or browsing needs that may not be shared by others. For MyFlix.com, we might use "Kid's Korner, Mom's Lounge, Dad's Lounge"

FIGURE 3.25
WHAT IS *THE MATRIX*?

A useful site will have to employ a variety of organization schemes to support different styles of searching and exploration. This page shows the depth of possibilities for classifying the DVD version of the movie *The Matrix*. Some classifications will be useful for the target profile, others will not. Each has implications on cost and time needed to create.

Ambiguous Schemes

Topic or Subject (+ Alpha)

Genres
- Action & Adventure
- Adult
- African-American
- Anime
- Art House
- Classics
- Cult Movies
- Comedy
- Documentary
- Drama
- Foreign
- Gay & Lesbian
- Health & Fitness
- Horror
- Independent
- IMAX
- Kids & Family
- Music Video & Concerts
- Musicals & Performing Arts
- Mystery & Suspense
- Science Fiction & Fantasy
- Soundtracks
- Special Interests
- Sports
- Studio Specials
- Television
- War
- Western

Subgenres
- Alien Invasion
- Biker Films
- Buddy Films
- Caper
- Chase Movies
- Costume Adventures
- Docudrama
- Escape Films
- Gangster Films
- Horror
- Love
- Melodrama
- Monster Movies
- Odd Couples
- On the Road
- Parody & Spoof
- Police & Detective Films
- Political Thriller
- Prison Films
- Psychological Thriller
- Slapstick
- Sports
- Sword & Sorcery
- Treasure Hunts

Exact Schemes

Alphabetical
- Title
- Director
- Cast names
- Studio
- Distributor

Chronological
- Date of theatrical release
- Date of DVD release

Geographical
- Country of origin

Standards
- ISBN
- MPAA rating
- Format (DVD, VHS)

Using standard schemes has value for future development, because you may want to combine the content with someone else's.

Numerical
- Price
- Popularity (number of page views)
- Purchase (how many bought)

Continuum
- Critics ranking
- Users ranking

Other attributes
- Movie summary
- Official movie URL
- DVD extras
- Sound options
- Language options

How will this information be classified? Does it need to be broken down in some special way?

Subjectivity

To create the topic list above, an IA would need to consider existing genre models (walk into any Blockbuster and you will genres in action). Naming a genre is tricky. Some names, like Art House, are very ambiguous. Does Art House mean artistic, foreign, independent, cult, or all of them? It's also easy to add genres that aren't really genres at all, such as Disney or Studio Specials. Maintain the integrity of a scheme to avoid confusion.

FIGURE 3.26
PUTTING IT ALL TOGETHER

All of this organization must to-gether in a way that makes the most sense to the customer. It helps to visual-ize the interaction design while still in the information architecture phase.

PRODUCT PAGE

MyFlix.com

| DVD | Video | Players | Forums | About | Help |

| MY COLLECTION | BEST SELLERS | NEW RELEASES | BARGAIN DEALS | USED SALE | DVD FORUMS |

SEARCH

All Products ▼

GO

Advanced | Tips

MY CART 🛒

Qty	Item	Price
1	X-Men	$11.45
Shipping		$5
Total:		$16.45

CHECKOUT

BROWSE GENRE

Action/Adventure
Comedy
Disney
Documentary
Drama
Family/Kids
Foreign/Art
Horror/Suspense
Music/Musicals
▶ Sci-Fi/Fantasy
DVD Players
DVD Forums

▶ DVD > Sci-Fi/Fantasy > Popular

PRODUCT PHOTO

The Matrix (1999)
List Price: $25
Our Price: $15
You Save: $10 (40%)
Availability: 24 in stock
Rank: ★ ★ ★ ★ ★

Trailer: RealVideo 56K | 300K | Help

Other Available Formats:
VHS, VHS widescreen, VHS subtitled in Spanish, Theatrical

Movie Details
Rated: R for violence and language
Starring: Keanu Reeves, Laurence Fishburne, Carrie-Anne Moss
Director: Andy & Larry Wachowski
Read More

DVD Details
• Region 1 encoding (US and Canada only)
• Color, closed-captioned, Dolby, anamorphic widescreen
• Commentary by Carrie-Anne Moss, Zach Staenberg and John Gaeta
• Isolated musical score with comentary by composer Don Davis
• Behind-the-scenes documentary "HBO First Look: Making the Matrix"
• Hidden special effects documentaries
• Follow the white rabbit to nine behind-the-scenes featurettes
• Production notes, theatrical trailer(s)
Read More

ADD TO CART

QTY 1

MAIL A FRIEND

myfriend@yahoo.co

RELATED

COMPACT disc DIGITAL AUDIO   COMPACT disc DIGITAL AUDIO

• Limited Edition Collector's DVD
• Original Score
• Music from the Matrix

© MyFlix.com | Company Info | Partners | Contact Us | Store Locator | Privacy Policy

Breadcrumbs
Reinforce notions of hierarchy and schemes. Helps customers remember how they got to their current location.

Relationships
A commerce site usually needs to show exact and ambiguous relationships between products. A relational database will help deliver this powerful association.

Product information
Content related to the product must be chunked and organized into a scannable list. This may be done in the database, or manually ordered by an editor.

as our audience categories. Also, we might include a members-only Adult section that is password protected.

- **Metaphor:** This is the most difficult of all schemes to pull off effectively because metaphors are clouded by various interpretations. Usually, a company is trying to re-create the offline experience when it uses a metaphorical scheme. For MyFlix.com, we might use Marquee, Now Showing, Viewing Room, Vault, Concessions, Ticket Booth, and Café for our metaphors.

Most commerce sites use a combination of exact and ambiguous schemes to satisfy the browse and known-item exploration methods. The key is to maintain each scheme's integrity. For example, it would be confusing to customers if you presented the following scheme on MyFlix.com:

- DVD
- Martial Arts
- Studios
- Dad's Lounge
- Gift Guide
- Viewing Room
- MyFavs

Use familiarity and simplicity as guiding principles. There is nothing familiar about this hybrid scheme. No glue holds it together. Before deciding on your schemes, it's helpful to consider all of the possible schemes (See Fig. 3.25) and a holistic view of how the schemes come together (See Fig. 3.26).

Structure

Whereas schemes are the street signs of the Web site, structure is the system of roads that allow the customer to get where they want to go. Every commerce site uses a combination of three structures to help users search and explore (See Fig. 3.27). These are:

Hierarchy

Sometimes called the "top-down" approach, a hierarchy follows the "general leads to the more specific" concept used in family trees, animal kingdoms, military commands, product catalogs and so on. Users can easily be comfortable with a hierarchical Web site because it is a familiar real-world model.

MyFlix.com click path example:
Home > Products > Movies > DVD > Sci-Fi > The Matrix > Keanu Reeves

One choice logically progresses to the next. A hierarchy's value depends on its breadth and depth. If it's too wide, too many choices are pushed to the top and customers are overwhelmed with choice. If it's too deep, the customer will have to make too many choices

Hierarchy (top-down)

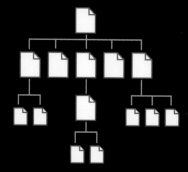

Relational Database (bottom-up)

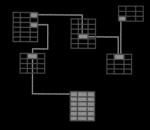

Hypertext

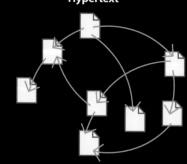

FIGURE 3.28

Hierarchy + Hypertext

Only one way to find something. Relationships between items is fixed by hierarchy.

"I want to buy The Matrix on DVD"

Movies

DVD

Genre

Sci-Fi

Alpha List

thematrix.html
"Do they have other Keanu Reeves movies?"

? To answer this question in a strict hierarchy, you would need to manually create a Keanu Reeves page, list all his movies, then link that list manually back to all the movie pages. Are you going to do this for every actor? Ouch!

Hierarchy + Hypertext + Database

Creating many relationships between items offers alternative ways to find something.

"I want to buy The Matrix on DVD"

Movies

DVD

Hey. What's this movie Devil's Advocate about?

Devil's Advocate
Oh, Keanu Reeves is in this film.

Keanu Reeves Filmography

The Matrix

"I want to buy The Matrix on DVD"

Search

Matrix

Choice List

The Matrix
"Do they have other Keanu Reeves movies?"

Keanu Reeves Filmography   **Choices**

! In a hypertext environment that is driven by hierarchy and supported by a relational database, users can follow logical associations and relationships. But don't kid yourself. Creating a well-formed database takes a lot of work, from the IA team, content team, and the technology team.

FIGURE 3.29
FLOWCHART FOR MYFLIX.COM

KEY

| Static | Dynamic | Secure |

It may be useful for your team to color code this flowchart to aid the development process. Static pages will need manual attention.

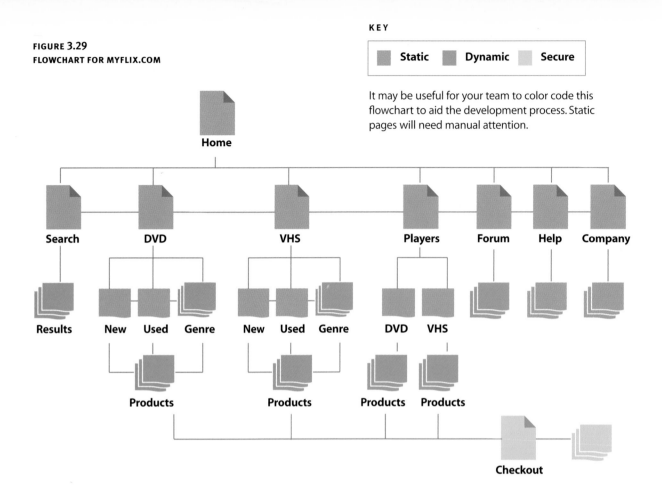

Some people use the term "site map" to refer to flow-charts. We prefer flowchart because helps distinguish it from the "site map" that will presented to the customer on the Web site. Flowchart reduces ambiguity.

to get to the bottom. Experts in this field recommend four or five levels as the limit for a hierarchy to prevent customer frustration.

DVD > Sci-Fi > The Matrix > Keanu Reeves

Make sure that you set limits to how items can be multiply categorized. If you don't, the hierarchy loses relevance.

The drawback of a hierarchy used as the sole structure of a Web site is that there is only one pathway to the information.

Relational database

Sometimes called the bottom-up approach to structure, a database is the storage place for the information classified by ambiguous and exact schemes. Without a database, every page would have to be hand-coded with HTML and manually assigned a location in the hierarchy and then manually linked to related pages. Multiply that by 5,000 products and you'd be lucky to launch a site in six months, much less be able to maintain it. Having a database supporting a hypertext structure enables a customer to follow non-linear relationships with relative ease.

Home > The Matrix > Sci-Fi > Star Wars > DVD > Box Set > The Godfather

A database is not a panacea for structure. It takes a good tech team to create a database that will support effective exploration. It also requires the appropriate schemes to be chosen and strict data entry based on those schemes.

Hypertext

This structure is integral to a Web site. It's nonlinear and works to complement the hierarchy and the database structures.

Home > The Matrix > Sci-Fi > DVD > Forums

When used alone, a customer can get lost in hypertext. In Chapter 4, we'll show you how to add context and "breadcrumbs" navigation so they don't lose their way.

In Fig. 3.28, we show how our MyFlix.com customer might search for the movie *The Matrix*. As always, consider a complete view of the customer experience. Does your structure support their goals?

A map of the site

Once an IA has determined the schemes and the structure, he or she establishes a flowchart (See Fig. 3.29), the beginning of a navigation system. Flowcharts provide a partial view of the hierarchy, but don't show the labyrinth of possible hypertext relationships, which would be visually overwhelming and, therefore, useless. A flowchart is helpful to your team because it shows a unifying view of structure and relationships of information. It also gives the development team a portrait of which pages may need manual attention and which ones can be published directly from a database.

With the flowchart in hand, an information architect next considers which hypertext relationships are most useful to the target profile. The IA also creates wireframes, a draft of the type of content which will be needed on each page. These basic steps fall under the heading of interaction design, which we cover in depth in Chapter 4.

---

[1] Kristof, Ray and Satran, Amy. *Interactivity by Design: Creating and Communicating with New Media*. Published by Adobe Press, 132 pages (1995.). The authors operate a design firm, Ignition, whose clients include: Apple Computer, Hewlett-Packard, Macromedia, and Pepsi-Cola. Learn more at www.ignitiondesign.com/

[2] Sonderegger, Paul. Forrester Research. *Why Most B-To-B Sites Fail*. Dec. 1999.

[3] Cooper, Alan. *The Inmates Are Running the Asylum: Why High Tech Products Drive Us Crazy and How to Restore the Sanity*. Published by Sams, 261 pages (April 6, 1999). It's worth noting that Cooper uses the word "personas" instead of "profiles."

[4] "We shape our tools, and thereafter our tools shape us." From *Understanding Media: The Extensions of Man* by Marshall McLuhan. (New York, McGraw-Hill, 1964).

[5] Argus Associates was founded by Louis Rosenfeld and Peter Morville. These two guys have written just about everything worthwhile on Information Architecture. Their 1998 book *Information Architecture on the World Wide Web* is a bible on this subject. Published by O'Reilly. (204 pp.)

chapter 4

INTERACTION DESIGN FOR COMMERCE
How customers control the experience

Interactions are everywhere—when we open a door, pour a cup of coffee, or press buttons on a remote control. These interactions are familiar but not always foolproof. As Donald Norman points out in his book *The Design of Everyday Things,* to err is human. "Humans do make mistakes," Norman writes, "but with proper design, the incidence of error and its effects can be minimized."[1]

To reduce error and enhance the possibility of buying success, commerce sites use interaction design to explore the experience in rigorous detail, before a single button is designed or line of programming code is written. Interaction design is the process of identifying what information will go on each page, what tools the customer will be given to control their experience and how the site responds to customer actions. It's the secret ingredient that separates a good commerce site from a mediocre one.

Ultimately, applying good interaction design principles should make for happy customers.

Happy customers find the products they want, get their password by e-mail when they forget it, and can add and remove items from their cart with ease. Customers are not designers, they're shoppers. They might put up with a site that has an ugly color scheme, but not with one that has a cumbersome or illogical checkout process.

Drawing upon customer profiles and other deliverables from the information design phase, interaction design tailors actions and outcomes to anticipate customer needs and create a rewarding interactive experience. Since all interactions have presentation, technical and usability consequences, interaction designers must consider what every link, form, field, and button does. Only by attention to detail can you avoid what information architects call "cognitive friction"—the difference between the way something works and the way the customer anticipates it will work.

Fundamentally, interactions are enabled by technology, and controlled by the customer via the interface. While interaction design is primarily the responsibility of the information architect, it's rare that one individual has the multidisciplinary background to solve every interaction problem and create a detailed and realistic experience. More frequently, you need a small team composed of an information architect, a technologist, a graphic designer, a content specialist, and, if possible, a usability specialist.

It's imperative that graphic designers understand the relationship between interaction design and presentation, because both are needed to satisfy the goals of the customer (See Fig. 4.1). As Norman says, "... Appearances are only part of the story: usability and understandability are more important, for if a product can't be used easily and safely, how valuable is its attractiveness? Usable design and aesthetics should go hand in hand: aesthetics need not be sacrificed for usability, which can be designed in from the first conceptualization of the product."[2]

Customer-Centered Design

To design an experience that is most likely to accommodate customer needs and tasks, you should be familiar with a few universal principles of human nature that apply to inter-action design.

- **Principle of Least Effort:** Formulated by Harvard linguistics professor George Zipf, this principle says that it is human nature to want the greatest outcome for the least amount of work. Zipf showed that behaviors that are useful are performed frequently. Frequent behaviors become quicker and easier to perform over time. The very existence of these quick, easy behavior patterns cause individuals to choose them, even when they aren't necessarily the wisest, or even most logical choice.[3] Usability expert Jakob Nielsen has devised a law of user experience that echoes this sentiment: "Users spend most of their time on other sites. This means that users prefer your site to work the same way as all the other sites they already know."[4]

Interaction

- Should we put a speedometer on the dashboard of our cars?
- What should be the starting and ending mph?
- Should it read in mph or km/h?

Presentation

- How can I visually reinforce important information feedback?
- Should it look like the speedometer in most cars?
- Should it be in the center of the dashboard?

- **Mental shortcuts:** To cope with increasing demands on our time and attention, humans create mental shortcuts to decipher and react to common situations. Psychologist and author Robert Cialdini says that clever salespeople take advantage of this inability to analyze all of the information that we encounter. No customer will accept blatant manipulation, but psychological tactics that work offline can be equally effective online. For example, many sites present a top-sellers list on their home page, triggering an automatic mental response: "If it's on the top-seller list, it must be good." Web sites need to use information (both visual and textual) that will trigger these shortcuts and persuade customers to navigate and explore in certain ways. Figures 4.2 and 4.3 show how two retailers use shortcuts to motivate and persuade their users.[5]

- **Rule of tenacity:** Customers have different tenacity levels—the level of willingness to hang in through adversity— depending on how many alternatives are available. When something is really important, customers will do anything to get it. Consider the difference between buying a book and shopping for a specialty item. For most books, comparably priced Web site alternatives exist, so the customer's tenacity level is low. When seeking specialty items such as fine art or skydiving equipment, the tenacity level increases. Customers will put up with poor site architecture, an inefficient search, and even slow download speeds to reach their goal.[6]

Far too often, companies use tenacity as an excuse for sloppy service. It's not uncommon to hear an executive say "Anyone who really needs our products will be willing to figure it out." This attitude is an open door for competition to walk through. Don't test your customers' boundaries of patience. Your team should strive to architect experiences that follow a customer's natural desire for least effort.

To better understand your customer's tendencies, conduct a field study (covered in Chapter 6). Get out of the office and watch some of your target customers in their environment. Observe how they browse and buy products on other sites. If possible, take a video camera. Your team needs to witness how customers react to different types of navigation, carts, and structures.

Scenarios

"In the beginner's mind there are many possibilities, but in the expert's mind there are few." —Shunryu Suzuki[7]

Web designers have a hard time accepting that they are not the customer. Because a designer is intimately engaged in the inner logic of a site, it's natural to feel that customers are just as knowledgeable. The result, however, is that you become blind to obvious customer interaction needs.

To get inside the customer's mind, information architects create scenarios based on observations of customers during field studies and the portrait of their target profile. A scenario is a hypothetical, but plausible narrative of how your target profile would use a site to complete a series of tasks. As customer experience specialist Peter Merholz says, "Scenarios are powerful because they force the designer to think the way customers act—not rationally, but impulsively and emotionally."[8]

FIGURE 4.2

This home page detail of the online jewelry retailer Blue Nile shows a few examples of targeting mental shortcuts. Under Recently Purchased Diamonds it says, "Over 10,000 couples have purchased diamonds at Blue Nile." This shortcut is called "the principle of social proof." When a customer sees that other people are doing something, then it must be okay for them to do so as well. Prominent logos along the bottom are shortcuts that suggest Blue Nile's reliability and trust.

FIGURE 4.3

Handspring uses the basic trigger of monetary discounts and special offers to persuade potential customers to buy their products. Do not dismiss this as "just marketing." The interaction design team used this content as incentive to get customers into the site quickly.

The best scenarios come from a consideration of a Web site's goal statement and its target profile. To illustrate the point, we will use a fictional retail Web site called MyFlix.com—a business-to-consumer (B2C) seller of movies and movie players. MyFlix is a new online division of SuperStar Video, a major national chain of movie rental stores. They are dominant in the field of rentals, and are looking to unload a massive inventory of previously viewed movies through online auctions. They also sell new movies in their stores and want to expand those sales online.

MyFlix.com's target profile is Chris, a self-professed movie junkie. He is thirty-eight years old and lives in Detroit, Michigan. He owns two DVD players, a VHS player (but hardly uses it), a large Sony Wega TV (with a Bose Surround Sound system) and four other TVs. He has a satellite dish fully loaded with all the movie channels. He is married and has two kids, ages four and eight. He downloads a file of DVD releases into his Palm Pilot each month. He has a PowerMac G4 computer, with a DSL connection. He has been using the Internet to buy merchandise for two and a half years. He lives five minutes from a SuperStar Video store, and rents there often, but never buys DVDs there because "the prices are too high."

One scenario for this profile might read something like this: "It's Monday morning at work and Chris is using his Palm Pilot to review the new DVD releases that will be available on Tuesday. He is specifically intrigued by the new Superbit collection of movies designed for high-end, home entertainment systems. At DVDiscuss.com, he reads an advance review about this collection that says *Air Force One* is the best example of incredible sound and image. Next he goes to MyFlix.com, because he heard about the site at the video rental store. He sees a list of new releases and their prices on the home page, and easily finds his movie. The price, $19.95, is rock bottom. He clicks on the buy button next to *Air Force One,* which immediately takes him to a shopping cart page. On this page he is shown four other Superbit films that he might want to buy ..." The scenario continues through checkout and the fulfillment process.

Scenarios should cover the most likely reasons a target profile would come to a site. Your team will need to create a variety of scenarios that cover different possible customer tasks. For example, MyFlix.com might explore scenarios for Chris that include browsing for gift DVDs, or how Chris would follow up on a previous purchase.

MyFlix.com task list

Retail tasks
- Find a product I know I want
- Buy a product I want
- Browse products I might be interested in
- Get recommendations on products that might interest me
- Keep a list of products that interest me
- Follow up on a product that I want, but that is out of stock
- Send someone a product as a gift
- Keep track of a product that I ordered
- Return a product that I ordered
- Redeem a gift voucher
- Update my personal information

Forum tasks
- Register to join a forum
- Browse posts I might be interested in
- Reply to posts
- Be notified when someone responds to my posts
- Get recommendations on posts that might interest me
- Keep a list of posts that interest me
- Send someone a copy of a post
- Keep track of posts that I read
- Update my personal information

Auction tasks
Buyers
- Find a product I know I want
- Browse products I might be interested in
- Verify authenticity of a seller
- Bid on a product I want
- Track bidding process
- Set up account for buying products
- Keep track of a product that I bought
- Update my personal information

Sellers
- Set up account for selling products
- Sell an item or group of items
- Upload information and images about products
- Track bids, sale of items
- Process sale of items
- Ship/fulfill order of sold items

Global tasks
- Get help, self service
- Get live help, customer service
- Provide feedback
- Find out what is on your Web site

MyFlix.com task flow for "Buy a product I want"

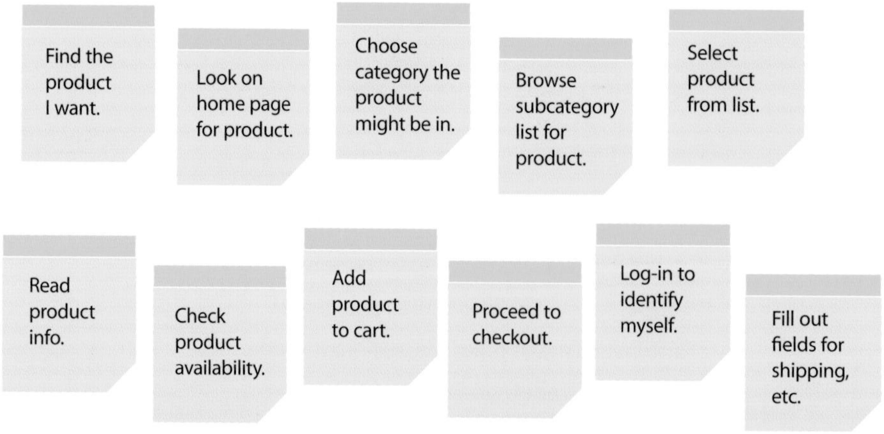

FIGURE 4.4: TASK ANALYSIS

With a task list in hand, information architects can begin to uncover the interactions in a task flow.

Much can be learned about customers through scenarios. They show how customers make decisions, what influences product choice and how customers expect a Web site to work. Scenarios are also important measurement tools for later stages of the design process. Refer to these scenarios as you develop a Web site to see if each design decision is relevant to the target customer's goals.

Task analysis

Based on scenarios, an interaction team specifies the tasks a customer must complete. Begin by making a list of all tasks represented in the scenarios. Take a holistic view of the experience. Examine the relationship between tasks and look for possible ways to minimize the customer's need to repeat them. Looking at this list, your team should ask questions like:

- Are the tasks on this list mutually exclusive? For example, will customers want the retail browse and the auction browse experience to overlap?

- Can we save our customers time and effort by not making them repeat tasks? For example, should we have one universal log-in for all areas of the site? Is that technically feasible?

- How seamless does this experience need to be? Should these tasks all be possible in one site, or should they be divided into three subsites? Will customers want to leave one experience for the other, or will they expect the experience to occur within one site?

- Which tasks on this list will be new to your customers? What familiarity or expectation will they bring to each task?

The team uses this list as a basis for outlining how a customer moves through a set of tasks to achieve a specific goal. The start with the most essential task, such as "buy a movie," and break it down into subtasks. For example, in order to buy a movie, the customer must first locate it (browse or search), add it to a shopping cart and then complete a checkout procedure.

In Fig. 4.4, we show a possible list of tasks for MyFlix.com and a task flow for buying a movie. Because task flows are based on scenarios, it's a customer-centric—not business-centric—way of looking at the commerce experience.

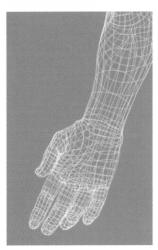

FIGURE 4.5
A wireframe of a hand made using Curious Lab's software program Poser.

Some design teams call wireframes page schematics, others call them storyboards.

Customer experience specialist Merholz says that keeping the customer's perspective in mind at this stage has other benefits. "Too often, site architectures are designed to support and categorize the content itself without looking at how the customer actually moves through the process. This leads to tidy hierarchical site structures that often bury what the customer really wants."[9]

Review the site flowchart that was created by the information architect in Chapter 3. Consider the following questions:

• Will the site's hierarchy support the task flow that has been outlined in this analysis?

• Does the site architecture force customer experience down a path that does not fall in line with their expectations?

Make revisions to the site's flowchart accordingly.

Wireframes

The term "wireframe" comes from 3D modeling software (See Fig. 4.5). Animators and 3D illustrators first devise a skeletal outline of figures and shapes, and only later map texture, color, and light onto the wireframe. Animators work on wireframes first to avoid wasting the computing power and time the later steps require. Similarly, Web commerce teams use wireframes to avoid costly mistakes in technology development and presentation design.

A wireframe is a sketch of the information, navigation, and transaction elements that might appear of each unique page within a site. Wireframes show the hierarchy of information and elements on a page but do not dictate exactly how or where something should be placed. They provide the pieces of the puzzle that can then be rearranged and reorganized by the presentation design team. From the wireframes, the team will create experience models—detailed diagrams of what is happening on the back- and front-end for every customer action.

Simple wireframes may just show just the content layout and navigational organization of key pages within a site. Complex ones include copy, functionality, links, navigation, and graphical content in a spatial relationship format. There is no industry standard for the methodology of creating wireframes. Some designers prefer handwritten sticky notes, or text-only HTML modeling, while others use somewhat detailed line art illustrations. Figure 4.6 shows the different types of wireframes that can be built.

FIGURE 4.6
TYPES OF WIREFRAMES

Wireframes are not templates, nor are they presentation design. They are an inventory of what content, navigation, and functionality the page will support. A leader in the field of information architecture, Argus Associates, defines three types of wireframes of increasing complexity and detail. They are abstract, low-fidelity, and high-fidelity.

Abstract

Logo
Global navigation
Local (category) navigation
Search box
Product photo

Product info
Buy button
E-mail-to-friend button
Related products

Make it with ...
• Sticky notes
• Paper sketches
• Text-only HTML

Consider ...
Everything that must be present on the page for the customer to complete a task.

Low-fidelity

Brand	Banner Ad	
Log In	Product Photo	Product Primary Info	Cart Container
Search			
Global Nav.			Add to Cart
Local Nav.	Product Secondary Info	Customer Reviews	E-mail/Save

Make it with ...
• Page layout or illustration program.
• Paper sketches

Consider ...
Mapping out priorities of content and navigation and their relationship to each other.

High-fidelity

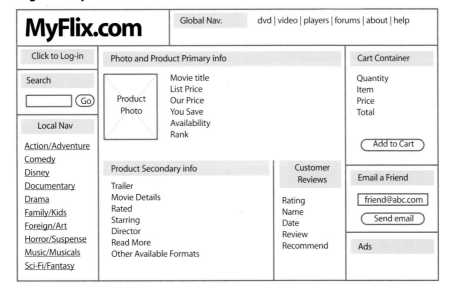

What you make it with ...
• Page layout or illustration program
• Paper sketches
• Rough HTML mock-ups

Consider ...
Showing a granular level of details for each component of the page, including elements like buttons.

High-fidelity wireframes show a more refined hierarchy but are still a long way from a fully developed design.

An information architect and a usability specialist begin the wireframe process by outlining the site with simple page-by-page sketches of information and functionality.

Special considerations are then made for technology, content, and presentation design. The technologist contributes possibilities and limitations given the proposed back-end solution. The presentation designer provides input on what front-end technology to use, navigation schemes, page layout and creative ways to move a user through a site or to display information. Content specialists provide the information a given page could present, and might also take notes on additional information that might still need to be created.

Every unique page type must be represented with a wireframe. Since you will be using templates to produce a commerce site, start by wireframing page types, such a home, category, subcategory, product, and search. Then consider wireframes for

variations of those pages. Pages that are parts of a process, like checkout, will also need to be wireframed (See Fig. 4.7).

In his book *User-Centered Web Design*, John Cato develops a model that describes how we interact with our world, and provides a good guideline for building wireframes. It's called the AUA model—awareness, understanding and action. People build an awareness of their environment, then move to an understanding of it. We then choose our actions from the available options.

In Fig. 4.8, we show how Cato's model is useful for determining what goes on each page. Customers must gain awareness of the information and control elements on the page and an understanding of the page content. They then compare it their reason for being on that page and determine the choices available there. Finally, customers take action. When the Web site responds, the AUA model starts anew.

FIGURE 4.7: **WIREFRAME UNIQUE PAGES**
You don't need to create wireframes for thousands of site pages. Because the Web site will be produced with templates, you can break up the site's wireframe design into discrete categories of page types.

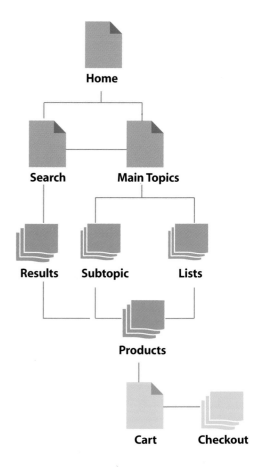

The site flowchart is a great starting point for unraveling what pages must have a wireframe. From this flowchart, you can make the following list:

• **Home Page**	• **Search Page**
• **Topic Page**	• **Search Results**
• **Subtopic Page**	• **Cart Page**
• **List Page**	• **Each Checkout Page**
• **Product Page**	• **Help**

John Cato's model of interaction design is based on the idea that everything we do in relation to our environment is an evolving attainment of purpose based on awareness, understanding, and action.

Each wireframe seeks to answer:

1. What do our visitors want to know here?
2. What do our visitors want to be able do at this point?
3. What should our visitors feel at this point in the process?
4. Where might our visitors want to go next?
5. How could we make it easy for them to do that?
6. What feedback should be provided after they've done it?

Wireframes are concerned with ...

Awareness

Before customers can interact with something, they must first be aware of the information and action. If something is hidden or poorly located, then there is no awareness. Presentation design is a major factor in awareness.

Understanding

Customers measure the reason for being on the site or page and determine through awareness and understanding if the options suit their needs. Purpose may change throughout the experience.

Purpose

Customers measure the reason for being on the site or page and determine through awareness and understanding if the options suit their needs. Purpose may change throughout the experience.

Choices

The customer discerns what options are available on a given page that help them achieve or get closer to their goal. Experiences can go really bad here, if an expected choice is not available.

Experience models define ...

Action

A choice that the customer makes to move toward their goal.

Experience models

An experience model is an extension of the wireframe. We like to think of them as interactions that are called upon and sometimes repeated throughout the experience. These interactions are explored in granular detail as schematics and given to the tech team as well as the presentation designers. In Figure 4.9, we show an experience model of an Add to Cart button.

For example, you can create a basic experience model for Search that will apply to the entire site. You would then adapt the model to the needs of different pages, such as home, category, and product. For each page, you might ask: "Will the page have pull-down menus that allow a customer to constrain the parameters of the search? What will the pull-down menu options be?" This level of technical and content detail takes a fair amount of time to develop, but the result is a clear portrait of how the customer will control the experience. Having a core model that is then repeated for different pages helps build a consistent experience.

Wireframes and experience modeling provide guidelines for the tech team as well as the presentation designers, so they can all understand each page's navigation, content, and transaction requirements. The wireframing process has a harmonizing effect on the project, because it gives everyone an indication of how different components come together for a reliable and useful customer experience.

This how an information architect breaks down the call-and-response of interactions.

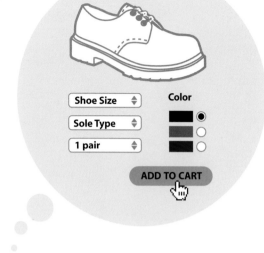

① **Examine wireframe**

Information architect reviews
wireframe of the purchase box.

> Shoe-size options
> Sole options
> Color options
> Quantity
> Add to Cart button

② **Explore possibilities**

IA works with tech, design, and usability
to explore possibilities such as:
• Show a picture of shoe added to a
  shopping cart.
• Reload the page with a message that
  says "This item was added to your
  shopping cart." Add a Proceed to
  Checkout button to the page.

*When a customer clicks
on Add to Cart, what will
happen next?*

③ **Diagram the model**

Programs like Microsoft's Visio are used to create diagrams that detail
the possible outcomes of a customer's action.

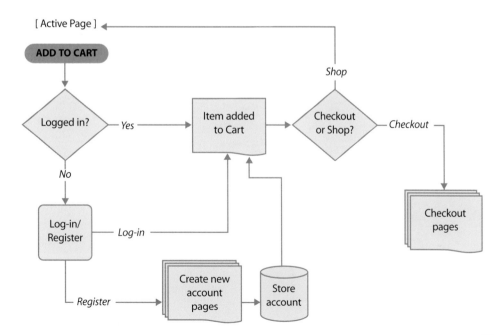

Components of Commerce

Many commerce sites have paid the price for poor usability and interaction design. From these failures and from others' successes, usability experts have identified some best practices for the interaction design of commerce sites. In this section, we cover the best practices for navigation, search, shopping carts, checkout procedures, forms, personalization, and accessibility.

Navigation

In a mall store, a customer looks at a shelf and knows how many different products are available. Stores have predictable layouts, and signs label different departments when needed. At checkout time, you head to the registers at the front of the store.

Online, there are no consistent and reliable ways to get similar information. Given the Web's lack of conventions, the interaction designer is also charged with developing a good navigation scheme to help customers make sense out of a site.

Good navigation shows a visitor their location in the site's structure. It provides a reliable base when everything else changes. Good navigation reinforces the purpose of the site and how to use it. It makes content easily accessible.

On most commerce sites, there are three different types of navigation at work: global, local, and contextual (See Fig. 4.10).

Global navigation

Breadcrumbs

FIGURE 4.10

Local navigation

Contextual navigation

Global navigation

Global navigation gives the customer a picture of the overall organization of the site such as major sections or product categories. It is a reliable guide that is available on every page, usually at the top or left side. Global navigation enables lateral navigation across the site's hierarchy.

Usability specialists agree that global navigation should consist of the following items:

- **Site logo:** Every page should have a logo to identify what site the customer is on. Usually, the logo is hyperlinked to the home page. No matter where the visitor ventures on the site, they should have a quick way to get back to the beginning.

- **Major sections:** After the information-design phase, logical site groupings should be obvious, but there may be too many options. To be consistent with the "chunking principle," sites should limit major sections to a maximum of nine items. Any more makes it difficult for the customer to quickly make sense of the choices. Pick the most appropriate items based on the customer's tasks and offer a link to a site map that supplies the rest.

- **Link to the help section:** Customers might run into something they don't understand and your team didn't anticipate. A simple link to the help section might retain customers that might otherwise leave out of frustration.

- **A way to search:** If a customer is unable to find what they want through browsing, they should be able to search. Although their chances of finding what they want are not guaranteed, it's an important option to offer. We cover searching later.

- **A way to view the shopping cart:** In a bricks-and-mortar store, customers always have a cart or basket in hand. On a commerce site the customer should be able to access their cart at every moment.

Some usability experts suggest not putting a lot of navigation choices on inside pages. That suggestion might work if customers always entered a site through the home page. But many customers enter by clicking on a link that lands them on category or product pages. Customers must be able to quickly orient themselves in the new site. Breadcrumbs are a great way to provide such context simply.

Breadcrumbs

Breadcrumbs augment global navigation and provide an efficient way to indicate where the customer is on the site. Breadcrumbs show the path from the home page to the current page. To be effective, breadcrumbs should be kept simple and be nested above or below the global navigation bar.

Local navigation

Local navigation complements global navigation. It provides more specific options that would overwhelm the customer if they were always part of the global navigation. Typically, local navigation defines the hierarchy of a category page.

For example, the local navigation components of an automotive category area wouldoffer subcategories like accessories, batteries, brakes, and so forth. Local navigation gets customers browsing by offering them more specific information targeted to their interest.

Contextual navigation

Contextual navigation guides customers through content related to the product or service. Amazon uses contextual navigation in brilliant ways. Every book, DVD, toy, or power tool is surrounded by contextual navigation that reveals the amount of information available for a given product.

FIGURE 4.11

Amazon.com's space-efficient tab-style global navigation has been widely adopted in the commerce world because tabs are easy for customers to understand.

FIGURE 4.12

Christie's pull-down style menu of global navigation gives customers access to deep layers of category and subcategory content from any page on the site.

Successful navigation schemes make content accessible to the customer. They are sensitive to customers' information needs and goals. When a navigation scheme fails to get customers to the content they want, they turn to the search function.

Search

The search engine has become one of the standing elements on many commerce sites. Some commerce sites even forego a large product promotion, opting for a large search box instead. With the predominance of search boxes on commerce sites, you'd figure they are the answer to a successful site.

Unfortunately, that doesn't appear to be the case. Usability experts Erik Ojakaar and Jared Spool have found that visitors to a site are 77 percent more likely to find the content they want when they don't use the search engine.[10]

These experts also found that visitors go to search only after they could not find what they wanted through links. Search is not a panacea for poor navigation design.

Therefore, according to Spool and Ojakaar, the best commerce site designers try to keep their visitors from having to use search at all. Not to mention, a well-thought-out navigation scheme can be more valuable, and less expensive, than a sophisticated search engine.

But since most customers expect a search to available on a commerce site there are some interaction guidelines to make the search engine more useful to your customers:

- **Keep the search box in the same place.** Making it part of the global navigation will keep it from moving around from page to page.

- **Make the search box easily recognizable.** Don't make it fancy. Use the word "Search," not "Find" or "Browse." The box should make it clear what will be searched—the entire site or just within a category.

- **Understand how your customers use search.** Focus search interaction on how customers will probably use the information. Do they need highly detailed descriptions? Will they use search to browse products?

- **Display results sensibly.** Consider grouping search results in logical categories. If someone types in "shoe," display results under headings "Women," "Men," "Running," etc.

- **Provide understandable feedback.** Display the original search query prominently, show how many pages retrieved, make it easy to revise the search, and make it obvious when the search found nothing.

- **Add navigation that encourages browsing.** Again, get your customers to browse. Add contextual navigation like related products or categories to the results page.

gettyimages™ creative   Take advantage of the benefits. Register now. Already a member? Sign In

images   motion   audio   fonts   spotlight   services   my account

advanced image search | CDs | catalogs | my lightboxes

◄ Page 2 of 1059 ►   Go to page : [   ] [Go]

ec6457-001
Stone
(Rights-protected)
Calculate Price

AA042402
PhotoDisc
(Royalty-free)
Calculate Price

944597
The Image Bank
(Rights-protected)
Calculate Price

ngs0_0465
National Geographic
(Rights-protected)
Calculate Price

smithc0011c
Illustration Works
(Rights-protected)
Calculate Price

jf6946-001
Hulton|Archive
(Rights-protected)
Calculate Price

fpx22452
FoodPix
(Rights-protected)
Calculate Price

ab67205
FPG International
(Rights-protected)
Calculate Price

E010049
EyeWire
(Royalty-free)
Calculate Price

040183
The Bridgeman Art Library
(Rights-protected)
Calculate Price

AA036891
Artville
(Royalty-free)
Calculate Price

wa5139-001
Allsport Concepts
(Rights-protected)
Calculate Price

◄ Page 2 of 1059 ►   Go to page : [   ] [Go]

Search Options
"beach"
12703 images found.
◉ New search - all brands
○ Search within results
[   ]
[Search]
Search tips

Show these images only
12703 images found.
Show these images only:
☑ Horizontal   ☑ B&W
☑ Panoramic   ☑ Color
☑ Square
☑ Vertical

Images on CDs:
☐ Show only images on CDs
   (RF brands only)

Select one or more image brands:
Active Brands - 12703
Allsport (RP) - 37
Artville (RF) - 69
Bridgeman (RP) - 49
EyeWire (RF) - 633
(To select more than one option, hold down 'ctrl' or 'cmd'.)

[Show only]

[Show All Results]

Set search preferences

Legend:
(RP) rights-protected images.
(RF) royalty-free images.

Rearrange images

Rearrange images
[12 per page ▼]
[Default order ▼]
[Rearrange]

Carts and Checkout

The checkout process is the most common cause of failure on commerce sites, causing 40 percent of customers to abandon their carts. According to research by the usability experts at Creative Good, these shopping cart problems amount to $3 billion in lost sales each year.[11]

Creative Good says there are three common interaction design problems with checkouts that result in buying failures:

• Confusion over the difference between "New" and "Return" customer log-in options. Many first-time shoppers mistakenly fill-in return customer log-in fields.

• Asking for personal customer information at inappropriate times, such as before a customer begins to shop or put items in a cart.

• Ineffective error messages such as "An error has occurred" or "You made a mistake on this form."

Looking at sites like Amazon.com and taking advice from usability experts, it is clear that proven information and interaction principles exist for designing a successful shopping cart and checkout process. (Fig. 4.14 shows the typical process that most carts follow.) Experts say that your team should follow these guidelines:

• **Make the cart accessible on every page.** Make it easy for the customer to view the cart and return to the shopping process. Insert a cart icon or "view cart" link into your global navigation.

• **Carts should be simple.** The shopping cart should include the option to easily add or remove items and change the quantity desired. Let a customer know if the product is in stock before they enter the checkout process. Providing too many other options could distract from these key tasks.

• **Show related products.** Suggest items similar to ones already in the cart or accessories for the chosen item. For example, if a customer chooses a portable radio, suggest batteries, headphones, or carrying cases.

• **Simplify ordering options.** Well-defined features need no explanation. If anything in your process requires lengthy explanation, it's probably too difficult for the customer to use. The ideal ordering process gets customers to the merchandise and their purchases as quickly as possible. Clearly label options. Customers don't want to read a lot of instructions. They look for an action to take that will bring them closer to their goal.

• **Make the shopping cart more forgiving.** Provide obvious navigation options for

Shop

Cart

Checkout process

| Log-in screen |
| Shipping info |
| Shipping method |
| Gift options |
| Billing info |
| Confirm order |
| Thank you! |

FIGURE 4.14 SHOPPING CART AND CHECKOUT

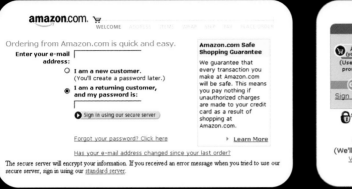

FIGURE 4.15

FIGURE 4.16

place to do business. Provide links to privacy policies and third-party verification services. Good commerce sites promote security throughout the shopping experience. In Fig. 4.16, Amazon.com promotes their safe shopping guarantee under the Add to Shopping Cart button. Amazon.com reinforces the security message with an explanation of the guarantee in Fig. 4.15.

- **Differentiate customer paths.** New customers must register before checking out. Return customers merely need to log in. These are distinctly different experience paths. Don't combine new sign-up forms with return customer log-in forms. Clearly separate them on the page, so that new users don't fill out log-in forms and wonder why there is a problem.

- **Don't make the customer log in to use a cart.** The appropriate time to ask customers to log in is the first step of the checkout process. Asking customers for all their registration information any earlier is prohibitive to the shopping experience. Does a grocery store ask you for a driver's license every time you put a bag of chips in your basket?

- **Keep order forms simple.** Make filling out forms as quick and painless as possible. For repeat customers, automatically fill in fields with their existing customer information. For example, fill in the shipping

returning to shopping pages. Make sure the customer's cart will be correct even if the browser's Back button is used. If an error occurs, the site should call attention to the mistake with a clear, simple, and polite message.

- **Allow items to be saved for future purchase.** Amazon lets customers save their choices in their cart for up to ninety days. Keeping the cart alive even after it has been abandoned lets customers change their mind and return to the checkout process. Amazon also provides "wish lists" as an option for customers to store items they can share, review, or buy later.

- **Let customer review past purchases and recipients.** This function prevents customers from having to reenter addresses for family and friends.

- **Visually show the process.** Once customers are in the checkout process, remove navigational interference. Replace navigation with a process bar that lets the customer know what to expect and where they are in the ordering process. An easy way to do this is by numbering and labeling steps at the top of the page. Make it clear to the customer which steps are already completed and those that remain. In Fig. 4.15, you see that Amazon.com has removed their tab navigation and replaced it with a graphic that clearly outlines the steps of checkout.

- **Be secure.** It's standard operating procedure for businesses to store user addresses and credit card data securely. But your team will need to reassure the customer that the site is a credible and safe address fields with the Bill To address. Use the customer's e-mail address as the log-in ID or user name. Their e-mail address is easy to remember and is a vital piece of information that the site needs anyway.

Frustrated customers will leave their carts full in the checkout line. They will be equally frustrated at a Web site when faced with forms that make them think they've completed a sale when in fact they've only registered on the site, or with fields that don't accept phone numbers typed in different ways. Good forms are hallmarks of an effective interaction design.

Forms

Commerce sites rely on forms for many critical interactions in the experience: searching, sign-up, log-in, shopping cart, and checkout.

But as interaction design specialist Adam Baker reminds us, people don't like filling out forms in the real world. Although viewed as a nuisance (i.e., taxes, registration, banking) they are a necessity of doing business. Customers especially don't like filling out forms online. When designed poorly, Web forms are distracting, time consuming, and take control away from the user.

Your team's interaction, presentation, and usability specialists must work together to carefully create simple, clear, and logical forms that lead customers to a rewarding experience. Baker has devised an insightful set of guidelines for form design:[12]

- Forms are mechanical by nature, but humans are not. Simplify the form until it has the fewest number of options, all of which are essential to each task.

- Use controls, such as radio buttons and pull-down menus, for the same purpose that they are used in a customer's operating system. The behavior of these controls will already be familiar. Remember: radio buttons are used to select a single choice among a set of options; check boxes are used when multiple choices are allowed.

- Collect information in bits and pieces at times that a customer will find appropriate. Asking for too much information up front appears confrontational. For example, don't make customers give a mailing address to create a new account or become a member. Collect that information during the checkout process.

- Determine the minimum amount of information necessary for each task, so customers don't become frustrated or overwhelmed. Do not ask for information that isn't pertinent, such as "How did you find out about our Web site?" while on the cart or checkout page. This question is best left for after the checkout has been completed.

- Ensure that the customer will never have to provide the same information twice. This rule is equally applicable to a unique visit as a repeat visit. For example, if the customer has stated a shipping address in previous purchases, just ask them to verify their preferences upon return. Don't make them fill out the form again.

- Test the form with the target profile to make sure it's relevant to the task at hand. Eliminate anything that isn't practical. Resist the temptation to add lengthy instructions to patch a usability problem. Shoppers rarely read instructional text. If a form requires a lot of explanation, then it needs further simplification.

In Fig. 4.17, we show examples of how to keep forms appropriate to the task without overwhelming the customer with choice.

CONFUSING

Available colors

Black   Maroon   Purple

Shoe Size ⬍   Color ⬍
Sole Type ⬍   1 pair ⬍
Ship this item to: Me ⬍

ADD TO CART

CLEAR

PURCHASING OPTIONS

SHOE SIZE   QTY
Pick one ⬍   1

SOLE TYPE
Standard ⬍

COLOR
● ○ ○

ADD TO CART

The first example has too many choices, all hidden behind pull-down menus. The revision makes options more clear and defaults to the most likely choices.

CONFUSING

Select a Password Hint
Enter a personal question that will help you remember your password (e.g., What is my mother's maiden name?) If you forget your password, we'll ask you your personal question.

type question here

CLEAR

Log-In Assistance
To help us confirm your identity if you forget your password or user name, please select and answer one of the following questions:

What is your pet's name? ⬍

answer

The first example makes the customer stop and think up a question. Besides, it's poorly written and vague. The clear example has a set of pre-chosen questions. The language is polite and explicit.

CONFUSING

SEARCH

enter keyword

Entire Site ⬍

Price Range ⬍

SEARCH   HELP

CLEAR

SEARCH

All Products ⬍

enter keyword   **GO**

Search tips & help

A customer can't type a keyword before they understand the search constraint. Buttons are also fighting for attention. The clear example places the search constraint first and minimizes cursor movement by placing the execute command next to the text field.

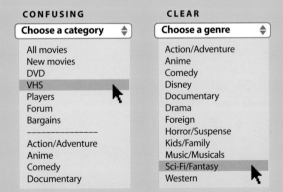

CONFUSING

Choose a category ⬍

All movies
New movies
DVD
VHS
Players
Forum
Bargains
_____
Action/Adventure
Anime
Comedy
Documentary

CLEAR

Choose a genre ⬍

Action/Adventure
Anime
Comedy
Disney
Documentary
Drama
Foreign
Horror/Suspense
Kids/Family
Music/Musicals
Sci-Fi/Fantasy
Western

Pull-down menus work best when presenting an ordered list of known or expected options. The confusing example forces the user to decipher the meaning of this list and hunt-and-peck through it to find a relevant choice.

FIGURE 4.17
THE FUNCTION OF FORMS
It only takes one bad form to kill the shopping experience. Consider the difference between the following forms.

Personalization

Allowing visitors to customize or personalize the buying experience adds another layer of complexity to designing effective interaction design.

To create personalized experiences, companies analyze customer data and predict the most appropriate products, advertising, and merchandising. Companies hope personalized features like tailored e-mail, wish lists, customer-account access, and product recommendations will improve service, increase revenues, and help to retain customers.

When a customer's personal information, transaction history, and clickstream data are dynamically matched with available inventory and product information, a personalized customer experience is created. (See Fig. 4.18) Commerce sites also use relevance engines from companies such as Autonomy. This technology distills patterns from product data, transaction histories and other disparate pieces of information to reveal potential matches for the consumer.[13]

Personalization has a strong effect on the process of interaction design. Each experience model and wireframe must be designed to accommodate different content and form display alternatives based on the personalized customer information (See Fig. 4.19).

The best personalization requires the least amount of customer effort. Ideally, no additional work should be involved. Amazon.com's The Page You Made is personalization based on items the customer clicked on during the current and recent site visits. When a customer chooses this page, they get several recommendations similar to products they previously viewed.

Two-thirds of Web users say that they are "extremely" or "very" concerned about their privacy. Because personalization usually involves a fair amount of confidential information, interaction design teams must address customer concerns by providing links to privacy policies.[14]

FIGURE 4.18: HOW PERSONALIZATION WORKS

Customer information and business content are combined to create unique, and (hopefully) relevant shopping options — almost like having a shopping concierge.

Customer
information

Product
relationships

Personal data,
preferences

Clickstream
What the customer has
done during this visit

Transactions
Previous and current
purchases

Matching engine
Makes predictions about
what the customer
might want

Jane's
Gift Guide

Products
Information and
categories

Ratings
From other customers

Transactions
From other customers
offline and online

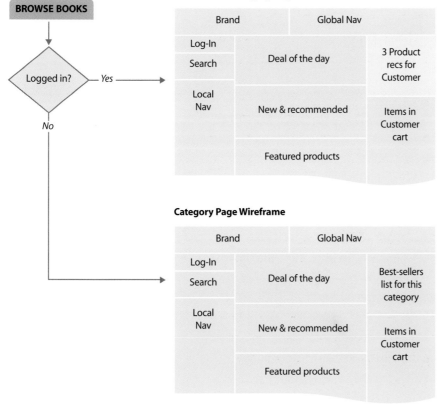

Personalized Category Page Wireframe

Brand		Global Nav	
Log-In	Deal of the day	3 Product recs for Customer	
Search			
Local Nav	New & recommended	Items in Customer cart	
	Featured products		

Category Page Wireframe

Brand		Global Nav	
Log-In	Deal of the day	Best-sellers list for this category	
Search			
Local Nav	New & recommended	Items in Customer cart	
	Featured products		

BROWSE BOOKS

Logged in? — Yes

No

FIGURE 4.19: MODELING PERSONALIZATION

Wireframes need to account for the possible content changes during a personalized experience. This will help the graphic designer understand which components need to be relatively the same size so that they can be swapped or moved around. In the example to the left, the three product recommendations need to be the same depth as the best-sellers list, if the cart is stay in the same place on the page.

Accessibility

Interaction design is the process of constantly asking, "What happens when… ." By asking this question, you flush into the open as many contingencies as possible. One of the contingencies you should consider early in the process are customers whose mental or physical disabilities would prevent them from having a positive shopping experience on your site.

Most companies are doing business on the Web to expand their potential customer base. There are more than 750 million people worldwide with a disability that could impact their Web-surfing experience. Designing for them is not just the morally right the thing to do. It makes good business sense. Another compelling reason for adopting accessible design is that many countries, including the United States, have passed or are considering legislation requiring that Web sites meet certain accessibility guidelines.

The World Wide Web Consortium's Web Accessibility Initiative has an in-depth set of guidelines and best practices, including scenarios of people with disabilities using the Web.[15] Michael Paciello's book *Web Accessibility for People with Disabilities* is also an excellent resource.

Completing Interaction Design

Wireframes represent the definition of an experience—how a site should work and how it should meet customer expectations. Hopefully, the wireframes your team creates during this phase represent an easy-to-learn, functional, and memorable commerce experience. These are the qualities of a usable design.

As the project moves into the presentation phase, the graphic designer's challenge is to make the experience outlined in the wireframes understandable and identifiable, while retaining usability.[16]

A good visual design, like a Lamborghini Diablo, is instantly understood. Sure, the chassis alone would send the message that the car is fast and handles well. But with the added visual cues of its bright yellow body and sleek design, the possibility of a great driving experience is immediately understood.

Through several stages of design and prototyping, you will arrive at a style that not only complements the interaction design, but communicates the site's value to the customer.

[1] Norman, Donald. *The Design of Everyday Things.* (Currency/Doubleday, 1990)

[2] Ibid.

[3] Zipf, George K. *Human Behavior and the Principle of Least Effort.* (Addison-Wesley, 1949).

[4] Nielsen, Jakob. "End of Web Design." (July, 2000). http://www.useit.com/alertbox/20000723.html

[5] Cialdini, Robert B. *Influence: Science and Practice.* (Allyn & Bacon, 2000, 4th Edition)

[6] Zona Research. Zona Market Bulletin, "The Need for Speed II." Issue 5, April, 2001.

[7] Suzuki, Shunryu. *Zen Mind, Beginner's Mind* (Weatherhill, 1988).

[8] Merholz, Peter. "User-Centered Information Design." Netscape.com. http://home.netscape.com/computing/webbuilding/studio/feature19980729-2.html

[9] Ibid. You might want to check out Peter's Web site, www.peterme.com, for excellent thoughts, links and essays on information architecture and customer experience.

[10] Ojakaar, Erik and Spool, Jared M. *Getting Them to What They Want: Eight Best Practices to Get Users to the Content They Want (and to Content They Didn't Know They Wanted).* (User Interface Engineering, 2001).

[11] Rehman, Amir. "Holiday 2000 E-commerce: Avoiding $14 Billion in Silent Losses." (October, 2000). http://www.creativegood.com/holiday2000/

[12] Baker, Adam. "Effective Use of Forms on Websites." (March, 2001). http://www.merges.net/theory/20010301.html

[13] Autonomy. http://www.autonomy.com/

[14] Forrester Report, "Retail & Media Data Overview" (Nov., 2000).

[15] W3C's Web Accessibility Initiative. http://www.w3.org/WAI/
Scenarios: http://www.w3.org/WAI/EO/Drafts/PWD-Use-Web/

[16] In his book *Experience Design 1* (New Riders, March, 2001), Nathan Shedroff explains, "Sometimes the roadblock to people being successful in an experience, isn't that they don't understand how to use the experience but that they don't understand what to expect from it or why it might be valuable to them —concerns that designers never consider since they can't imagine their audience not understanding what they are trying to accomplish." Find more on-line at: http://www.experiencedesignbooks.com/

chapter 5

PRESENTATION DESIGN FOR COMMERCE
Putting a face on the user experience

Although the Web is a relatively young medium, it already displays many design conventions. Commerce sites, especially, are becoming more similar to each other— and for good reason.

Unlike other types of Web sites that are free to push the boundaries of creative expression and technical experimentation, commerce sites are hypersensitive to the bottom line. In the marketplace, if one design or interactive approach boosts sales, then naturally many sites will fall in line and adopt a similar approach.

For example, hundreds of sites may look like Amazon, but few work like Amazon.

Amazon's interaction design, not its graphic identity, has been the cornerstone of its success. Yet, the visual identity that we associate with Amazon has been adopted as a standard because it is identified with how successfully Amazon applied it to customer goals.

Conventions are not dirty. They are a necessity of doing business, and there can be negative consequences if you break them without good reason. Instead of trying to push the envelope, a commerce site designer must start with familiar visual cues. If these familiar conventions don't satisfy customer's goals, then it's time for you to innovate.

Creating a Visual Identity

"Those are my principles, and if you don't like them... well, I have others." —Groucho Marx

As with any project, you will have to balance your design principles with the principles of the business and the preferences of others. But design is subjective, sometimes dreadfully so. Everyone has an opinion—marketing VPs, CEOs, even programmers. They will all tell you in which direction the design should point.

When confronted with these pressures, focus on visual identity and purpose. Protect the soundest ideas established during the review process from being lost amid dozens of proto-types and requests from management ("I think this icon should be in cornflower blue, don't you?"). Do justice to the work that has preceded the presentation phase—customer profiling, information design, wireframes and experience models.

The wireframes produced in Chapter 4 serve as your guidelines for creating this identity. They represent the inner logic of the site—the why, what, and how of business. Your goal is to make that inner logic visible in a simple, understandable way.

It is your mission to translate the tangible and intangible—market surveys, profiles, intuition, and technology—into something that is easily recognized and useful. Always remember that the measure of success for a commerce site's visual identity is not its sheer beauty, but its functional appropriateness to task and brand. If the site also earns design accolades, well, you've hit one out of the park.

The most important tool you have is the one between your ears. There is no recipe for choosing a style for your site. If there was, designers' work would have no value. While certain elements of commerce style have been commodified, you can still create a unique, engaging experience for your target audience. The elements that should influence your choice of style are brand identity, content, and customer tasks.

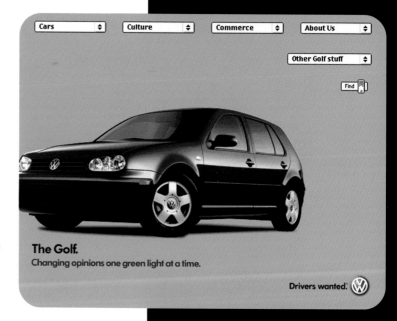

FIGURE 5.1

Volkswagen has very strict branding guidelines. They have a unique typeface, logo, and style of photography that is consistent across all marketing initiatives, including its Web site. The company's light, airy, clean style of design pervades everything they do. Imagine how ridiculous this site would look if it adopted the style of Amazon or Yahoo!

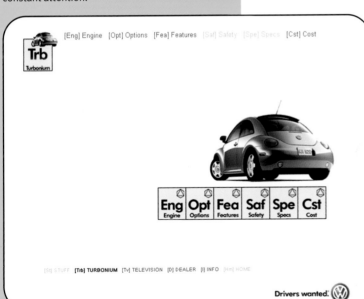

The Impact of Brand Identity

A company's trademark and its supporting identity system will have a significant impact on the design of your site. The company has official logos, colors, typefaces, and content that currently represent the brand. You will have to adopt and interpret these elements to some degree in order to tie the Web site to the offline enterprise.

Customers don't come to a site to see the brand, they come for a brand experience. Don't carry the company's look so far that you're forced to make bad design decisions. When color and design are stressed for the sake of the identity rather than the customer best interests, the corporate look gets in the way of usability. A site can express the right amount of personality by using the logo and corporate colors as an effective accent rather than as a sledgehammer (See Fig. 5.3).

Metaphor is another option for translating identity online. Metaphors are useful when they unify items that are part of a collection or when they communicate a familiar concept, like the shopping cart.

Sometimes, though, even well-intentioned metaphors are extended beyond their usefulness. For example, a movie rental company might make its navigation bar out of a marquee. Instead of being instantly recognizable as navigation, the marquee may be perceived

FIGURE 5.3: BRAND BALANCE

A designer's job is to interpret an existing brand as an online experience. Only by considering the Web's limitations and advantages, along with customer goals, can you balance identity and usability.

Here are two prototypes showing different approaches:

Prototype 1: Too much

Bold colors that work well in an identity system can be visually overwhelming when used in the same ways that you would in print. This prototype puts more emphasis on the brand than the content. "Scoop" category is unclear.

Prototype 2: Just right

Bold colors are used to accent content and control elements. Logo is less prominent but clearly identifiable. Navigation labels are more obvious. Page elements like Deals and Browse reinforce the site's retail nature.

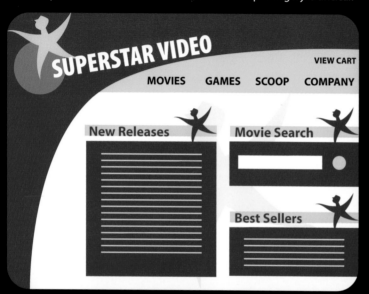

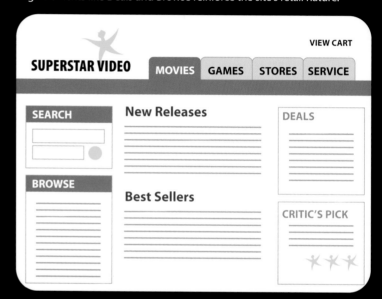

Corporate materials:

Logo

Corporate colors

Annual report

FIGURE 5.4: TOO CLEVER

FIGURE 5.5 : IMPACT OF LOGO SHAPE ON PAGE STRUCTURE

The fixed shape of a company logo can have a noticeable impact on the structure of your page. When sketching possible layouts identify objects that are fixed in size or cannot be reduced below a certain dimension.

Horizontal logos work well on most Web pages, since computer monitors have a horizontal format. Pairing up navigation with the logo is a logical combination.

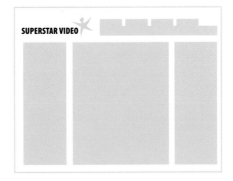

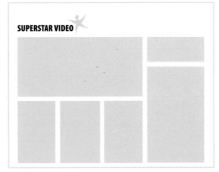

A square logo usually forces a horizontal navigation bar to be deeper than necessary. It's better to run the navigation column beneath a square logo.

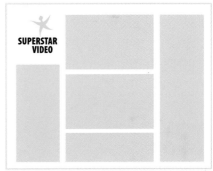

Vertical logos always force a vertical format on the page. If you attempt to regain a horizontal structure, you might get a gratuitous amount of white space. This will eat up a chunk of your precious screen real estate.

as decoration or illustration (See Fig. 5.4). The designer's need to look clever or to make the site more lighthearted leaves the customer's goals in the back seat. Bottom line: it's better to stick with a more literal interface and design than to go overboard with metaphors.

Whether you use a metaphor or not, you don't have much say about a company's logo shape or style. The trademark is the most easily recognizable company symbol. It should be treated with some amount of reverence and usually carries with it strict guidelines for usage. Before you waste time developing your ideas, get a clear understanding of any logo usage guidelines from the marketing department. Since you might need to alter the logo for the site, make sure you seek approval from the marketing

department before incorporating the company logo in the design.

Logos with sans-serif faces and highly graphic logotypes fare best on low-resolution monitors. But you might be dealing with a logo that is more figurative, like a scratch-board illustration (See Fig. 5.5).

When faced with a figurative trademark, you might consider creating a modified version for the Web that is simpler. If that's not an option, you will have to display the logo larger, which could make the design seem unbalanced or add to download time. Many sites use letter marks, like Yahoo! or Amazon (See Fig. 5.6), which can be used as versatile labels across the site. Letter marks scale to smaller sizes well and download quickly.

FIGURE 5.6: LETTER MARK LOGOS

Impact of Content

The true test of a design is how well its style matches the content. By this time, you should have a clear idea of the quality and types of content you'll be supplied. In Chapter 3, we showed you how to take a content inventory. If you've done one, you know what the product photos will look like and how long the descriptions that accompany them will be.

With these parameters in mind, experiment with designs that suit the nature and style of the content. To a large degree, the content of your site may mandate a certain style. If the content doesn't meet the quality demands of the design, its limitations will eventually undermine the customer's shopping experience.

For example, consider the image quality of the photos found on eBay. The people selling the items (not professionals) usually take their own photos of the product. The photo quality varies widely, along with the amount of information provided. For most items on eBay that's fine. Why have a professional shoot a picture of a ceramic owl saltshaker if you're only going to get $12 dollars for the sale?

Christie's, on the other hand, is a high-end auction site that has hundreds of expensive antiques, paintings, sculptures, and other collectibles. Buyers expect a higher-quality experience and need better information to make a purchase decision. Professional photography and detailed information about the piece are not just nice to have on the site—they are essential for buyers (See Fig. 5.7).

CHRISTIE'S LotFinder®

Log In ▶ Your Account ▶

Search Options [?]

SEARCH ▶

16 October 2001

HOME | SALE CATEGORIES | AUCTIONS | SELLING | PUBLICATIONS | OUR SERVICES | ABOUT CHRISTIE'S | HELP

Japanese Art

Overview
Contact Information
Specialist Profiles
Exceptional Prices
Consignments
Auction Calendar
Related Books

Exceptional Prices

Kawase Hasui (1883-1957)
May Rain at Sanno Temple, 1919
Sold for NLG5,000
($2,075)
October 1999
Amsterdam

From the series *Tokyo Junidai (Twelve subjects of Tokyo)*

Go to:

1 2 3 4 5 6 7 8 9 10 11

1

2

3

4

5

6

7

8

9

10

11

Back to Home | Site Map
Terms & Conditions | Privacy Policy

© Christies 2001
Contact Us

FIGURE 5.7

Christie's must use professional photographs to substantiate the quality of a product up for auction. Otherwise, customers would be left questioning the condition of the products. Its interface and design must also meet a higher standard. They are simple, stylish, and present an image of sophistication.

Sometimes, photography is good enough to carry the design. Handspring's sleek, stylish product photography defines their Web site design. They keep typography and the color palette restrained so that their products jump off the page (See Fig. 5.8).

Words can affect visual style just as much as images can. Most sites that sell flowers have very literal and bland text, like: "Do you love flowers? Get our great looking bouquets delivered fresh every month for a full year."

Flowerbud.com (see the case study on pp. 198–201) infuses just the right language to extend its personality into the sale: "Can you get too much of a good thing? For those who subscribe to that notion, may we suggest flowers once a month for a full year? A beautiful array of our growers' finest, shipped direct to the recipient the same day they're harvested."

Flowerbud uses a descriptive and active writing style that suits their audience and their other content. It is short, readable, and consistent in tone. The visual design reinforces this friendly tone with calligraphic lettering and watercolor art elements.

When developing content, consider the tradeoff between style and performance. While they are not mutually exclusive, they are rarely complementary. For example, a sports car site might benefit enough from a rich multimedia experience to be willing to sacrifice quick download times and universal browser support. If a company knows their customer well, it might be a smart tradeoff. However, few sites have the production talent to pull this experience off. Making the tradeoff without production support only result in mediocre media on a sluggish site.

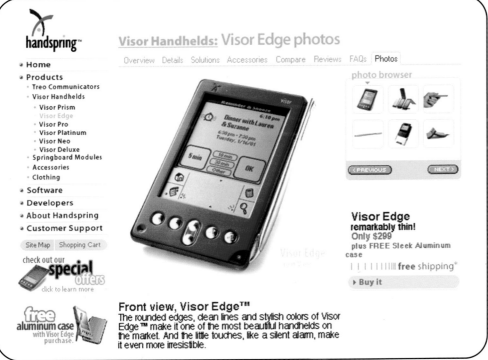

FIGURE 5.8

Ornate typography or heavy use of Handspring's brand colors (blue, green, orange) would have distracted from this clean product photography. Despite being image intensive, Handspring's site downloads fast.

Impact of Tasks

In Chapter 4, we stressed the importance of understanding tasks and goals through good interaction design. These factors also help to define the overall look and feel of the site.

Imagine walking into a bank and having to watch a two-minute commercial before you could make a deposit. You would quickly become frustrated. The same reaction will happen online. On a banking site, no customer wants to be subjected to a two-minute animated Flash intro or a 400-pixel-wide photo of a smiling sales rep behind a desk. Customers want to log in, make a deposit, pay a bill, update the balance and get out.

Your design must be practical. This is why so many sites make the Checkout section of a Web site free of sales and marketing interference. Once the customer has committed to buy, the only task left is to move them through the purchase steps.

As always, being appropriate to task doesn't mean creating a bland design, void of personality. When selling wedding rings, retailer Blue Nile not only must educate its customers about diamonds, metals, and settings, but move them gently through the buying process. Blue Nile maintains a effortless shopping experience with rich attention to details and addressing customer concerns (See Fig. 5.9).

Many commerce sites have products, such as computers or shoes, which the customer must build or customize before they checkout. Since this task is different from the browse-and-find process that may dominate the site's overall design, it may require a unique approach to presentation (See Fig. 5.10).

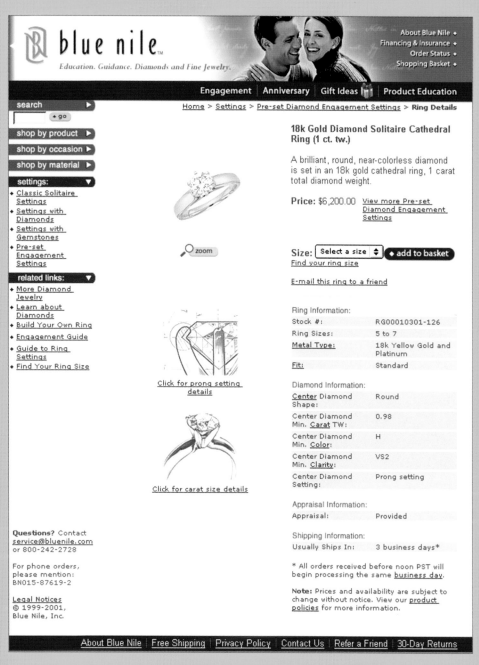

FIGURE 5.9

Blue Nile's "ring detail" pages are information intensive but appropriate to the task. If customers are going to spend $6,000 on a ring without even trying it on, they are definitely going to need a wealth of specific detail to feel confident about their choice. Clicking on "zoom" reveals a 400-pixel-square picture of the ring.

Cases
Custom Case Builder Status:

Type · Color · Material · Finalize

Shipping and Return Information

Follow these 4 easy steps to create your one-of-a-kind Visor case.

Follow these 4 easy steps to create your one-of-a-kind Visor case.

Step 1. Pick a case type.

Step 2. Choose a color.

Step 3. Pick a material.

Step 4. Add your initials if you like, confirm your order, add to your shopping cart, and you're done.

Step 1 Pick a type:

Deluxe — it's quick and easy with a paper pad and slots for cards.

Select

These cases fit Visor, Visor Deluxe, Visor Neo, Visor Platinum and Visor Pro. Not for use with Visor Edge or Visor Prism.

Slim — for a quick and easy open and close.

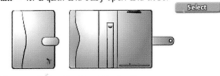

Select

These cases fit Visor, Visor Deluxe, Visor Neo, Visor Platinum and Visor Pro. Not for use with Visor Edge or Visor Prism.

Zipper — it's the most secure way to go.

Select

These cases fit Visor, Visor Deluxe, Visor Neo, Visor Platinum and Visor Pro. Not for use with Visor Edge or Visor Prism.

FIGURE 5.10

Presenting a customer with a list of all the available Handspring cases would be overwhelming. Instead, Handspring chunks the browsing experience into steps that narrow the product choices. First the customer picks a style, followed by a color. The customer then receives a selection of the most appropriate products.

Cases
Custom Case Builder Status:

Type · Color · Material · Finalize

Step 2 Choose a color:

Blacks	Blues	Browns
Select	Select	Select

Grays	Greens	Orange & Yellows
Select	Select	Select

Cases
Custom Case Builder Status:

Type · Color · Material · Finalize

Step 3 Pick a material:

Click the case material you want. And get the big picture

Select	Select	Select	Select
Aqua Marine Belting Leather $61.95	Blue Abbey Nubuck * $59.95	Generation Blue * $53.95	Old Blue Alligator Embossed Calf * $61.95

Cases
Custom Case Builder Status:

Type · Color · Material · Finalize

Step 4 Finalize your order:

Type: **Zipper**
Color: **Blue**
Material: **Old Blue Alligator Embossed Calf**
Dimensions: **3 3/4" x 5 3/4" x 1 1/2"**
Basic Price: **$61.95**

 Or call 1-888-565-9393

These cases fit Visor, Visor Deluxe, Visor Neo, Visor Platinum and Visor Pro. Not for use with Visor Edge or Visor Prism.

Familiar Friends

There are many fine books that go into great detail about graphic design on the Web. *HTML Artistry: More than Code by Ardith Ibanez; Designing Web Graphics by Lynda Weinman; and the Web Style Guide by Patrick Lynch.*

Books basically all follow the same design model with one column of body type on each page. Chapter labels, footnotes, and page numbers are found in standard locations. Such predictable design elements project an image of tradition and authority.

The information architecture of a book is familiar and has been proven functional over the years. Contents and index pages tell the reader where to look for specific content.

Early Web sites (and even some current ones) mimicked similar aspects of print design. To a certain degree, this made good sense. Principles of grid, color, and typography still apply, since the majority of Web-page elements are still built of words and images.

However, computer-based interactive experiences impose unique parameters on grid, color, and typography. The following set of figures explains what a commerce designer will need to consider.

Someone once said that design is nothing more than lining up something with something else. All graphic design, from Egyptian hieroglyphs to Web pages, is based on the linear grid. Invisible rows and columns provide the skeleton for words and images and determine their interrelationships.

Flexibility

Many designers don't like flexible grids because they undermine the very thing a designer covets: visual control. But because a Web page appears on a variety of different monitors and browsers, it's almost inevitable that the page will have to resize to fill the available space.

Tables

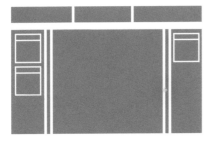

HTML is not a page-layout language, but it does come with an indispensable design tool to maintain a grid structure—the table. Web designers use tables to impose strict order or allow flexibility to support a variety of monitor sizes and operating system conditions.

HTML tables can be stacked (placed on top of each other) or nested (placed inside of each other) to accommodate a variety of grids.

Width

Before allowing a page to expand horizontally, decide which part of the table lends itself to flexing. Usually this is the content in the center. Flexing navigation or the search box causes buttons to shift unpredictably.

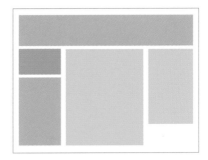

Horizontal flexing can cause readability issues if the page gets too wide. Control elements can lose proximity to each other.

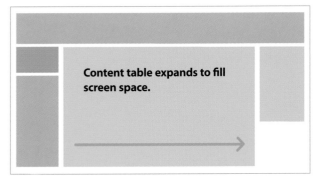

Content table expands to fill screen space.

Depth

Web pages have no inherent vertical limits. But research shows that Web visitors rarely scroll down below the first screen, and almost never below the second. Odds are that information presented on the second or third screen will not get the attention you desire. When designing product pages with large amounts of information, break the material into additional pages rather than allowing it to scroll.

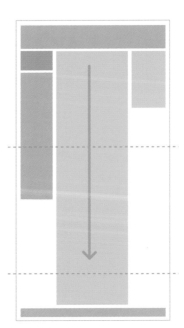

Navigation
Content/products
Search

Even though most commerce sites use similar design and navigation elements (like tabs and search boxes) grid layout can vary greatly to add order, simplicity or activity. A commerce site might employ a variety of grids depending on the task and information that needs to be presented. For example, a checkout area usually has a different grid from a product page.

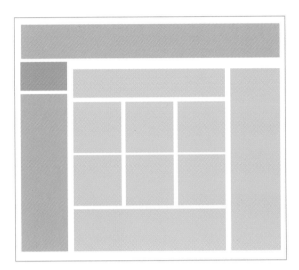

Familiar L-grid layout
This grid is the most common on the Web because it can easily be designed to flex to the full width of any size of screen.

Navigation surrounds content on three sides
Right side navigation can reduce the distance a user must move the cursor from the navigation to the scroll bar. However, on a smaller screen, the right side navigation can be hidden.

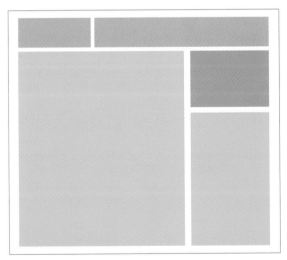

Top navigation only with two-column content area
This style emphasizes content. Many commerce sites use this type of grid on step-driven pages like checkout or build-a-product.

Asymmetric layout
Good for adding energy and a hip feel. The downside of this style is that it's not very forgiving. Content must exactly fit the design.

FIGURE 5.13: THE COLOR OF COMMERCE

The right color scheme on your commerce site can help boost interactivity, provide harmony in your design, add personality and show consistency. But choosing from millions of available colors can be overwhelming. Starting with one of these schemes will guarantee color harmony and reinforce the identity of your site.

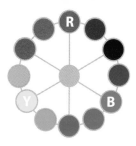

The basics
The color wheel shows the relationships between colors. All colors are based on three primary colors (red, blue, and yellow).

Monochromatic
This is the easiest scheme. Chose one color and make a few variations in its saturation and brightness. Monochromatic colors work especially well in tables or buttons.

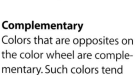

Complementary
Colors that are opposites on the color wheel are complementary. Such colors tend play off each other. Use one as a background, and the other as an accent color for important buttons or directional purposes.

Analogous (Adjacent)
Choose three adjacent colors on the wheel. Adjust with different values of brightness. Analogous schemes are found often in nature (shades of blue found in the sea) and effectively create mood.

splash.com

Triad (Equidistant)
Choose three colors that are equidistant from each other on the color wheel. Black and white can be added for different shades.

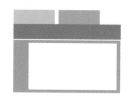

Split complementary
Choose three adjacent colors on the wheel and add the complementary color of the middle hue. The complementary color helps add balance.

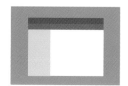

FIGURE 5.14: WEB-SAFE COLORS

Most of your customers probably have monitors and computers that can display thousands of colors or more. But there are many people out there who have old equipment or who use incorrect settings for their monitors.

The 216-color Web-safe palette brings color consistency to site design. Web-safe colors are designed to appear nearly the same across browser and computer platforms.

While you need not go overboard and use Web-safe colors on every graphic, you might consider using colors in a limited way for interface elements, buttons, or logos. (The orange arrow Amazon uses is a Web-safe orange color #FF9900). That way, you can be guaranteed that your important elements are as readable as possible, no matter what browser or computer combination your visitor has.

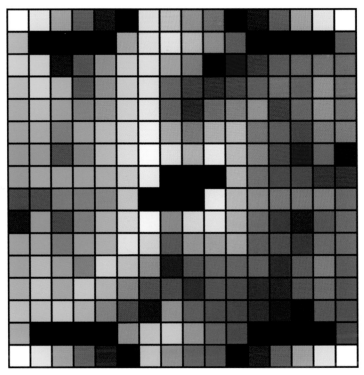

Web-safe color palette

Original logo

Nearest Web-safe equivalent

Dithered equivalent

Take advantage of dithering

Mixing two or three of the original 216 Web-safe colors together in different patterns (dithering) can produce nearly 10 million different colors.

Programs like Adobe's Photoshop or sites like ColorMix.com can easily convert high-fidelity color into a dithered pattern (right). The advantage of doing this is that browsers will try to approximate missing colors on their own, usually with shoddy results.

Dithering also provides a pixelated texture rather than smooth, flat color. The more active palette might provide the kind of early '90s Web feel you've been looking for.

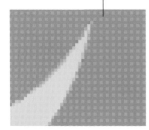

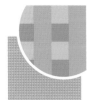

New color made from three Web-safe colors.

FIGURE 5.15: COLOR-BLIND DESIGN

It's poor business sense to exclude anyone from your site. About 9 percent of the population has some form of color blindness. In the most common form of color blindness, red and green hues look the same.

In general, it is difficult to come up with a scheme that guarantees complete accessibility to people who have color vision problems.

One sure way to make your site more accessible is to increase the brightness contrast between foreground and background colors.

For additional information on color blindness and Web design, see visibone.com.

Normal vision
Most people see a full range of colors and have the ability to make fine distinctions between hues and different levels of gray.

Color blindness
An example of what the color wheel can look like to individuals who have the most common form of color blindness.

Actual
What might seem to most people like clear color differences and obvious cues can leave people with color blindness stumped.

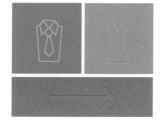

Simulated
Notice how the bright red arrow and pink background turn to grays. The arrow nearly disappears.

Providing more brightness contrast between foreground and background colors will help all visitors navigate better.

Provide redundant clues like texture, labels, or consistent location to help reduce confusion.

Use fonts designed for monitors

When you get down to the pixel level, only typefaces that have been specifically designed pixel by pixel will read well.

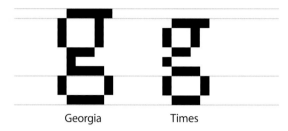

Georgia   Times

If you want to use a serif face, choose Georgia. Notice how a typeface designed for monitors is slightly larger and cleaner in shape. Georgia has a larger x-height and bigger counters.

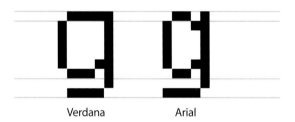

Verdana   Arial

For sans serif, we recommend Verdana. Even a one-pixel difference can have an impact on readability. Verdana's extra pixel of width provides for larger counters.

Choose pixel-fonts

Look at other pixel-based fonts, such as Sevenet and Mini, for use in graphic image navigation bars or control elements. They offer wonderful readability at small sizes, usually 7 or 8 pt.

Sevenet   Mini

Prioritize font choice

HTML font tags allow designers some control in defining a hierarchy of type choice for the customer.

`<FONT FACE = "Verdana, Arial, Helvetica, san-serif">`

With this code, the visitor's browser will first look for Verdana. If it doesn't find that, the browser will look for Arial, then Helvetica. If none of those exist, it will use the default sans serif face chosen by the browser. To make your list, consider what is typically found on most computers:

PC Fonts	Mac Fonts
Arial	Helvetica
Book Antiqua	Palatino
Courier New	Courier
MS Sans Serif	Geneva
MS Serif	Times
Symbol	Symbol
Times New Roman	New York
WingDings	Zapf Dingbats
No equivalent	Chicago

Cross-platform

Common PC web fonts widely available for Mac: Arial, Georgia, Trebuchet MS, Verdana

Maintain contrast

Some commerce sites seem to go out of their way to make even appropriately sized type hard to read by reducing the contrast between the lightness of type and background.

Switzerland   Switzerland

High contrast   Low contrast

FIGURE 5.16
WEB TYPOGRAPHY

Even though people mostly scan online, it's important that what they do read is legible. Getting type right (or just read-able) can be a chore. Here are some suggestions for increasing readability of your Web page.

FIGURE 5.17
USING STYLE SHEETS

The designer's first responsibility is to make sure that type is presented in the most readable way. Cascading Style Sheets (CSS), when supported by the browser, provide excellent control over a type's style, leading, and size.

Presentation logic

Style sheets for Web pages work similarly to style sheets in page layout programs, in that they allow the designer to separate appearance from code. If Handspring wants to change price color from green to blue or orange on all their pages, they would only have to change the attributes in the style sheet document. Without style sheets, a designer would have to make this change to each individual page.

Maintain structure

Cascading Style Sheets can be applied to standard HTML tags like <H2> or <B> changing the way they look. The advantage of applying CSS to HTML tags is that the structure of the document is retained. Incompatible browsers will still show your type as having varied size and style, which will keep the page readable to visitors.

STYLE SHEET

H2 {font-family: "Myriad", color:#1E73B2, size: 15pt}

WITH CSS

<H2> —— New Products
<b> <font size=-2> —— Digital Answering Machine

<font size=-2> —— Never have to take phone messages again with this amazing product $59 (US).

WITHOUT CSS

<H2> —— **New Products**
<b> <font size=-2> —— **Digital Answering Machine**

<font size=-2> —— Never have to take phone messages again with this amazing product $59 (US).

Display typography

Like color, use your site's signature display face in small but effective doses and combine it with photography to save space. Amazon uses decorative type to highlight category pages and sales of special items. Grouping of type with image can help keep download times fast. Display type is best used for page or content labels, as in this example from online jewelry retailer Blue Nile.

Display type used for accent combined with HTML text.

When used sparingly, these display type labels help add style without making the page slow.

The Face of Interaction

Even with the best possible design and content of any single page, a commerce site will fail to sell anything without a clear and consistent interface. The interface pulls together individual pages and creates a coherent experience. On every page, the interface must be answer three questions for a customer, "Where am I?," "What can I do here?," and "Where can I go from here?"

The hypertext nature of the Web allows pages to link, making every Web page an interface. So a major goal of Web-interface design is to provide a sense of order. You provide this order through navigation and control elements. Links, pull-down menus, and buttons are the tools that allow the visitor to explore, choose, and act.

In recent years, Web-interface design has moved from the provenance of designers to become a discipline of its own. Interface design requires a lot of planning and testing to make sure the navigation can accommodate the tasks of the customer. The following three figures explain the components of an interface.

FIGURE 5.18

PRIMARY NAVIGATION

The components of navigation will appear on all parts of the page. Most sites use a main horizontal navigation bar to give site visitors a way to access the main sections of a site. Sometimes popular lower-level categorizations are exposed here. There is no compelling evidence to support one design over another. However, some methods are simply more familiar to customers than others.

TAB STYLE

TAB STYLE WITH SUB-CATEGORY TEXT LABELS

VARIATION ON TAB STYLE WITH SUB CATEGORIES

TEXT LABEL STYLE WITH BREADCRUMBS

PULL-DOWN MENU

DROP-DOWN MENU A LA OPERATING SYSTEM

Looks familiar

Graphic buttons are identified best when they are shaped like a pill, because that is the shape associated with operating system buttons.

Works familiar

Graphic buttons can behave like links. When the customer mouses over the button, the cursor changes from an arrow to a hand. This feedback signals the user that the element is clickable.

Bigger is better

Fitt's law states that the time it takes for users to mouse to and click on a button is related to the size and distance of the button. Important and frequently used buttons should be larger.

A smaller target is more difficult to click on with a mouse.

Larger targets don't require precise mouse control.

OS default

> **Checkout**

Benefits
No additional time for download. Are familiar to customers because they are defined by the client's operating system.

Drawbacks
Can change dimensions depending on client's operating system. Designer has no method of distinguishing button types—they all look the same.

Text link

Checkout

Benefits
No additional time for download. Are familiar to customers because every site visitor understands the function of a text link.

Drawbacks
Can change dimension and readability depending on client's browser setting for type. Because it's text, it can sometimes move around on the page and be in an unpredictable location.

Graphic

Benefits
Designer has complete control over style, size, color of button, and typeface.

Drawbacks
Some graphic buttons can confuse customers with their design. It may not be apparent that they are buttons. Graphics also add to page download time.

Rollover

Benefits
None. If your buttons are consistent in look and behavior, the visitor should quickly understand what they are, making the rollover version unnecessary.

FIGURE 5.19
CUSTOMER IN CONTROL
Commerce sites are filled with buttons. Good buttons reveal their purpose at first glance and behave in predictable ways.

FIGURE 5.20
WHAT'S IN A NAME?

The appropriate use of
language is fundamental
to the success of all good
interfaces. In fact, it may
be more important than
how it looks. If someone
doesn't understand what
the word means, they
certainly won't care about
the typeface or color.
Work with the information
architect, who should
understand taxonomy
and language better than
anyone on the staff.

Don't be cute or clever

Explicit and familiar terms are more usable. In the tab navigation, what does Buzz mean?
What does New refer to—new movies or new information on the site?

UNCLEAR

SPECIFIC

Most appropriate

The text used in a button or link is just as important as its appearance and behavior.
The text indicates where someone is going and what the button will do.

On the Internet, the labels on these buttons are used synonymously. Yet each term has
distinct connotations and different interpretations. When choosing words for buttons,
use terms that are the most appropriate to the task and the least ambiguous. In this case,
the best choice is Search.

Say what you mean

This is a commerce site, not a video game. It's the job of the designer and the
information architect to make sure that your interface elements make sense. Which
one of these links are you most likely to click on?

[+]   Magnify   See larger photo

Effective interfaces for commerce sites should:

- **Have clear navigation.** One of the biggest complaints is that site visitors can't find their destinations. Your interface should use clear and consistent navigation elements and always let the visitor know where they are within the site.

- **Be efficient.** Navigation should focus on getting the customer to what they want in the easiest manner possible, rather than accumulating page views.

- **Be simple.** Don't complicate an interface with graphic design or interactivity just for the sake of doing so. As interface design specialist, Alan Cooper, has said, "No matter how cool your interface is, less of it would be better."[1]

- **Leave breadcrumbs.** Breadcrumbs keep a visitor from getting lost and help provide context for how the page they are viewing fits within the larger scope of the site. Breadcrumbs also provide an easy way for a visitor to jump up a number of levels without having to resort to the browser's back button.

- **Be familiar.** Use conventions like tab navigation. They are not innovative or unique, but they work well and are easily understood by most site visitors.

- **Be consistent.** Consistency is more important than look. Be strict about consistent use of control elements, graphic style and behavior. Customers expect the interface to remain constant throughout the site.

Consistency is the cornerstone of usability. The more things stay the same, the less a customer will have to learn. This leads to a transparent interface—one that doesn't require thought—allowing users to fully concentrate on the task at hand.

The Value of Modular Design

Templates excel at helping you maintain a consistent look and interactivity. They harness the processing power of your site's computers to automate the production of HTML pages. The concept, as described in earlier chapters, is simple—join databases of words, images, and numbers with powerful scripting languages to generate dynamic and highly responsive Web sites.

But most important, templates allow a site to process the content separately from the design. This separation provides a tremendous number of advantages for a commerce Web site.

Division of labor

Templates allow a natural division of labor within a team. Designers are freed from more mundane tasks like writing font tags and can focus on presentation and interaction issues. Web producers can translate the design into HTML and scripts without being asked to understand design fundamentals. Site editors can concentrate on supplying quality content instead of becoming HTML jockeys. With editors not entering errant code, programmers have less to debug and can focus on boosting the site's performance. When people are allowed to focus their talents, the site inevitably benefits.

Static HTML

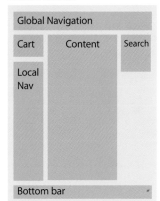

Global Navigation

Cart | Content | Search

Local Nav

Bottom bar

Limited Template

Global Navigation

Cart | Content | Search

Local Nav

Bottom bar

Modular Template

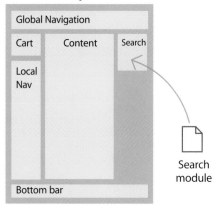

Global Navigation

Cart | Content | Search

Local Nav

Bottom bar

Search module

FIGURE 5.21
MODULAR TEMPLATES

Modular pages require more planning and coding but offer the rewards of easy updating, more dynamic content, and consistent customer interaction.

Benefit: Unlimited control
Drawback: Time-consuming to build and update.

Each page needs to be hand-coded with content nested as part of the presentation. Each page will have to be updated manually.

Benefit: Dynamic content
Drawback: Updating these types of templates can be time-consuming.

Only a small amount of content is dynamically generated or inserted. Even a little content can result in large productivity gains and improve the customer's experience.

Benefit: Easy site-wide changes, personalization quick to implement.
Drawback: Highly structured.

Modular approach breaks page into small, discrete pieces that can be built or modified individually. Content is separated from design code.

Intelligent modules

Template modules can be programmed to change based on the page that inherits them. Below is an example of a search box module that offers more specific choices depending on the page it appears on.

Home page

SEARCH

All Products

enter keyword **GO**

Advanced | Tips

Category page

SEARCH

All DVDs

enter keyword **GO**

Advanced | Tips

Subcategory page

SEARCH

All Sci-Fi

enter keyword **GO**

Advanced | Tips

Easy and quick updates

Changing something on one Web page is not difficult. Changing something on every Web page is. When January 1 nears, your Web team won't want to spend their holiday scrolling through lines of HTML to change all the copyright dates. Templates allow a designer or even an editor to make that change in one file and have it apply to an entire site.

Most content-management systems provide simple interfaces for editors that allow them to modify content without ever having to use as much as an ‹a href› tag. These systems archive changes, which is helpful in tracking errors or coordinating workflow (for example, when many editors must approve content).

You can also use templates to publish content on a scheduled date or after a specific approval takes place. For example, the Web team of a site selling a line of new toys can input all the database information but hold publication until the big product release date.

From one come many

Templates can hold many scripting instructions, making it possible to have one template transform into many different-looking pages. It can seem like magic when you see two or three of your design templates blossom into a full site, with hundreds of pages filled with content and working links. Keep your templates to manageable number. Usually, a commerce site can be defined in about ten templates (home, category, product detail, search, shopping cart, checkout, order status, etc). On the other hand, don't overdo your template efficiency. While it's possible to have one template play Superman and handle multiple rolls, the template will start to bloat with code and become unwieldy.

You will soon discover that scripting languages used by templates provide you with a creative freedom unattainable in other media. In print, a single version of your work is produced and distributed. Templates, however, are assembled in real-time and can respond instantly to the types of visitors, what they are doing, the content they access and many other factors. For example, a template can let you change the car on the home page of an auto-maker's site by determining a visitor's probable geographical location from his or her IP address. Such capability opens up tremendous possibilities and suggests that design can play a more dynamic and vital role than is has traditionally.

Consistency

Templates provide the best way to create a site with consistent identity and interactivity. Without templates, maintaining a site would require many different people, each responsible for different sections of the site. It probably would not take long before each section began to diverge in look and feel. One designer might label a button Search while others use Go! Such inconsistencies cause needless visitor confusion and can easily be eradicated with templates.

Modular design benefits

The best templates take a highly modular approach. Modularity rewards you with consistency, reinforces the interactive experience and makes development easier (See Fig. 5.21).

In a modular design, pages are made up of discrete units of code, content, and graphics. Splitting a page into smaller pieces means you can concentrate on creating each component without having to entangle its code with the rest of the page. Modularity makes it not only easy to assemble but to debug.

For example, you can build one module for the search button that includes all the HTML, JavaScript, and graphics. Once the module exists, every template that requires a search box can simply retrieve and load the search button code in the appropriate place. Later, if you need to change every search box on the site, you would only have to modify a small file containing a minimal amount of code.

Modular components aren't just design elements like search boxes. You might need a JavaScript code to "sniff" the customer's browser for compatible plug-ins like Flash. Again, structuring your code and design in a modular way will make for a plug-and-play page.

There are multitudes of possible page variations based on different combinations of words, images and data. This template-driven code can have unintended results. In combination, two or more dynamic page elements can conspire to embarrass or cause confusion. For example, a major commerce site designed a personalized store for their customers. Instead of calling it something bland like My Store, they added the personal touch and used the customer's name. Unfortunately, any name longer than six characters was truncated. See Fig. 5.22 for the scary results.

As a designer, you might be concerned that a modular approach will make pages that look like a patchwork of information spit out of a database. Poorly designed sites do look that way. Sites that follow a process and center their design on the customer's goals can look as alive as any handmade HTML. In this next section, we examine what makes for compelling templates across the major commerce categories: home, category, product, search, and checkout.

FIGURE 5.22: UNINTENDED CONSEQUENCES
One of the dangers of dynamic content is that it might not display as intended. Here's an example of a site that used a customer's name to label a personal store. But in this instance, the result was a major gaffe.

Template snafu
In the effort to highlight a personalized store, designers put a button in the navigation column. The template was designed so that names longer than eight letters, like Christopher, were truncated to fit.

Welcome to Christ...'s Store
(If you're not Christ..., click here.)

The truncated version carried over to the page title, which could have accommodated the full name. In this instance, the retailer should have used MyStore in the navigation, and designed a template to accommodate longer names.

The home page

The home page is a strange beast. Unlike other page types, there are no conventions for what should appear on a home page or how it should look. This is because home pages are political animals within an organization. Everyone in the company, from sales to marketing to the CEO, will want a say in what's on it. They will probably also want a piece the real estate to be dedicated to their interests.

Try to put all that corporate pressure aside and consider the customer's point of view. For the customer, a commerce home page should answer:

• What kind of site is this?

• What can I do here and how do I get started?

• How many and what type of products are you selling?

• Why should I buy from your site, rather than my other options?

• Will this purchase be easy and secure?

To answer these questions, you will need to:

• Establish company message/identity

• Add elements that promote trustworthiness

• Establish the breadth and depth of the site and its inventory

• Move customers to their destinations (transaction, help, information) as quickly and efficiently as possible

You will decide how much of the page to devote to each of these concerns. If the company is not a well-established brand, then you may need to use a little more space on the brand and trust. If the company has a frequently changing inventory, then you may want to focus a large part of the real estate on what's new and available.

Successful home pages get visitors started on their task right away, either through category links, search boxes or featured products. As we explained in Chapter 3, knowing what your customers want and how they view your site's offerings should drive the solutions.

When designing a home page template, examine which parts of the page can be used elsewhere on the site. For example, many home pages establish the site's main navigation and search components. These modules can be reused in other templates.

Introducing... trēo. talk. organize. connect.

Jeff Hawkins talks Treo

▶ Learn more about Treo

places to **go**

- International Sites
- Products
- Software
- Developers
- About Handspring
- Customer Support

Site Map | Shopping Cart

- **Where** to Buy
- **Shipping** & Ordering Info
- **Product** Registration

FREE!
Documents To Go
with the purchase of any
Visor Handheld

click here to learn more

Affiliates Program
$$Sign up today! GO

things to **buy**

Visor handhelds
check out our newest models—
plus free shipping

click here for details

Special Offers
free cases, GameFace & more
with Visor handheld purchase

click here for more great deals

Visor Prism
was $399, now only $299
same fabulous color, great new price

click here to learn more

Super Savings!
Save 20% on a variety of
popular Springboard™ modules

click here to learn more

FREE aluminum case
with Visor Edge purchase
plus get free shipping!

click here to learn more

news to **know**

win a **free**
trēo autographed
by Jeff Hawkins
sign up for our e-newsletter today

Coming Soon!
Jeff Hawkins keynote at Comdex

10/15/01
Handspring Unites Phone, Messaging
And PDA In New Treo™ Communicator

10/15/01
Visto Corporation to Power Wireless Email
Application for Handspring Treo
Communicators

10/01/01
Handspring And DataViz Offer Popular
Office Software For Free With Purchase
Of Any Visor

Springboard
module news
GO

Affiliates | E-Newsletter | Feedback | Handspring Policies | Help | International | Where To Buy
Copyright © 1999-2001 Handspring

FIGURE 5.23

Product manufacturers like Handspring typically use their home page to reinforce the marketing message of their products and their company. Handspring knows that there are plenty of other Web sites that are selling their products. So their site caters to potential buyers who came there to learn more about their PDAs and other products, not necessarily to buy one. Understanding this fact about their target audience, Handspring only dedicates about 20 percent of this page to online sales.

FIGURE 5.24

The home page of this fine-art auction house highlights new inventory, because the products up for sale are always changing. Christie's uses the home page to establish its core site navigation, along with a sophisticated color palette and crisp photography.

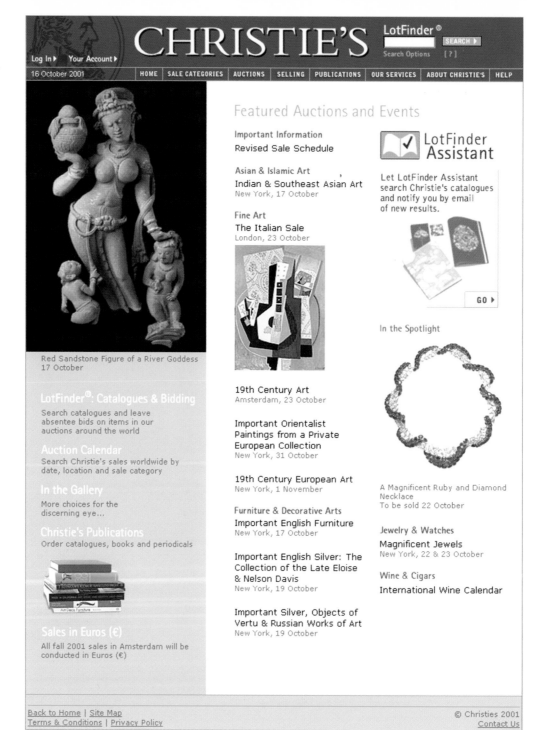

blue nile™
Education. Guidance. Diamonds and Fine Jewelry.

About Blue Nile ◆
Financing & Insurance ◆
Order Status ◆
Shopping Basket ◆

Engagement | Anniversary | Gift Ideas | Product Education

search
- Diamond Search
- Jewelry Search
  [ ] ◆ go

shop by product
- Loose Diamonds
- Settings
- Rings
- Earrings
- Necklaces & Pendants
- Bracelets
- Men's Watches
- Women's Watches
- Accessories

shop by occasion
- Gift Ideas
- Engagement
- Anniversary
- Wedding

shop by material
- Diamond
- Pearl
- Sapphire
- Ruby
- Emerald
- Gold & Platinum
- Silver

Questions? Contact
service@bluenile.com
or 800-242-2728

For phone orders,
please mention:
BN015-87619-2

Legal Notices
© 1999-2001,
Blue Nile, Inc.

Welcome to Blue Nile

The Platinum
Cathedral Setting ▶

 **Build Your Own Ring** ▶

Easily combine diamonds and settings to find the perfect match of quality and price, in a ring that's one of a kind.

◆ more

Voted Best Online Jeweler ▶
- "Best Value on Diamonds" - Fox News
- "Best Online Jeweler" - Forbes
- "Highest Customer Rating" - BizRate
- Read Our Customer Letters

? Diamond Buying Guide
Learn the four Cs of diamond quality, and receive a diamond price comparison chart. All you need to choose the right diamond.
E-mail: [ ] ◆ send
☑ Send me future news from Blue Nile.

Why Blue Nile?
Blue Nile is the leading online retailer of certified diamonds and fine jewelry.
- ▶ Free shipping
- ▶ 30-day return policy
- ▶ Outstanding quality and prices

  Gift Ideas ▶

Whether for a birthday, anniversary or just because, we have just the right gift for your occasion.

[Select a Gift ▼]

 Catalog & Diamond Guide ▶

This catalog features our most popular jewelry, and includes a detailed guide to buying diamonds.

- ▶ Catalog Quick Order
- ▶ Request a Catalog

 Pearl Pendants ▶

Celebrate graduation with our 14k gold cultured pearl and diamond pendant, $175.

◆ more

About Blue Nile | Free Shipping | Privacy Policy | Contact Us | Refer a Friend | 30-Day Returns

FIGURE 5.25

Since this online jewelry retailer does not have a widely-familiar brand name, it uses much of its home page to build identity. Starting with its slogan "Education. Guidance. Diamonds and Fine Jewelry." Blue Nile presents the personality of a trusted advisor. This site's designers understand the task at hand (buying fine jewelry for important occasions), and the anxiety that comes with it (price, quality, complex terminology).

FIGURE 5.26

Like most retailers, Amazon uses its home page to present the breadth of the site and depth of their inventory. They entice you to browse with navigation tabs, search boxes, category lists, and deals of the moment. Everything, it seems, is clickable. Amazon's page design has become so familiar that, even in a foreign language, the page's information and interaction design are understandable.

Products: Visor handhelds

- Visor Prism - Visor Edge - Visor Pro - Visor Platinum - Visor Neo - Visor Deluxe

- Home
- Products
  - Treo Communicators
  - Visor Handhelds
    - Visor Prism
    - Visor Edge
    - Visor Pro
    - Visor Platinum
    - Visor Neo
    - Visor Deluxe
  - Springboard Modules
  - Accessories
  - Clothing
- Software
- Developers
- About Handspring
- Customer Support

Site Map Shopping Cart

check out our
special offers
click to learn more

free aluminum case
with Visor Edge purchase.

Introducing... our
newest additions.

Visor Neo™ ▸Learn more   Visor Pro™ ▸Learn more

free VisorPhone
with service activation
click here to learn more

what is Treo?
- Why get a handheld?
- Why get a Visor?
- Which Visor is right for me?
- How does Visor compare?
- What is expansion?

premier

Visor Pro
- 16 MB memory
- amazingly fast
- rechargeable battery
Only $299
plus FREE Bi-Fold Leather case
▸Buy it ▸Learn more

Visor Edge
- remarkably thin
- rechargeable battery
- 8 MB memory
Only $299
plus FREE Sleek Aluminum case
▸Buy it ▸Learn more

Visor Prism
- 65,536 colors
- rechargeable battery
- 8 MB memory
was $399, now only $299
▸Buy it ▸Learn more

performance

Visor Neo
- amazingly fast
- alkaline batteries
- 8 MB memory
Only $199
plus FREE GameFace
▸Buy it ▸Learn more

Visor Platinum
- amazingly fast
- alkaline batteries
- 8 MB memory
Only $199 ▸Buy it ▸Learn more

value

Visor Deluxe
- a great starter
- alkaline batteries
- 8 MB memory
Only $169
plus FREE GameFace
▸Buy it ▸Learn more

Which Visor™ is right for me?
Check out our handy Recommendations Guide to find the perfect fit.

The ultimate in handheld expansion.
Transform your Visor handheld into almost anything, with optional Springboard modules.

Check out our great Special Offers

Check out Handspring's many cool products:
Visor Prism   Visor Platinum
Visor Edge   Visor Neo
Visor Pro   Visor Deluxe

Documents To Go **FREE!**
for
with the purchase of any Visor handheld
(after mail-in rebate)

Affiliates | E-Newsletter | Feedback | Handspring Policies | Help | International | Where To Buy
Copyright © 1999-2001 Handspring

FIGURE 5.27
Since Handspring has a small number of products, it can create a visually stunning category page that's still marketing driven. Their PDAs are similar in look, so the products are grouped by number of features and price. The global navigation bar has expanded with additional choices.

Category page

A category page is the next level down from the home page in a site hierarchy. Think of the category page as the home page for a group of products. Your task is to decipher what home page properties must be inherited, or modified. You must also ask what properties were absent on the home page that must be established at this level for the remainder of the experience.

A category page's first purpose is to restate the global navigation and indicate the visitor's place in the site. This is usually done with some type of minor modification to the global navigation bar, and then substantiated with breadcrumbs and a page label.

Customers browse the category page to narrow the parameters. Therefore, present them with a list of subcategorizations that give the customer an indication of whether or not they are getting closer to their target product(s).

As with the home page, categories usually include some special deal content, new product announcements, and contextual search capabilities. Because category pages are somewhat less political than home pages, it might be beneficial to start your prototype work on this level.

FIGURE 5.28

The strategy on this category page is simple: present a list of subcategory options, all directed at specific buying tasks. The list of top-selling products presents a taste of what lies beneath the subcategories. Breadcrumb navigation appears in the upper-right hand corner, showing customers their place in the site hierarchy.

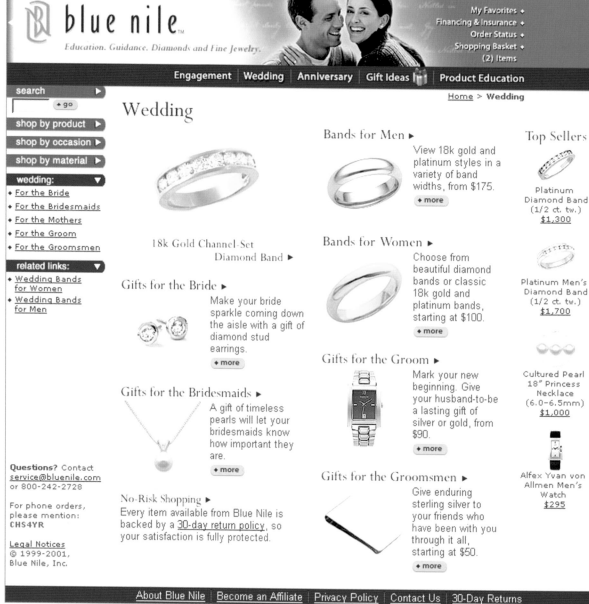

CHRISTIE'S

LotFinder®

Search Options   [?]

Log In ▶   Your Account ▶

22 October 2001

HOME | SALE CATEGORIES | AUCTIONS | SELLING | PUBLICATIONS | OUR SERVICES | ABOUT CHRISTIE'S | HELP

Old Master Paintings

Overview
Contact Information
Specialist Profiles
Exceptional Prices
Consignments
Auction Calendar
Press Releases
Glossary
Related Books

Overview

▲
Rembrandt Harmensz van Rijn (Leiden 1606-1669 Amsterdam)
Portrait of a Lady aged 62
Sold for £19,803,750
December 2000
Word Auction Record for any Dutch Old Master Painting, and for the Artist The 2nd most expensive Old Master Painting
London, King Street

◄
Rembrandt Harmensz van Rijn (Leiden 1606-1669 Amsterdam)
Portrait of a bearded man
Sold for $12,656,000
January 2000
New York, Rockefeller Center

Masterpieces by the most famous artists from the 14th to the early 19th century have appeared in Christie's auctions, including Rembrandt, Raphael, Cranach, Titian, Velázquez, Hals, de Hooch, Canaletto and Fragonard. Prices range from $1,000 to Christie's world auction record of $35.2 million for Pontormo's *Portrait of a Halberdier* (1989).

Read More >

Old Master Pictures
31 October 2001
About this sale >

Property from the Collection of the Late Nelson & Eloise Davis
October 2001
About this sale >

Arts of France: Paintings, Furniture, Tapestries and Porcelain
26 October 2001
About this sale >

Property from the Collection of the late Andre Meyer
26 October 2001
About this sale >

Old Master Pictures
2 November 2001
About this sale >

LotFinder®

🔍 LotFinder®

Search Catalogues Online and Bid >

Suggested Reading

Rembrandt By Himself
edited by Christopher White
Description >

Back to Home | Site Map
Terms & Conditions | Privacy Policy

© Christies 2001

Contact Us

FIGURE 5.29

A subcategory page, like its parent page, exists to lead customers closer to their goal. Christie's shows subcategorical navigation on the left, and related auctions on the right. The center well is dedicated to testimonials —customers who bought items in this category. These success stories insinuate, "You, too, could own a Rembrandt."

Product page

The product page should close the sale. The goal of just about every other page on the site—home, category and search—is to guide customers to the product page. Once there, information and presentation design attempt to influence the customer to make a purchase.

Smart product pages have a clear hierarchy of information. Start with the most important information at the top: product photo, name of product, price, and availability. This information answers the customer's primary questions: Is it the right product? Is it the right price? Is there one in stock?

Next, list the secondary product information—the details (like battery life, compatibility, or materials) that distinguish that product from similar ones. Secondary information is valuable for expensive or technical items where there are a host of factors in a buying decision.

Add organization devices like chunking and bullet lists to prevent the volume of product information from becoming overwhelming. For example, Handspring delivers detailed information on its PDAs in seven pages. Each page is cleanly designed, highly graphic, and sprinkled with very digestible snippets of information. Of course, each page has a buy button (See Fig. 5.30).

FIGURE 5.30
Handspring's global navigation on the left highlights where a customer is on the site. Bright orange breadcrumbs reinforce that location. The tab navigation underneath the breadcrumb showcases the depth of information available for the product. This treatment suggests a portal approach to the product—anything a customer could possibly need to know is at their fingertips.

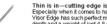

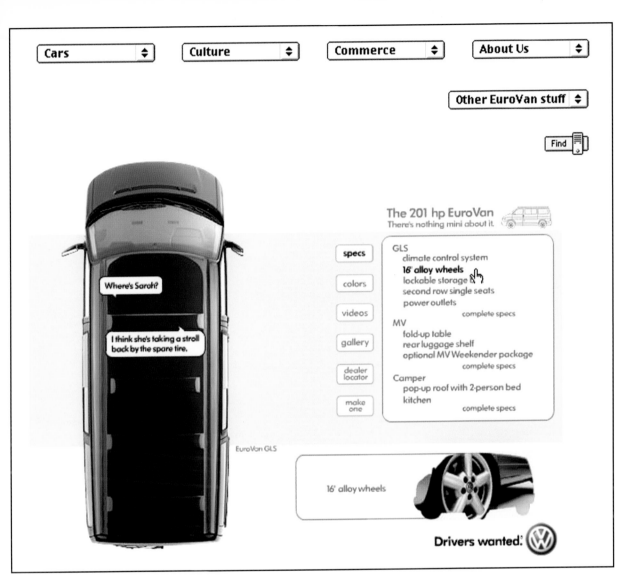

FIGURE 5.31

VW uses their product pages to showcase the personality of each of their nine car models. Customers come to VW's site to learn about the cars and to find places to buy them. This Flash mini-site for a EuroVan nicely balances the goals of the company and the task of the customer.

After reviewing a product, most customers will do one of several standard actions — buy the product, leave it and continue shopping, bookmark the page, or look for more information about the product on some other site. The best product pages anticipate these actions and clearly label options. Most contain an Add to Cart button placed in a prominent position. Add to Cart suggests the shopping experience can continue with no interruption.

The product page should never be a dead end. It should provide ways to browse other products. Keep your pages uncluttered and provide an abbreviated category list of links to other related products. Remember, the more people browse, the more likely they are to buy.

FIGURE 5.32

This DVD product page from Amazon is jampacked with information, but it's very scanable. All information is broken into chunks. The upper-left box contains a set of links to show the depth of additional product information—reviews, reader comments, and related links. The Add to Cart button follows Fitt's law—the most important button is the largest.

blue nile™
Education. Guidance. Diamonds and Fine Jewelry.

My Favorites ◆
Financing & Insurance ◆
Order Status ◆
Shopping Basket ◆
(2) Items

Engagement | Wedding | Anniversary | Gift Ideas | Product Education

Home > Men's Watches > Alfex for Men > Watch Details

search ▶
◆ go

shop by product ▶

shop by occasion ▶

shop by material ▶

men's watches: ▼
◆ Alfex
◆ Baume & Mercier
◆ Chase-Durer
◆ Ebel
◆ Festina
◆ Kenneth Cole
◆ Seiko
◆ Skagen
◆ Spoon
◆ Swiss Army
◆ TAG Heuer
◆ Wired

related links: ▼
◆ About Alfex
◆ Alfex Warranty
◆ Alfex for Women
◆ How to Buy a Watch
◆ Women's Watches

Questions? Contact
service@bluenile.com
or 800-242-2728

For phone orders,
please mention:
CHS4YR

Legal Notices
© 1999-2001,
Blue Nile, Inc.

🔍 zoom

View more Alfex for Men ▶

Click for buckle details

Alfex Yvan von Allmen Watch

This men's watch features a brushed
stainless steel bezel with gently beveled
edges, quartz movement, and a mineral
crystal. It is water resistant to 100 feet and
has a black matte leather strap with a
brushed stainless steel buckle.

Price: $295.00

Add this product:
[to your shopping basket ⇕] ◆ add

E-mail this watch to a friend ▶

Watch Information:
Stock #:   ZS63800700-2162
Series: Yvan von Allmen
Model #:   5424.01
Metal Type: Stainless Steel
Clasp: Buckle
Bracelet Material: Leather
Face Color: Silver
Crystal Type: Mineral

Shipping Information:
Usually Ships In: 1 business day*

* All orders received before noon PST will
begin processing the same business day.

Note: Prices and availability are subject to
change without notice. View our product
policies for more information.

About Blue Nile | Become an Affiliate | Privacy Policy | Contact Us | 30-Day Returns

FIGURE 5.33

Grouping and prioritiza-
tion are hallmarks of this
Blue Nile product page.
A prominent photo, brief
summary, and price take
center stage. Additional
product details rest confi-
dently below, all focused
on maintaining their
theme of educating the
consumer. A breadcrumb
and subcategory naviga-
tion help the customer
understand how they got
there and where they can
go next.

FIGURE 5.34

On most product pages, the description is the most prominent. On Christie's it is the last, because the customer is assumed to be an educated collector. Details that speak to the product's quality and heritage, such as history of ownership and exhibition are placed higher on the page. Temporal auction information is critical to the purchase and is, therefore, prominent.

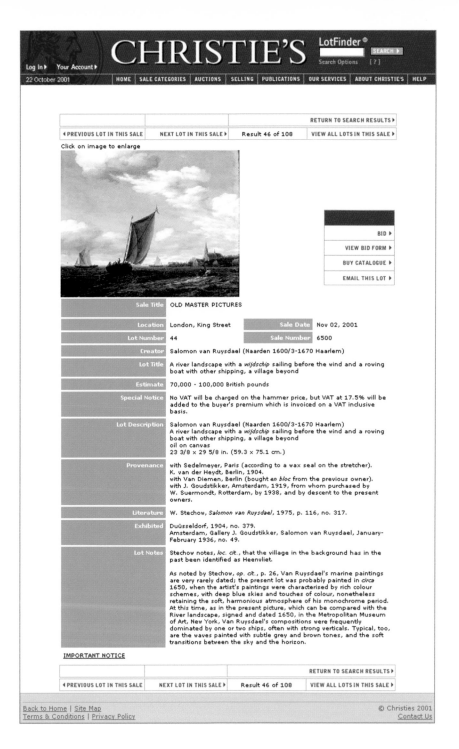

Search pages

Building an effective search results page is easy. Building a good search engine is not. Examine the project wireframe and experience models for what information and interaction controls need to be on the page. Your design goal is to maintain and support the interaction design and technology thinking already completed.

Regardless of your site's specific needs, there are a few principles that all search result templates should follow:

- Allow the customer to focus on the results. Remove as much interference from the page as possible. The global navigation is all a search result page should inherit from the site.

- Search results require a unique grid because the search page is essentially a display of a list. Easy-to-use lists are always organized in tabular form, with clear rows and columns.

- Clearly organize product name, price, and other primary information to make it easy for the customer to scan and compare data.

- Display the customer's search choice, i.e., "You searched for 'Jeans' in "Women's Clothing."

- Include the search box so that customers can execute a new search. Many sites include the current search term in this keyword field to make it easier to refine the search.

- Clearly label the total number of results and how they are sorted, i.e., "We found 234 results, sorted by price."

- Make it easy to see that the list can be re-sorted by different parameters, such as price or availability.

- Search results are dynamically built pages, so your templates should be as lightweight as possible to deliver the results quickly.

Though not a principle, we consider the inclusion of images of the product in search results almost a must. The physical characteristics of a product are an essential part of identification and comparison. However, this will make the page download a bit slower. If your technology allows, offer customers the option to include or exclude images on results.

FIGURE 5.35
DYNAMIC SEARCH

Blue Nile search results page for diamonds contains a Java applet (mini program) that lets customers dynamically reduce the number of choices. With a few clicks on the slider bars, a customer could narrow 6,000 results to ten ideal options. Customers can save different diamonds for later comparison.

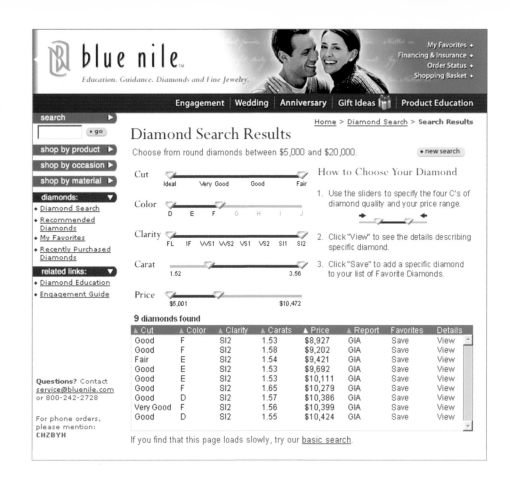

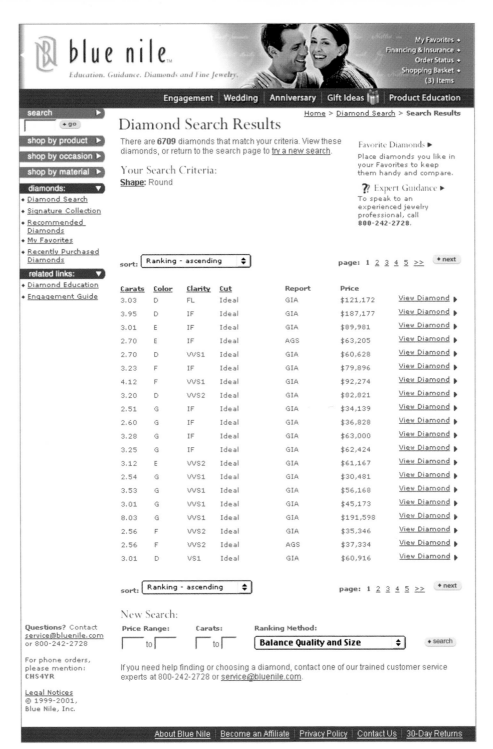

FIGURE 5.36
STANDARD SEARCH

If a customer's browser does not support Blue Nile's applet, they are given a more traditional list of results. The results page is clear of visual clutter. The list of results are well-spaced and sortable by category, which make for easy scanning and comparison.

FIGURE 5.37

All search results on Christie's, whether keyword or catalog triggered, appear in this nicely organized structure. The spacious design allows customers to focus on results. Photographs make it easy to browse and identify items. Time and place of auction are critical to making the bid. Notice the absence of estimated price. If you have to ask, you can't afford it.

FIGURE 5.38

A perfect example of a no-nonsense cart page that enables customers to easily review and modify items. Handspring breaks their airy style and places the cart in a blue background to provide visual focus.

Cart and checkout pages

The shopping cart is the first page of the checkout process. It is a simple container of a customer's purchase choices. This page should keep track of every item a customer is interested in buying, the availability of the items, the quantities ordered, and a running total of price. A cart usually has a few controls that allow the customer to remove items or modify the quantity of items.

Good cart pages allow customers to choose between proceeding to the checkout process or returning to browsing. Intelligent carts look at the choices a customer has made and offer a few additional buying suggestions.

Once the customer moves into the checkout environment, virtually all site navigation should be removed to eliminate distractions. The navigation should be reduced to a series of explicit steps. Other than the fields and forms, the only page elements should be instructions that help the customer fill out the proper information.

Anxiety may be high for some customers. There is always a perceived risk to privacy and personal information. This anxiety makes them more sensitive to mistakes. The HTML in your checkout section must be bullet proof. Any mistake, a broken image or link of any kind, could kill the deal.

FIGURE 5.39

Buying a wedding ring is an emotional purchase. The photograph on Blue Nile's cart page provides more comfort and reassurance on this significant expenditure than would the typical invoice list style. Since the customer had to make a lot of decisions to find the right diamond, setting, and metal, the photo reassures the customer, one last time, that this is the right ring.

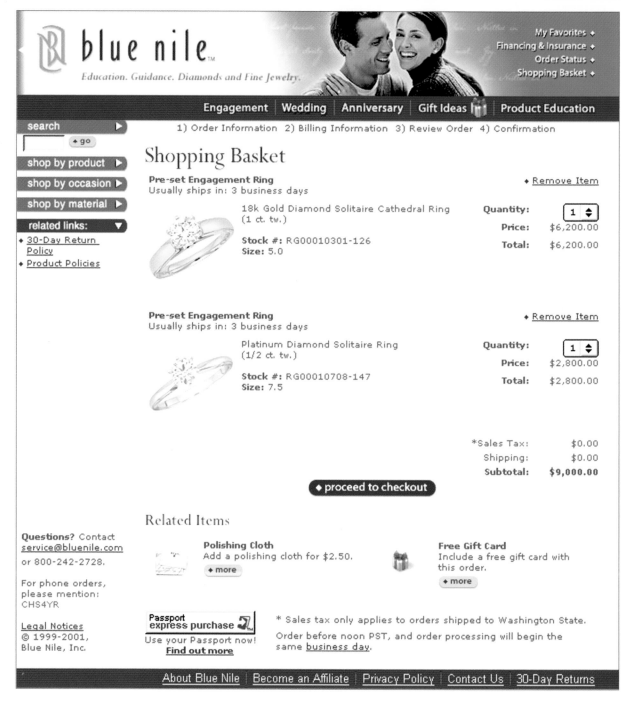

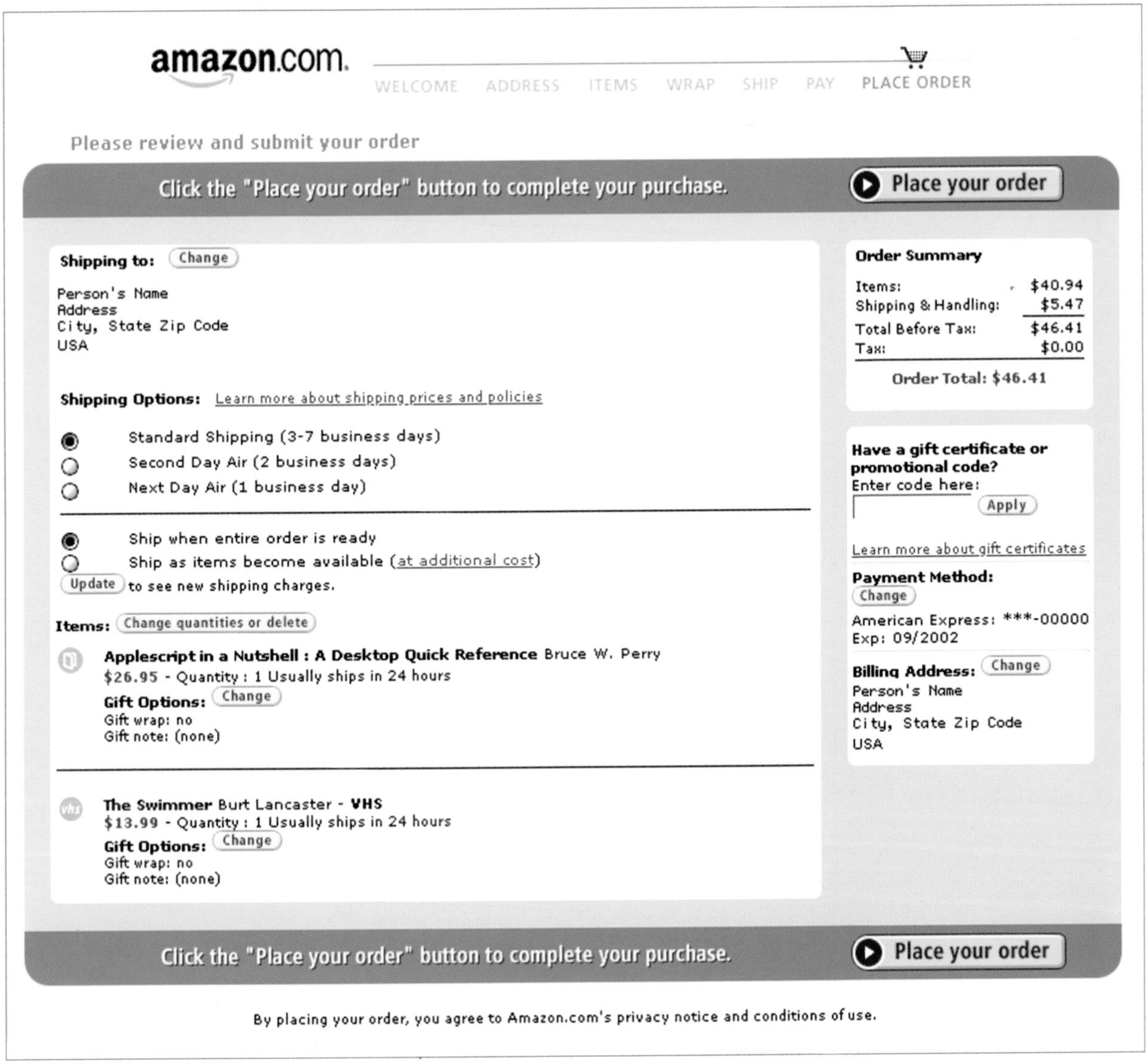

amazon.com.

WELCOME   ADDRESS   ITEMS   WRAP   SHIP   PAY   **PLACE ORDER**

Please review and submit your order

Click the "Place your order" button to complete your purchase.   ▶ **Place your order**

Shipping to: (Change)

Person's Name
Address
City, State Zip Code
USA

Shipping Options: Learn more about shipping prices and policies

- ● Standard Shipping (3-7 business days)
- ○ Second Day Air (2 business days)
- ○ Next Day Air (1 business day)

- ● Ship when entire order is ready
- ○ Ship as items become available (at additional cost)

(Update) to see new shipping charges.

Items: (Change quantities or delete)

Applescript in a Nutshell : A Desktop Quick Reference Bruce W. Perry
$26.95 - Quantity : 1 Usually ships in 24 hours
Gift Options: (Change)
Gift wrap: no
Gift note: (none)

The Swimmer Burt Lancaster - **VHS**
$13.99 - Quantity : 1 Usually ships in 24 hours
Gift Options: (Change)
Gift wrap: no
Gift note: (none)

Order Summary

Items:	$40.94
Shipping & Handling:	$5.47
Total Before Tax:	$46.41
Tax:	$0.00

Order Total: $46.41

Have a gift certificate or promotional code?
Enter code here:
[   ] (Apply)

Learn more about gift certificates

Payment Method:
(Change)
American Express: ***-00000
Exp: 09/2002

Billing Address: (Change)
Person's Name
Address
City, State Zip Code
USA

Click the "Place your order" button to complete your purchase.   ▶ **Place your order**

By placing your order, you agree to Amazon.com's privacy notice and conditions of use.

FIGURE 5.40

Amazon's checkout pages are a model of simplicity and efficiency. The shopping experience has been completely removed. Everything is focused on an error-free checkout process. On this page, a customer is asked to review all the information that has been entered in the checkout process. The Place Your Order button completes the transaction.

FIGURE 5.41

Like Amazon, Handspring
removes all navigation
on checkout pages
except for the steps to
complete a transaction.
This navigation shows
where the customer is
in the process, and how
many steps are left to
complete. Green is used
to highlight fields of
entry. Contextual instructions on the left-hand
side help to reduce
customer error.

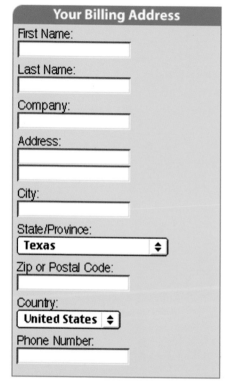

International | Affiliates | E-Newsletter | Handspring Policies | Help | Feedback
Copyright © 1999-2001 Handspring

FIGURE 5.42

Christie's Auction Calendar

Other pages

A commerce site may have other templates that need to accommodate unique tasks, such as forums, chat, or help. Treat them like all the other templates by asking which elements can be inherited or borrowed from existing pages, and what aspects of the task require special design consideration.

For example, Christie's Auction Calendar page (See Fig. 5.42) uses the same navigation bar and grid as the rest of the site. Subcategory links on the left side help guide the browsing experience. The list of auctions is organized similarly to a search results page, with pull-down menu controls to refine the results.

Prototyping the Look

All design is iterative. Not even Paul Rand or Saul Bass solve a logo or poster design problem on their first attempt. Prototyping for Web design is no different than for other media. It's a process where you design, test, and evaluate possibilities. Prototyping is also the best way to explore ideas before a company invests time and resources in them.[2]

Your first goal is to create a set of paper prototypes. Start prototyping with the wireframes. Using a drawing program like Adobe Illustrator, place fixed elements on the wireframes like search boxes, logos, and navigation.

Focus your efforts on working through a good number of ideas. Do not give in to the temptation of writing any HTML. Writing code at this point can slow down the process to a crawl. It's also irrelevant this early in the game.

These prototypes will be printed out and used for internal discussion purposes. Save all of your versions. Don't be shy about trying both conservative and outlandish ideas. This part of the process is devoted to exploring the full range of possibilities. Always print prototypes at real size. Larger sizes or thumbnails might distort people's perceptions of the design.

Prototyping a design should be an additive process. Don't throw lots of graphics and colors on the page until you account for of the interactive elements. Prototype in different shades of gray and use boxes for pictures until you get the proportions to your liking.

Once you have a design that's showing some promise, include some real images and control elements. Does the page feel cohesive or do some elements seem to be floating off on their own?

Fill in your stark prototypes with different color schemes. Since your design is already gray, try different monochromatic versions next. Cycle around the color wheel to get the full effect of the different moods and personalities that schemes can evoke. Try different colors as accents for directional items like arrows and buttons.

Next, try more complementary or analogous schemes. Post them on the wall and get people's reactions. Allow cubemates to write comments next to the designs.

Tip: Scan your paper prototypes into the computer. Add an image map of hyperlinks to the page. Begin to click around on the experience. How does it feel? Perhaps you will want to test paper prototypes this way because it puts the testing experience inside the computer.

Three is the magic number

Pick your three best approaches and develop at least one example of each of the five key page types—home, category, product, search, and checkout. This will give your test group an idea of the total experience. The initial tests can be made on a small group of employees and team members, but eventually you will need to test the paper prototypes on the actual target audience.

We cover usability testing in Chapter 6, but the main thing you want to take away from these sessions is a customer's understanding of the site. Do they get it? And, of course, does your site anticipate their tasks? Continue with paper prototypes until you, and the executive leadership, are satisfied with the results. Pick only one design to prototype.

The second phase of prototyping a commerce site is a basic HTML mockup. Some design elements, usually the finer points of typographic control and graphic exactness, simply don't translate well into HTML. This is when you start to poke holes in your design and figure out what will and won't work. Make sure you mock-up each of your five key page types in HTML. You might even code a couple extra category and product pages to make the prototype feel more like a complete site.

The HTML mock-up should be tested internally and with target users. Hopefully you've addressed concerns from the previous rounds of testing and your design is gaining acceptance. Continue with iterations of your HTML mock-ups until all parties, from CEO to customer, are satisfied.

Welcome to alpha

You are now at the point where your design must hook up with the back-end environment. Before you do anything further, sit down with the tech team one last time and make sure you have a clear idea about how they want templates to be built. It's different for every system.

Use these guidelines to help get you through the process:

- **Build pieces.** Break up your template work into chunks, much like your design. For example, design your navigation bar and search box templates first. These are pieces that all pages will need. They will be easier to tackle independently, rather than as part of a whole page.

- **Get representative content.** Make sure you have access to a database with real content to test your templates. Fake content is never as good as the real thing, and usually leads to coding mistakes.

- **Test incrementally.** Don't code an entire template with two hundred database requests for content and then test it. Code one request and test until it's correct, then move to the next request. This method helps keep the template-building process manageable.

Once you've built all the templates, it's time to publish an alpha version of the site. The alpha site will be rough, but once it exists, technology, content, and design personnel will use it to work out the integration kinks. And there will be kinks. Some technology or content might not come together as predicted. When making compromises put the customer and their tasks first, and the project will be a success.

The presentation-design phase is not yet complete. As site launch nears, further rounds of testing will require your keen insight for a few last tweaks in the design.

---

[1] Cooper, Alan. *About Face: The Essentials of User Interface Design.* (Hungry Minds, 1995).

[2] Berkun, Scott. "The Art of UI Prototyping." http://www.uiweb.com/issues/issue12.htm

chapter 6

SITE LAUNCH AND MAINTENANCE
Fear. Testing. And measuring success.

le sociology professor and author harles Perrow knows something about our Web site—it will fail. What's more, e knows your site will likely fail in ways at you never dreamed.

his book, *Normal Accidents*, Perrow de- cribes how complex systems like nuclear ower plants, space shuttles, or airliners are special characteristics that make em inevitably prone to failure.

errow's argument: As we build more com- icated systems, made up of smaller parts esigned to reduce risk, we actually increase e likelihood of making bigger mistakes. ecause elements of complex systems are terrelated, failures in one part can create nexpected failures in many other places.

dmittedly, your commerce site is not a ace shuttle or nuclear power plant, but does share similar characteristics. ommerce Web sites are much more com- icated than your average brochure-ware eb site, and they're more mission critical.

re you getting anxious yet? Here's the ightening part: Soon, people will be coming your site wanting to buy something.

hen they buy, they will ignore your arning signs and disclaimers, forget to pe in their zip code or hit their back but- n several times at the worst possible moment. At each muddled step, your site will either fly or crash and burn.

Unlike a botched sale in the real world, when the inevitable happens your site won't respond with a caring voice or follow up with a phone call. Most often, the site displays a cryptic message or a broken image icon.

Anytime something breaks on your site, you can be sure that you, the designer, will get the first call. It might not be fair, but as the designer you will be summoned to answer questions not expected of others. No one would mistakenly ask the Oracle database administrator the difference between leading and kerning. But it's not beyond anyone to ask you to decipher a Java servlet error.

To be sure, there will always be a few bugs that were unforeseen or overlooked. But that shouldn't have you running for cover. With thorough planning and testing, you can begin fixing problems well in advance of launch—long before the first 404 Error Not Found can surface.

In this chapter, we will take you through the proper preparation and deployment of a site using different types of user and func- tionality testing. This analysis will give you the confidence to take your Web business public. As well, we will provide advice on managing site growth and evolution.

During the development of a Web site, designers must continually clarify their responsibilities to their team. The designer must also know a little bit more about everyone else's role than others know of theirs. Manage people's expecta- tions of you, and manage expectations of your own abilities.

Usability Testing

For a Web site to be successful, its users must have a revelation within a matter of seconds. You want to strive for the "aha" and avoid the "huh?" You can achieve this goal only with usability testing.

No one needs a manual to use a book, newspaper, magazine, or brochure. Online, however, standards of usability are in flux as the medium, the technology, and the online audience (and their habits) continue to develop. A usability test will help prevent confusion with your site's method of navigation, structure, information, and shopping cart.

For a commerce site, usability is critical because it can have a direct impact on revenue. The claim you may have heard about how company A increased revenue by several thousands of dollars through usability testing is just an urban legend. There's no guarantee that usability will make your online business successful, but it will help prevent it from being a complete failure.

Surely, if the shopping cart system doesn't make sense to a user, the purchase is dead. If the search engine doesn't work, the purchase is dead. If the JSP code breaks, the purchase is dead. Though commerce is mission-critical, time-to-market pressures tend to rush or bypass these

FIGURE 6.1 (ABOVE): JCREW CATALOG
It's familiar. Pick a bikini. Dial a phone number. Buy it. No usability testing required.

FIGURE 6.2 (BELOW): JCREW WEB SITE
Unlike anything you've ever used. Make anywhere between 25 – 50 decisions just to buy one bikini. Cross your fingers and hit "Submit." Usability testing mandatory.

Though they look similar, usability results are sure to differ. A designer's anecdotal evidence or personal opinion is irrelevant. Only a usability test with real customers will reveal the best approach.

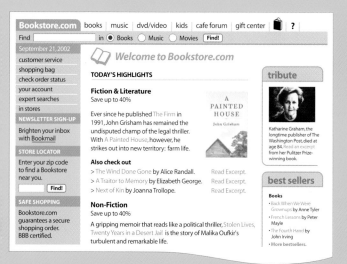

What's wrong with this picture? Possible usability questions:

1. Is the top-bar navigation apparent and clear?
2. Do customers understand the bag icon?
3. Will customers want to search across all categories?
4. Is the link to customer's account information buried?
5. Is the link color too light to read?

What's wrong with this picture? Possible usability questions:

1. Does the lack of link colors or underlines confuse customers?
2. Is the advanced search button lost?
3. Do customers understand the options in the Quick Search pull-down menu?
4. How would the customer review their last order or any account information?
5. Does the similarity of the Add to Cart and Read Excerpt buttons confuse customers? Should we change their color or position?

valuable usability tests. Critical mistakes in such areas can create costly redesigns and redeployments.

You should also recognize usability's influence on building loyalty. The easier a site is to use, the more positive the emotional connection to the experience. Poor usability makes users feel frustrated, befuddled, and humiliated. They blame themselves.

It's easy for a designer, who is intimate with the Web site, to buy into the fallacy, "Users are stupid." Jakob Nielsen, one of the world's top usability gurus, explains the reality. "If many people make the same mistake, the conclusion is not that people are stupid but that the design is wrong."

Types of usability tests

Focus groups: Many graphic designers have tested their print products on a focus group. A facilitator leads a group of customers through a directed discussion about the product, while the marketing department typically observes behind a mirror. Usability testing is similar. A single person is led through a series of tasks on a Web site. Cameras record each step while designers and product developers watch through the mirror or on a remote TV.

A focus group, like surveys and questionnaires, is good for identifying needs, opinions, or feelings. This type of testing belongs early in the design process, when users' goals and needs are still uncertain. For Web usability, however, focus group testing is not recommended. People in groups tend to say what they want to be true or what they think you want to hear, rather than what they actually do.[1]

Field study: A direct observation test is conducted while the user is at their own computer, not in a lab. According to the Nielsen/ Norman Group, "field studies are one of the most effective ways to learn about your users' goals and needs. Watching users in their own environment gives you the real picture of what they're trying to accomplish, and their obstacles to success in their current way of working."

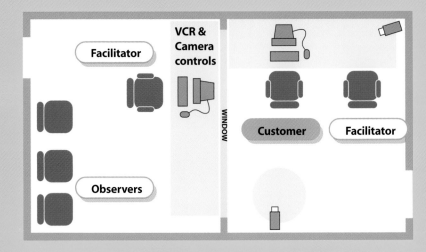

FIGURE 6.4: PROFESSIONAL USABILITY LAB ROOM
One camera records the customer's screen, the other records the customer's body language and movements. The test facilitator can sit beside the customer or behind an observation window.

Lab test: The traditional and most sophisticated method of usability testing occurs in a usability lab (See Fig. 6.4). In this controlled environment, tests of specific tasks take place, with full observation, recording, and reporting facilities. The obvious disadvantage to this method is cost, with charges as high as $20,000.

On a budget: It doesn't take a lot of dollars to discover what might be wrong with your site. Some experts advocate iterative usability testing with less-costly methods. Testing between three to five users, several times, in an informal setting with a video camera should provide a sufficient set of usability data. According to Nielsen, one test with five users can find 85% of the usability problems. Make your corrections, then test again.[2]

What to test

Usability testing is most effective when you use it to determine how much time a user needs to complete a task or series of tasks and how difficult the tasks seem. Testing also may be relevant for checking users' conceptual understanding of the site. Simply ask the user, "Do you get it?"

Remember that the point of testing is not to prove or disprove a design issue. It's to

FIGURE 6.5: WHEN TO TEST USABILITY

Begin testing usability as early in the design process as possible. The number of times you test will depend on the complexity of your site. According to Jakob Nielsen, testing 5 people per session will reveal about 85% of the usability problems. Make corrections, then repeat tests until you and your customers are satisfied.

	Planning	Paper prototype	Working prototype	First usable version	Beta test
Design phase	Information design	Interaction design	Presentation design	End of presentation or early build phase	Test phase
What to test	Competitor sites	Printouts of home page and labels of top-level categories and second-level templates	All pages you've completed to date	All pages you've completed to date	Each unique page
Format	Live site	Paper	HTML	Live site	HTML page
How to test	Key tasks	Names of things	Basic navigation	Key tasks	Key tasks
What you're looking for	• What do they like or dislike about it? • What goals are they able to fulfill? • How hard is it to do key tasks?	• Do they get the point of the site? • Does it seem like a site that would meet their needs?	• Can they accomplish the key tasks? • How easily can they find things?	• How quickly and easily can they accomplish the key tasks?	• How quickly and easily can they accomplish the key tasks?

Source: *Don't Make Me Think: A Common Sense Approach to Web Usability,* by Steve Krug

inform a designer's judgment, says Steve Krug of Advanced Common Sense. "What testing can do is provide you with invaluable input, which, taken together with your experience, professional judgment, and common sense, will make it easier for you to chose wisely—and with greater confidence."

When to test

Many companies make the mistake of testing usability only after launch, leading to thousands of dollars in redesign expense and lost revenue. The goal of testing is to correct as many problems as possible before the launch. Krug recommends two options,

depending on budgetary constraints:

1. Perform one expensive test when the functional prototypes are close to completion.

2. Conduct several small, inexpensive tests throughout all phases of the development process.

Who should conduct a usability test

Research by Web-usability veteran Jared Spool revealed that companies that hired outside usability firms were typically unable to increase usability by a significant factor.

In fact, the most usable sites were the ones whose planners had conducted in-house usability studies. Spool says that in-house designers truly understand the intricacies of their business and, thus, they are the only ones capable of seeing the subtle problems that have a huge impact on usability. He recommends that in-house personnel receive professional training on how to conduct usability tests. In lieu of training (hey, everything costs money), there are several books that tell you how to conduct a proper test: Nielsen's *Usability Engineering,* Krug's *Don't Make Me Think,* and Jeffrey Rubin's *Handbook of Usability Testing.*

Quality Assurance Testing

In June 1999, a software company used its error detection technology to scan 95 of the Fortune 100 corporate Web sites for coding mistakes and other functional glitches.[3] The results were remarkable: Almost 29 percent of the pages contained link errors and each page had an average of more than a dozen HTML coding errors. The report also noted, "$58 million per month in e-commerce sales are lost due to Web page loading failures."[4]

Whereas usability is somewhat subjective and concerns the quirks of human nature, quality assurance (QA) testing is a technical assessment—does it work?

A total quality assurance plan requires discipline and attention to granular detail. According to Lotus usability engineer Terry Sullivan, "The single most important step towards consistent Web page quality is the creation of a stable, predictable quality process for Web documents. Defining a quality regimen for Web documents that is both reliable and valid is an investment of time and energy that carries with it the potential for significant payback."

He suggests establishing a measurable standard and sticking to it. For example: "Pages should download fast" is not quantifiable. "Page size should be no larger than 100K, with HTML and images included" is not only measurable, but explicit.

FIGURE 6.6
BROWSER COMPATIBILITY ISSUES
This is how the designer intended the site to appear—elements on the screen align properly and the text is formatted in a readable style.

On a different browser, the design can shift or fall apart.

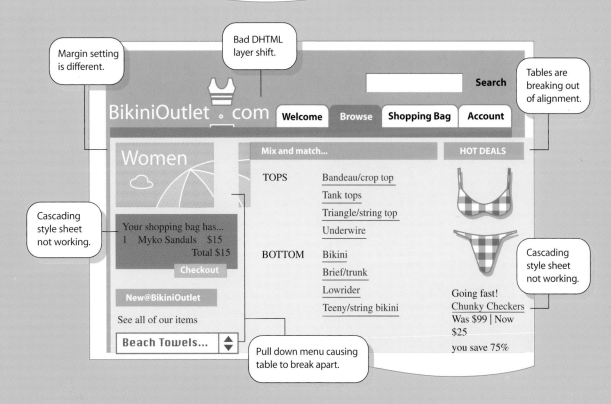

The designer's role

A Web designer may be called upon to perform or oversee the quality assurance testing of all code, functionality, and browser/ platform compatibility. Other QA tests examine the scalability of the back-end system. For example, stress tests measure the number of simultaneous users a Web server can handle. A page design that's too complex may limit the number of simultaneous users who can visit your site, so it's imperative to be familiar with these results.

During the prototyping of functional Web pages, a designer should test the design for variation of display between browsers. Examine not only different makes, such as Netscape and Internet Explorer, but also different versions and operating systems. Browser variation can be a design nightmare. To avoid headaches, create a user technology profile that represents your site's base level of browser support. For example, you may decide to only design and rigorously test for browser versions 4.x and higher. Remember that browsers are constantly being upgraded. A new

FIGURE 6.7 USE OF VARIOUS NETSCAPE BROWSER VERSIONS

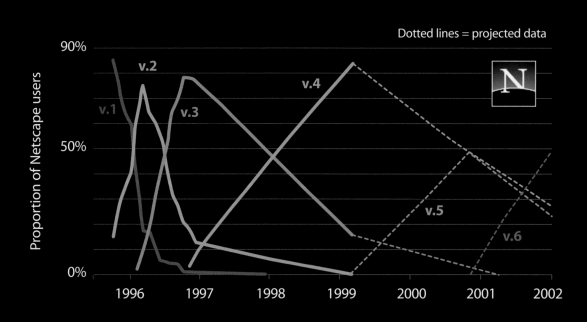

Source: Jakob Nielsen, April 1999, http://www.useit.com/alertbox/990418.html

Jill Smith
Age: 28
Job: Accountant

At-Work Profile

Dell Laptop, Pentium 4
OS: Win 2000
Browser: Explorer 5.5
ISP: Company
Connection: T1

At-Home Profile

HP 667mhz, Celeron
OS: Win ME
Browser: Explorer 5.0
ISP: AOL
Connection: 56k

version of Explorer can be adopted by a significant user base within a matter of weeks. Will your site still work for them?

It's easy to make the mistake of only testing your pages on your own browser and operating system. Web designers should run a copy of every major browser version on both PC and Apple Macintosh—using the latest operating systems—to check page appearance and functionality. HTML can render quite differently even in the same browser version, depending on the platform. DHTML does not work on some browsers. Try HotWired's Webmonkey for a comprehensive overview of the differences in browser features and their quirks.[5]

Do you want to be inclusionary and build pages for everyone, or can you go with your best design and forget about being accessible to every browser version? A commerce site designer needs to think hard about this tricky choice. Commerce sites rarely desire to exclude any potential customer. To sidestep the choice, they program multiple code variations into the back-end system. The technology team adds some server-side programming to detect site visitor information such as browser, operating system, monitor resolution, and connection speed. Once detected, the server dynamically delivers a version of the design compatible with the site visitor's environment.

What to test

According to CNET, the Internet and technology resource, a month of intensive, structured quality assurance testing is the minimum for the launch of a large-scale commerce site. A designer will not typically be asked to perform such tests, but you will need to know the results.

Typical structural testing includes:

- The purchasing process, from the shopper's point of entry to shipping preferences. If you can, play consumer, and buy something from your site.

- The fulfillment process, from setting the shoppers' expectations to seeing how well those expectations will be met.

- The credit card verification system, as well as the billing that follows.

- The server traffic load, including simulating peak demand.

- The site's impact on the back-end systems, such as databases and firewalls.

- Testing not only the computers, but the people and processes that support commerce systems. Think fulfillment, returns, exchanges, customer service, and technical support.

FIGURE 6.9: DESIGNING ERROR PAGES

QA testing will catch many mistakes, but not all. The inevitable 404—Page Not Found error can be handled quite gracefully. Even with errors, it's important to maintain a positive brand experience.

Bad This default message from the Apache Web server software tells the user nothing at all. This is a dead end.

Not Found

The requested URL /catalog/index.cfm?cat=DIN&src=shp

―――

Apache/1.3.16 Server at www.bikinirepair.com Port 80

Better Some sites customize the default message and sends users back to the home page.

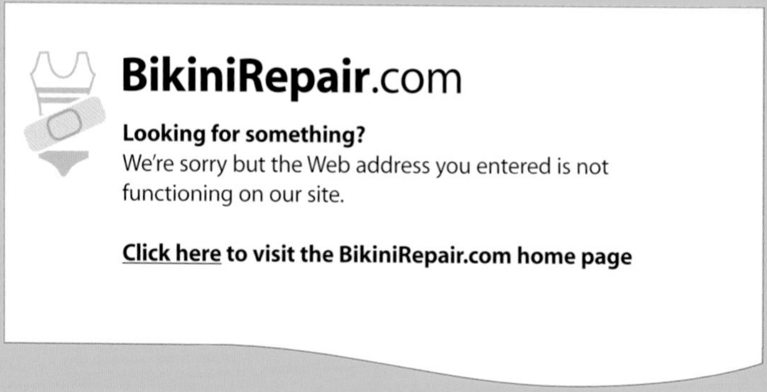

BikiniRepair.com

Looking for something?
We're sorry but the Web address you entered is not functioning on our site.

Click here to visit the BikiniRepair.com home page

Best It's better to provide a possible explanation for the error, then give the visitor several alternatives for finding the intended page.

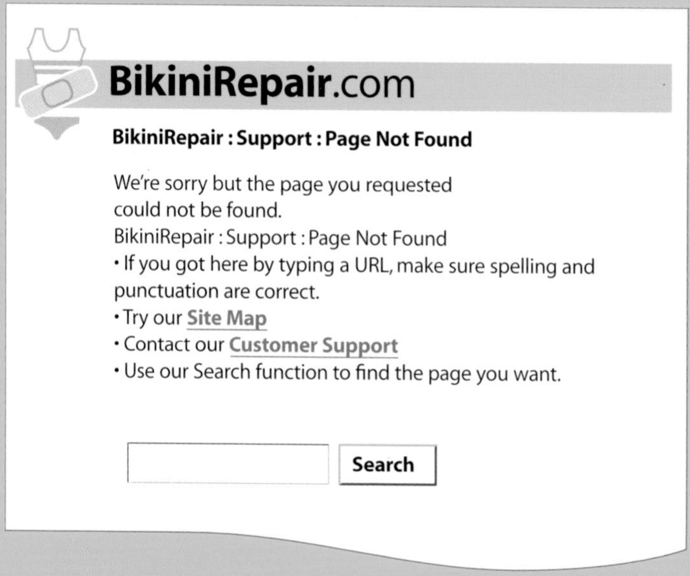

BikiniRepair.com

BikiniRepair : Support : Page Not Found

We're sorry but the page you requested
could not be found.
BikiniRepair : Support : Page Not Found
• If you got here by typing a URL, make sure spelling and punctuation are correct.
• Try our **Site Map**
• Contact our **Customer Support**
• Use our Search function to find the page you want.

[   ] **Search**

Other standard QA tests apply to commerce sites as well:

Speed: Much of the QA research on commerce focuses on the time it takes for a page to load in a browser and what effect that has on purchasing. A study by Hewlett-Packard on this subject revealed:

- If users habitually experienced poor or unpredictable (quality of technical service) at the site of a particular company, the company's products are viewed as inferior.

- Users made a connection between poor site performance and compromised security. "If it's slow, I won't give it my credit card," said one participant.[6]

Some QA tests, especially ones for testing speed, require special software. If you don't want to invest in the software and time, you can outsource them to companies like Mercury Interactive or Keynote Systems. Track these tests and their results so you can adjust your designs accordingly.

Content: Proofread all content, including graphically created text such as buttons and navigation labels, for spelling and punctuation errors. This step is easy for a designer to overlook.

Links: At least once a month and whenever a site is restructured, verify that all links work as expected. Some content publishing systems can automatically check links, which is a valuable time saver for large sites with hundred or thousands of links that make manual verification impossible. As well, someone should periodically verify that links to external sites remain active, and continue to contain content relevant to your site.

Graphics: Check that all graphic files are loading on every page. This applies not only to image files but also audio, video, and Flash.

Advertising: Check that all advertisements appear correct; and that links from the ads work. Because ads are often fed dynamically into a browser from a third-party Web server, they can often affect the speed of your page load. It's worth your time to investigate this potential delay.

Functionality: Verify that all interactive elements, such as search, shopping cart, and e-mail-a-friend, are working properly.

Browsers: With every significant update, perform an aesthetic and functionality review of your site, using multiple browsers. Don't forget to include a text-only browser and/or an AOL browser in this test.

Important note: Do not use the testing period to continue developing the site. Code must be "frozen," or left unchanged, before testing starts.

Before you deploy changes

During each round of fixes, maintain a checklist of every change to ensure that it satisfies the site's standards. For example, one change might increase download time to make it exceed the standard. Sometimes fixing a problem creates a new one. If a new problem surfaces, this checklist will also help you identify the culprit.

Beta Testing Site

In preparation for the 1994 launch of a Developer Network Web site, a team at Microsoft spent a summer developing, coding, and testing. Despite this careful groundwork, they were in for a bumpy ride.

The problem? A few days after launch, the MSDN team realized that updating the site quarterly wasn't nearly often enough to satisfy a hungry audience of Internet developers. The site was revised to update monthly, then weekly, and, finally, daily. It took MSDN about a year before they were updating content every day.[7]

This story from "A Brief History of Microsoft on the Web" is a common one. You seemingly have all the right design and technology, but something unexpected rears its head. Once you've made it through usability and QA testing, you've got one more step before you're ready for prime time—the beta test.

	What to check	
Performance	• **Check page download speed.** For example, does your home page load in four seconds or less on a 56k connection? • **How many simultaneous connections** can the site handle?	• **Send an e-mail message to the site.** Who gets the message — a person or auto-responder? How long does it take to get a response?
Brand identity/personality (experience)	• **Examine content elements, including names and descriptions.** How well do these match the company's brand and other merchandising schemes?	• **Look for a way to return an item.** Is this the quality of experience that customers would expect from your company? • **Search for a nonexistent or unstocked item.** What appears in search results? Are the results satisfying or embarrassing?
Finding a product or service (usability)	• **Check critical navigation elements.** Are they consistent and easily available? Is critical content available from the home page in one click? • **Check ease of navigation.** Does it take more than three clicks to find anything on your site? • **Follow links on the site.** Do you easily understand where you are? Can you locate your place on the site map from any random page?	• **Check the search results.** Do they provide enough information to allow a customer to move forward? Can the visitor resort them in a way that meets their needs (i.e., alphabetical vs. price)? • **Check keyword searches.** Do they anticipate misspellings or synonyms? • **Using a browser option, turn off graphics.** Can you still use the site? Look at content elements, follow links, explore the site completely.
Making a purchase decision (information design)	• **Is the necessary information available** when your customer needs to make decisions? • **Try to exchange an item.** Can you do this easily? • **Read the privacy policy.** Are you comfortable turning over your private, personal data to the shopping experience?	• **Try to input false information.** Can the site verify the credit card billing address or shipping address in real time? • **Examine customer options for flexibility.** Does the site let customers make comparisons or easily refine choices? Can customers save some search results or items for later review?
Placing an order (interaction design)	• **Time your checkout process.** Overall, is it swift and understandable? Does your design set up realistic expectations for the fulfillment process that follows? For example, have you presented a screen that tells the customer to expect e-mail updates on the order? • **Exercise the shopping cart.** Change the quantity of an item, then continue shopping: where did you end up? • **Does the site handle errors well** when an item is out of stock or you need to cancel the order? • **Abandon the cart and leave the site.** When you return, is your cart still available and does it contain the items you left in it?	• **Complete the required forms.** Are required fields clearly labeled differently from optional fields? Leave a required field blank. Are instructions clear about how to complete the required field? Previously completed fields should still filled with your data — are they? • **Check your customer decision points.** If the site notifies you about additional shipping charges after the order is placed, can you find a way to cancel the order? • **Check the order confirmation process.** How useful is the confirmation number for future information queries? • **Change the delivery address** after you've placed an order. Were you successful?

FIGURE 6.10
BETA CHECKLIST

The type of commerce site dictates many of the items on your checklist. Brainstorm with your team to develop a comprehensive checklist. Consider the goals and tasks of your customers when devising the test. Whenever possible, include measurable criteria.

What is a beta test?

During a Web site beta test, a fully functional version of your site becomes available to a modest number of volunteer users who are part of, or at least represent, your target audience. They act as willing guinea pigs to help you find weaknesses before you launch.

There are not many industries that have the luxury of releasing a product before all the bugs have been thoroughly worked out. How many travelers do you think would rush to board the beta version of a Boeing 747?

A beta, then, is a unique chance to take testing out of the lab and put it through the paces of a live user environment. A typical testing period lasts between three and four weeks, depending on the size of the site. This testing involves real customers, who can explore and react without fear of catastrophic consequences. It is also a valuable way to judge how well you have anticipated problems.

What should you test?

The beta test will identify not just technical problems but ones of performance, aesthetics, and usability. Problems uncovered through goal-oriented tasks (like finding a product, researching a purchase and placing

FIGURE 6.11: SQUAWK LIST
Use a spreadsheet or wipeboard to track problems that need to be solved.

Design Problem	Date in	Priority	Assigned to	Status
Search page presents wrong footer template	3.15.02	Medium	Ira Smith	Fixed 3.16.02
Broken image links on electronics category	3.17.02	High	Steve Jones, & tech team	Open
Tables are not aligning properly on product pages	3.17.02	High	Aly Sheva	Fixed 3.17.02
Rollover buttons don't work on some AOL browsers	3.18.02	Low	Ira Smith	Open
QTVR on product pop-up boxes doesn't work	3.19.02	High	Ira Smith, & prod. team	New QTVR needed

an order) will be your most pressing. Make sure your beta testers are explicitly asked to do these types of things.

After your beta test, assess whether your site is ready to go public. Decide which bugs must be fixed. If enough beta testers criticize your navigation model, face the situation and change it. Then, when the next iteration of your site is ready, invite the beta testers back for a quick one-week testing program. [8]

A spreadsheet is a helpful tool in managing this stage of development (See Fig. 6.11).

Enter in all of the problems that need to be investigated and give each item a date discovered, priority, status, and assigned owner. At the start of the day, print out a new copy for you and the team so that everyone is clear on the most important problems to solve and who is responsible for working on them.

The beta checklist should be backed up by a clear plan of action and have tasks assigned to different team members. You should know who will be responsible for different types of problems before they're reported.

Launching the Site

If you have performed usability, quality assurance and beta tests, then you are more prepared than 90 percent of all commerce Web sites. You are a rare breed, driven by excellence. Congratulations! Now you can flip the switch to go live with confidence.

Post-launch review

After initial launch, conduct or participate in a post-launch review. While the details are fresh in everyone's mind, get all the hits, misses, goods, bads, significants, and insignificants out on the table for discussion, and document lessons learned. This exercise becomes a powerful tool and a great lesson for site revisions.

Once your site is live, you will receive input about its success and failure from two sources: Web logs and site visitor feedback.

Web logs

A Web server keeps track of much of what a user does during a site visit—including every page or image request in something called a log file. When a request is unfulfilled, it's recorded in the failure report section of the log file. Analyzing these server logs can be a quick way to expose weaknesses in your site's navigational structure and to expose broken links.

FIGURE 6.12
CLIENT PAGE STOP TRENDS

As a page is downloaded, the browser renders images, loads applets, and builds tables. If this process is too slow, the customer may press the browser's Stop button. This chart shows the percentage of customers who stop the page before it has finished loading. You'll probably have to purchase this type of analysis.

Designer Alert!
Why are customers bailing out of the home page? Did you add a large graphic to the page on Friday?

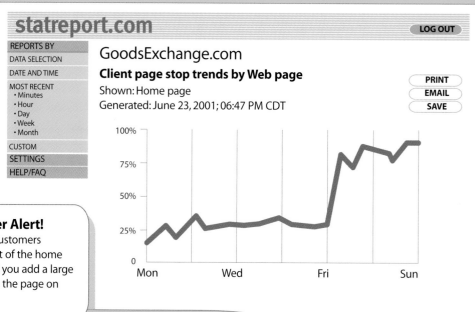

To interpret this wealth of data, you'll need an analysis tool that can interpret these cryptic files into charts about customers' browsing behavior such as visit duration and entry and exit pages (See Fig. 6.12).

Visitor feedback

A site can be swamped by user e-mails after a well-publicized launch. What you do with that e-mail is critical.

It's simple to interpret fifty e-mails that all say "I can't find Search" when the search link is on the home page. This is obviously a usability/design issue. But what do you do if you get an e-mail like this: "I don't like the way your search engine works. Why doesn't it work like Amazon's?" That's why someone must be in charge of the challenging task of interpreting and disseminating user feedback.

E-mails generally will fall into several common categories:

- Site bugs
- Praise or gripes
- Questions from the media
- Calls for help from a frustrated shopper or customer
- Usability issues
- A comment about another part of the company, such as a retail store
- Product questions or comments
- Transaction questions or comments

Make sure that you receive this feedback each week. Discuss it with the team working on the site. Talk through the toughest issues and establish a blueprint for future site revisions.

Customer service

Everyone on your team must respond promptly and politely to feedback, including team designers. Remember that your responses are an opportunity to win an interested customer with a great customer service experience. John Lyle Sanford, Executive Vice President—Design at Circle.com has developed such sites as drugstore.com, The Discovery Channel and Talbots.com. "Customer service is a part of your brand," Sanford says. "When you launch a Web site you get a lot of communication—most of it bad. How you handle that reflects on your brand."

Questions to ask: Who is responsible for collecting and parsing user feedback in your organization? Is it customer service, marketing or the tech team? How will this feedback be dealt with? Will it be discussed in a team meeting, or will be up to each department to interpret and react?

Revising the Site

A tremendous amount of thinking goes into redesigning and rebuilding a site. Like any large project, a site is a product of compromises and educated guesses. When it comes time to breathe new life into yours, keep these six rules of revision in mind:

Rule 1. Design for change. Use templates, be modular, and stay that way.

In Chapter 5, we showed you the value of templates. With templates, revisions are much easier. One of the cardinal sins of Web development is to design a site without considering how it will be revised. Revising your site is akin to changing tires during the middle of the Indy 500. Unless you've come prepared, you'll be in trouble.

Templates are a perfect way to head off problems. While a consistent layout might seem uncreative at the start, stick with it. The urge will be great at times to create something unique, but a clear and consistent layout is the mark of a pro and need not be boring. It's possible to stay fresh while using common elements to separate functions and content clearly.

FIGURE 6.13
BEAUTIFUL BUT NOT EASY TO REVISE

The Barney's New York site has been heralded for its elegant Flash design, but revisions on this site must be a nightmare. Typically, the more stylized the look, the more complicated the revision. However, Flash sites can be designed with modular templates that call a database for pieces of information.

Such effort pays off. From the customer's standpoint, a site that is consistently designed will be easier to navigate, remember, and will provide a more positive experience. For you and your team, a modular site is easier to evolve or grow. It also allows less experienced design team members to contribute because they can be trusted to execute their designs within the guidelines of an overall style.

When revising a template-based site, it is sometimes tempting to create a new template for unique content or a design problem. Avoid creating new templates— eventually you will have too many to manage. Get your design team into the habit of writing comments in their template code that clarifies what's important and what can be modified. If you have several designers, ask them to sign and date their code changes in the template.

```
   </tr>
 </table>

 <!-- Personalization Ends Here -->

 <!-- Navigation Top Bar Begins Here -->
 <map name="navTopMap">
   <area shape="rect" coords="15,0,110,15"...
   <area shape="rect" coords="15,0,110,15"...
 </map>

 <!-- Navigation Top Bar Ends Here -->
```

FIGURE 6.14 : COMMENT YOUR CODE

Adding comments to your code makes revisions easier for you and your staff.

Who will benefit from these changes? Keep that answer at the front of your mind and maintain team focus on the answer. Even if the revisions only affect hardware, software, or infrastructure, follow these rules of revision anyway.

Rule 2: Revise for a reason.

Revising a site can mean a substantial investment in time and money, and major site upgrades can stir your most loyal customers into a frenzy. They have become comfortable with your site's look, feel, and behavior.

Consider this survey from Jupiter, a research firm: One-third of the respondents reacted negatively to changes in site layout, functionality, and look and feel. Nearly one-quarter of them explored alternate sites as a direct result of the relaunch. "To prepare users for changes," Jupiter recommends, "sites should utilize such features as on-site postings, interactive tours, e-mails, and opt-in beta testing."[9]

One way to retain customer loyalty is to announce the coming change. Make clear what will be changed and why. This can be great way market to your site and its features. For example, you can design a mini tour and post it three weeks to month before launching the change. Ask people what they think, be prepared to react to their feedback, and offer to notify them when site changes will take effect.

You can enroll your top loyal customers as a new set of beta testers, and offer them secret access to the revised beta site. Set up expectations about how their feedback will be used, and offer them an incentive to participate and be open and honest with you about your proposed upgrades. A discount coupon good for thirty days after the new feature launch usually works as an effective incentive.

Rule 3: Always be able to undo what you've done.

Okay, so you made a change without applying Rule 2, and customer service tells you that the response to changes has been miserable. They ask if it's possible to go back to the previous version of the site. Anticipate this possibility by making a backup copy of the entire site before you execute any changes.

Rule 4: Keep up with changes in technology.

There's a popular proverb that goes "You can't step in the same river twice." For you, that river is the ever-evolving technology of your customers. Computers become obsolete, so they are always being replaced. Monitors get bigger and cheaper. Browsers are upgraded. New browser plug-ins are developed.

Don't be complacent. Stay in touch with changes in your site's visitor technology profile. It will be different than when you launched the site. You can find this information in your Web logs or in trend reports from research companies like StatMarket or eMarketer.

Rule 5: Don't launch a site revision at 5 P.M. Friday before a long holiday. Have a plan.

This might sound like common sense, but too many great vacations have been spoiled by ignoring it. You can experiment and test a site in a safe environment, but when the switch is thrown, make sure someone is around to help in case something unforseen goes wrong. We recommend launching a site revision on the lightest site traffic day of the week, with proper staffing scheduled.

BikiniRepair.com

Introducing Our New Outlet: BikiniBargains

Dear Loyal BikiniRepair Customer,
As someone who has had many bikinis fixed at BikiniRepair.com, how would you like an exclusive sneak peek of our new BikiniBargain Outlet? Don't answer yet – there's more! How do blowouts of up to 70% off on great styles sound?

Try it out, tell us what you think and you'll receive a free beach towel!

1. Go to: **http://www.bikinirepair.com/bargainpreview/**
2. Explore our Bargain store. Use the discount claim code below for an additional 10% off of bargain bathing suits.
3. Your exclusive access to these great deals won't last long. We're launching our bargain store to the public on July 21, 2002.

PS. We want our site to be perfect when we officially launch, so we'd really like to hear your suggestions. Please help us make our store better by writing to:
bargain-suggestions@bikinirepair.com

FIGURE 6.15: INVITATION TO A BETA TEST

Send an e-mail invitation to your customers asking them to participate in an exclusive opportunity to visit your store or a newly revised site. It's an excellent way to get beta testers and build loyalty.

Rule 6: Beta test big changes and keep testing.

"Brokerage Charles Schwab's main Web site for online investing customers crashed at 9:35 a.m. today, returning to service about an hour and a half later. The glitch was not due to a capacity overload ... but resulted from a glitch in a mainframe upgrade done over the weekend." (CNET— February 24, 1999)

Just as with your initial site launch, it's vital to keep your guard up when implementing site upgrades. Even small and seemingly insignificant changes, alterations, or relocations can produce unexpected results. A well-intentioned code update to an active server page could spell unexpected disaster. Remain vigilant and keep testing. Announce to customers that you are making changes for their benefit and request their help to track success.

[1] "The Use and Misuse of Focus Groups" by Jakob Nielsen http://www.useit.com/papers/focusgroups.html

[2] "Test with 5 Users" by Jakob Nielsen http://www.useit.com/alertbox/20000319.html

[3] Parasoft study: http://www.parasoft.com/press/releases/misc/for100rep.htm

[4] Citing Zona Research's "Need for Speed" report: http://www.zonaresearch.com/promotion/needforspeed/index.htm

[5] HotWired Browser chart: http://hotwired.lycos.com/webmonkey/reference/browser_chart http://hotwired.lycos.com/webmonkey/authoring/browsers/

[6] HP Labs: Integrating User-Perceived Quality into Web Server Design http://www9.org/w9cdrom/92/92.html

[7] "A Brief History of Microsoft on the Web" by Dave Kramer. This short article provides a wonderful selection of humble "we goofed" anecdotes. I guess it's easy to laugh about it now. http://www.microsoft.com/misc/features/features_flshbk.htm

[8] "Beta testing your Web site" by Vik Chaudhary. An excellent overview of the beta testing process. http://builder.cnet.com/webbuilding/pages/Business/BetaTest/index.html

[9] "Web Site Relaunch" Jupiter Research Report, November 15, 2000

chapter 7

REAL-WORLD EXAMPLES
Commerce design that works

Theory and discourse can only take you so far. At some point, good thinking and planning need to be turned into a site that sells.

The challenge of site design is inextricably linked to considerations of technology, interaction, and performance—an unforgiving canvas for the designer. While effective information architecture and a logical layout will aid customers, they probably won't entice them. For that, you need the seductive art of good visual design. As these seven case studies show, good design can transcend the vagaries of the development process to create an emotionally seductive customer experience.

What follows are a variety of sites—some with large staffs and budgets (such as Herman Miller) and others with only one or two behind the wheel (Audion). The graphic approach ranges from potently simple (Transportation.com) to lavishly intense (Flowerbud.com).

Regardless of their budget, staff, or approach, each remains effective because its design is relevant to its customer needs. These are not fad-driven designs. They are all fast, easy-to-use, thoroughly consistent, and packed with personality and meaningful user personalization.

We offer these case studies as both inspirational proof that great design can be created within the constraints of a commercial project and as a reminder of the smart details critical to commerce design. We believe these sites are among the best at execution and seduction.

Flowerbud.com

In the crowded field of online (and off) flower sellers, this site for a Portland, Oregon, flower grower stands out. The mom-and-pop proprietors hope to cater to those who share their passion for flowers, not those looking for a cheap bouquet deal. Graphic design plays a critical role in market differentiation. The site has a seasonally rotating inventory of less than a hundred products, which affords a deep level of graphic detail. Despite this visual intensity, the site is very fast.

A page for the moment

Flowerbud uses a poster approach to showcase the newest flowers of the season and a link to options for the upcoming holiday. This a perfect temporal anticipation of audience task. The left-hand side of the page features standing elements of the site, including the core navigation pull-down menu that is repeated throughout the site.

COLOR PALETTE

Earth tones

The colors naturally supports the site's theme; thick blocks of neutral tones contrast nicely with hyper-real flower photos.

TECHNOLOGY

Front-end
• JavaScript
• ASP

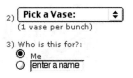

-- Ten, 32-inch stems per bunch.

-- Spectacular, perfume-like fragrance.

FLOWER DETAIL ▶

Scanability

Flower pages are easy for customers to quickly peruse: a brief description, bright photo, and a link to additional detail.

2) Pick a Vase: ◆
(1 vase per bunch)

3) Who is this for?:
● Me
○ enter a name

Easy choices

Forms have been prefilled with an instruction or a useful default. Order options are clarified with parenthetical comments.

Have personality

With its calligraphic headlines, earth-toned watercolor illustrations, high-quality photographs, and intelligent product descriptions, Flowerbud displays a personality that says "thoughtful, elegant, and experienced."

The writing on the site conveys precision, passion, and detail. With each flower description is a miniature history about the plant's origins and its place in our lives. The writing implies that the Flowerbud folks care about getting things right. Therefore, your order will get the same care and attention as they took picking and growing the flowers.

PRODUCT DETAIL

Flowerbud.com — *continued*

Signal a change in experience

Flowerbud makes a smart design choice by using color to signify to the customer, "you have entered the checkout process." Flowerbud's designer has minimized the intensity of the visual experience because the customer must now focus on making exact checkout choices.

Reveal last choice

In each step of a process, it's helpful to present the customer with an indication that the system has registered their last set of choices. In this case, the page restates the shipping options and quantity chosen on the product page.

Reinforce process

Every good commerce site explicitly presents the steps of the checkout process. As a customer proceeds through each step, a visual reminder is displayed to show progression.

Ask when appropriate

This is the perfect time to ask customers to identify themselves for billing purposes. But Flowerbud does not force customers to create a permanent account. Instead, they respect customer privacy by offering a permanent account as an option. Repeat customers with an account sign in to bypass the billing information step.

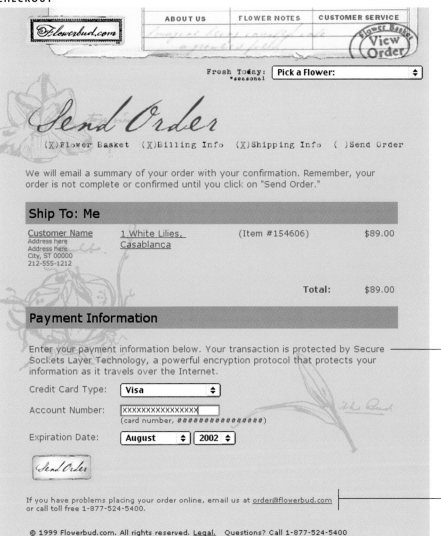

Double-check

The final step of most checkout procedures is a confirmation review of all data the customer has submitted. Flowerbud combines the confirmation and payment info to shorten the number of steps in the process.

Security

Flowerbud presents customers with a short message about the safety of completing a credit card transaction on the Internet.

Customers who experience a problem can use the e-mail link or call the toll-free number for offline help. Making it easy to contact a human being is mandatory for customer retention.

Say "thank you"

It's remarkable how many commerce sites fail to express their appreciation for a customer's decision to shop at their site. Sales people thank you in stores, so why not online?

In addition, customers need confirmation that their order was processed. Flowerbud reassures customers by telling them their order number and to expect a confirmation e-mail "within 24 hours."

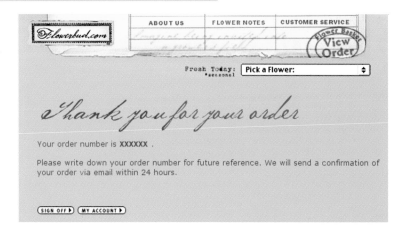

Transportation.com

This B2B global transportation-management company serves shippers and carriers with a broad range of traditional and Internet-based services. The site matches up shippers and their loads with the carriers' equipment and routes. It also handles tricky tasks like price negotiations and equipment auctions.

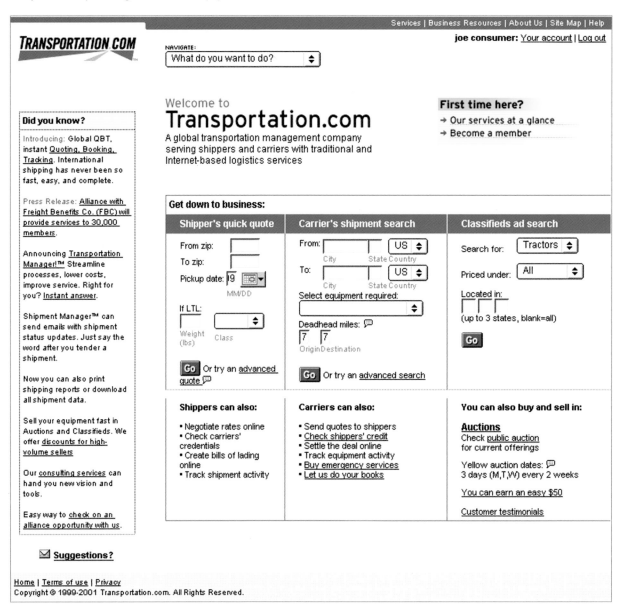

Get down to business

Sites that deal with complex tasks must visually scale back to bare bones and focus completely on the visitor's transaction—zero interference. Notice that this site is free of the generic promotional photography that plagues many B2B designs. This home page invites immediate action with a personality that's all brass tacks.

TECHNOLOGY

Front-end
- JSP
- DHTML
- CSS
- JavaScript

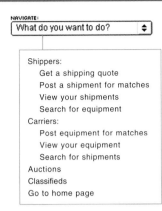

Command action

The site's primary method of navigation is one pull-down menu at the top of the page that asks, "What do you want to do?" The pull-down is grouped by the logical tasks of the participants so it is easy to find the area of interest. The language here is simple and direct.

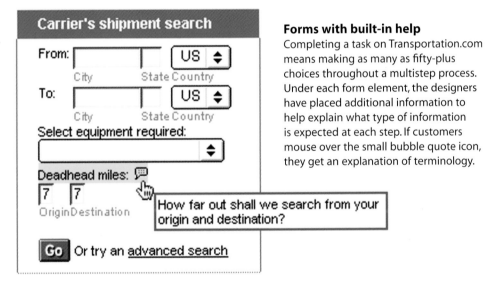

Forms with built-in help

Completing a task on Transportation.com means making as many as fifty-plus choices throughout a multistep process. Under each form element, the designers have placed additional information to help explain what type of information is expected at each step. If customers mouse over the small bubble quote icon, they get an explanation of terminology.

COLOR PALETTE

Actions

Since this Web site is heavily form-driven with very little graphic design, color is primarily used as a directional tool. Green identifies log-in or personal information actions. Blue identifies the process steps. Light yellow and gray are used for highlight and tone.

Transportation.com—*continued*

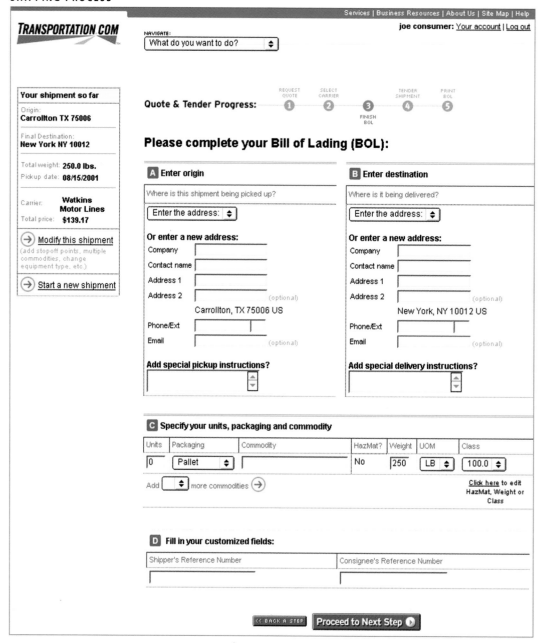

Process, process, process

There are many choices that have to be made to complete a shipping transaction. Transportation.com understands this and makes each page's process hierarchical. The progress bar displays the steps numerically, and alphabetical labels are used to assist the customer through the components of the step. This methodology is repeated for every task on the site.

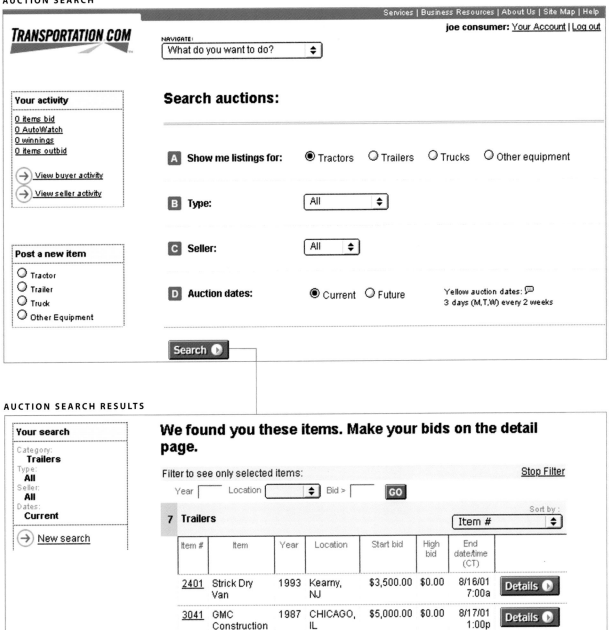

Grid consistency

A customer who has learned the shipping process doesn't need to learn many new things to take part in an auction. The left-hand boxes provide contextual help and display customer's choices throughout the process. The content area is organized by alphabetical steps. This religious allegiance to grid and signal consistency makes complicated tasks easier. Customers become faster and more efficient.

AUCTION PRODUCT PAGE FOR LOGGED-IN USER

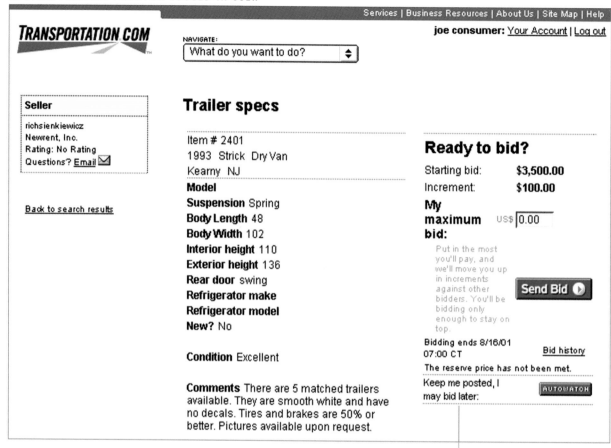

Services | Business Resources | About Us | Site Map | Help

TRANSPORTATION.COM™

joe consumer: Your Account | Log out

NAVIGATE:
What do you want to do? ⬍

Seller

richsienkiewicz
Newrent, Inc.
Rating: No Rating
Questions? Email ✉

Back to search results

Trailer specs

Item # 2401
1993 Strick Dry Van
Kearny NJ

Model
Suspension Spring
Body Length 48
Body Width 102
Interior height 110
Exterior height 136
Rear door swing
Refrigerator make
Refrigerator model
New? No

Condition Excellent

Comments There are 5 matched trailers available. They are smooth white and have no decals. Tires and brakes are 50% or better. Pictures available upon request.

Ready to bid?

Starting bid: **$3,500.00**
Increment: **$100.00**

My maximum bid: US$ [0.00]

Put in the most you'll pay, and we'll move you up in increments against other bidders. You'll be bidding only enough to stay on top.

Send Bid ▶

Bidding ends 8/16/01 07:00 CT   Bid history

The reserve price has not been met.

Keep me posted, I may bid later: **AUTOWATCH**

NOT LOGGED IN

Ready to bid?

Current bid: $5,000.00   Increment: $500.00
Bidding ends 8/17/01 13:00 CT

Please log in first:

Login ID: [   ]
Password: [   ]

Log In

Help, I forgot my password

Not a member yet?
Tell me more   I'm ready: sign me up

Identify when ready

Certain functions of a site naturally require a customer to log in first, but browsing through auction items is not one of them. When it comes time to bid on an item, the site needs to verify the customer and their buying information. Without verification, bids could easily be falsified. This template flexes to accommodate the user state (logged in or not) and determine the appropriate next step.

Icons with meaning

The icons on Transportation.com are designed for function, not decoration. To minimize download time they are small, but they provide useful information when moused-over or clicked.

Repeat experience

Yellow Global is the international shipping sister site for Transportation.com. If the customer has created a personal account on Transportation.com, the account and customer ID automatically carry over to the second site. The customer is also presented with an experience model that works just like Transportation.com. Replicate experiences whenever possible to breed familiarity and make a site friendly to repeat business.

Eziba.com

Named for the Persian word for beautiful (ziba), Eziba.com is an online catalog and global bazaar, offering an exclusive and constantly changing selection of authentic handcrafted items created by artisans from around the world. Eziba.com combines this retail product offering with exclusive-collection auctions and information about the origins of the products.

EZIBA
HANDCRAFTED ITEMS GLOBALLY SOURCED

SEARCH ▸
Enter key word, item name or number.

JOIN ▸
Enter your email address to receive Eziba news.

ACCENTS | ROOMS
GIFTS | JEWELRY
ART OBJECTS | KIDS

threads of life

EZIBA PARTNERS WITH PEDIATRIC AIDS FOUNDATION

SHOP

PURCHASE GIFTS AND HANDCRAFTED ITEMS

SHARING

EZIBA'S WORLD COMMUNITY INSPIRING STORIES FROM BEHIND THE SCENES

GIVING

EZIBA GIFTS GIVE BACK THE WHOLE WORLD OVER

SPECIAL

WHAT'S HAPPENING NOW! PROMOTIONS EVENTS AUCTIONS UPDATES

CATALOG SHOPPING   REQUEST A CATALOG

HOME   HELP   LOGIN   YOUR ACCOUNT   CHECKOUT   CATALOG SHOPPING   ABOUT US

For answers to your questions, please call us toll-free at 1-888-404-5108 or email customerservice@eziba.com
Privacy Notice © 1999-2001 Eziba.com, Inc. All rights reserved.

Get acquainted

Because they are an online pure play, Eziba's home page must establish the company personality. Folk-artsy icons denote the six product categories of the shopping area, while beautiful photography points the customers to other shopping alternatives. Eziba is a business that aims to do well while doing good around the world. Words like "sharing" and "giving" play to a consumer's like-minded sensibility.

COLOR PALETTE

Limited

One color is used to drive brand, to avoid competing with their image-laden design.

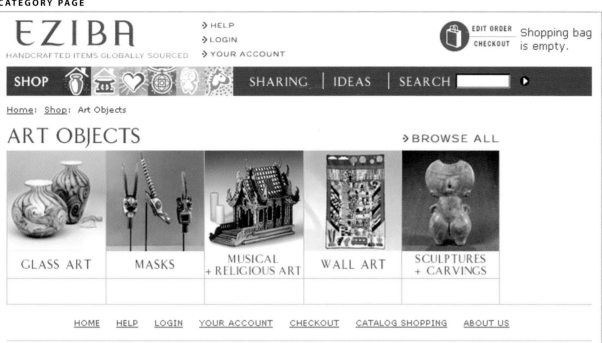

Home: Shop: Art Objects

ART OBJECTS

›BROWSE ALL

GLASS ART | MASKS | MUSICAL + RELIGIOUS ART | WALL ART | SCULPTURES + CARVINGS

HOME   HELP   LOGIN   YOUR ACCOUNT   CHECKOUT   CATALOG SHOPPING   ABOUT US

SUB-CATEGORY RESULTS

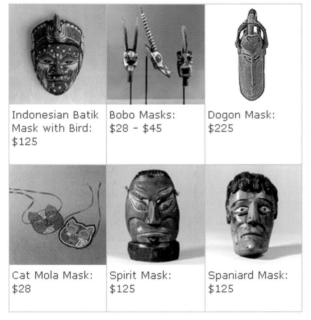

Indonesian Batik Mask with Bird: $125

Bobo Masks: $28 - $45

Dogon Mask: $225

Cat Mola Mask: $28

Spirit Mask: $125

Spaniard Mask: $125

Graphical browsing

Like many catalog sites concerned with style and product identity, Eziba uses graphical browsing to guide users through the site. Akin to window-shopping in a real store, Eziba provides very little product detail before the customer reaches the product page. This unobtrusive interaction is perfect for customers who base their choice in art and artifact on appearance alone. Up to six variations of size and angle are used for every image.

Eziba.com—*continued*

NAVIGATION

Breadcrumbs

Eziba uses the popular navigational aid of breadcrumbs to help customers know where they are on a site. It is sometimes easy to get lost during graphical browsing and this text reminder helps customers find their place. If a customer clicks on Shop they are taken to the site map below for a breakdown of what's in each section.

Visual confirmation

On many sites, customers put products in their bag and are forced to remember what's in it while they continue to shop. Eziba's solution is elegant as well as useful. Each time an item is added to the bag, a small thumbnail of the image is placed in the upper right-hand corner of the page next to the bag icon. If the visitor leaves the site before completing the purchase, these items will appear in the bag when they come back.

SITE MAP

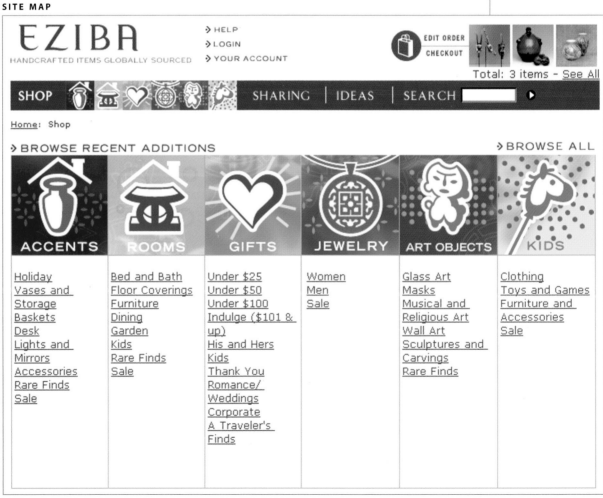

Women

1 2 3 4 5 6 7 next

Festival of Lights Hand Mirrors: $28

Caravan Lapis Necklace: $42

Bandorfer Wire Jewelry: $95 – $450

Vintage Sequin Bag: $42

Floral Yukata: $85

Pink Droplet Necklace & Earrings: $35 – $95

Amber Bezel Jewelry: $89 – $185

Onyx Inlay Earrings: $32

Glass Bead Necklace: $38

Get More. Get Eziba's latest catalog.

CATEGORY
Set Category ⬍

MINIMUM PRICE
$25 ⬍

MAXIMUM PRICE
$100 ⬍

REGION/COUNTRY
Set Region/Country ⬍

ITEMS PER PAGE
9 ⬍

update ▶

reset menus ▶

1 2 3 4 5 6 7 next

Customer choice

On category pages, customers are presented with a few representative products from the available inventory. On the left side of the page, Eziba's designer gives customers an elegant combination of pull-down menus to make it easy for a customer to re-sort or narrow the list of products to suit their shopping needs.

Eziba.com—*continued*

PRODUCT PAGE

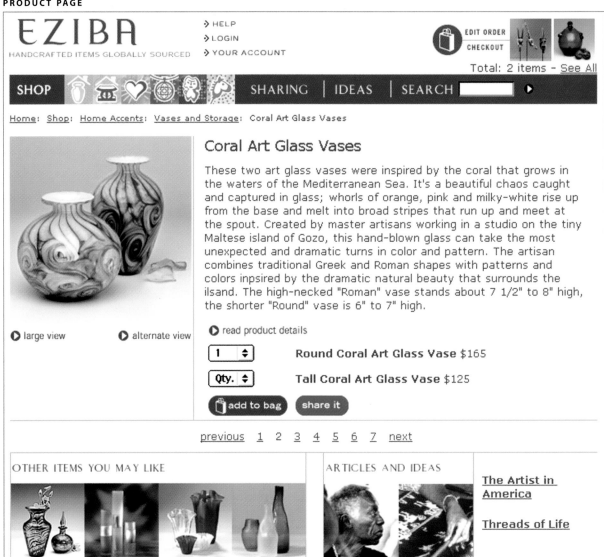

Standout photography

Eziba's images are gorgeous. In fact, these photos are the cornerstone of this beautiful design. But this beauty is not just skin deep. Toronto-based content consultant Joe Clark illuminates the thinking behind the design: "What were people saying about consumers' unwillingness to buy online because they aren't sure what they are getting? Beautiful documentation of this sort blows worry out of the water."
(www.contenu.nu/article.htm?id=1190)

Tell me a story

To sell each product, Eziba uses the power of narrative. They tell the story of the product by showcasing the artisans and explaining their creative intent. How many customers do you think ever heard of the tiny Maltese Island of Gozo? Nice touch.

EZIBA
HANDCRAFTED ITEMS GLOBALLY SOURCED

> HELP
> LIVE CUSTOMER SERVICE

CHECKOUT
Your total including tax and current shipping options is $443.00

| 1 BAG | 2 SHIPPING ADDRESS | 3 SHIPPING METHODS | 4 GIFTS | 5 BILLING | 6 CONFIRMATION | 7 INVOICE |

REVIEW ITEMS IN YOUR SHOPPING BAG

ITEM NAME	ITEM #	QUANTITY	PRICE	
Coba Bobo Mask	#1010236	1	$45.00	✖ remove
A Toast to Life	#1002130	1	$145.00	✖ remove
Round Coral Art Glass Vase	#1000037	1	$165.00	✖ remove
Day of the Dead Candleholders	#1002165	1	$58.00	✖ remove

➕ update quantities

◉ Ship all of these items to one address.
◯ Ship items to more than one address.

▶ continue checkout

For personal answers to your questions, please call us toll-free at 1-888-404-5108 or email customerservice@eziba.com
Privacy Notice © 1999-2001 Eziba.com, Inc. All rights reserved.

Explicit procedures

Like all good checkout pages, Eziba adapts its main navigation bar to show the customer the steps they need to follow to complete the transaction. This change helps to guide the customer's expectation of what's next. They also added a prominent Live Customer Service link, because help is most relevant at the checkout stage. Visual repetition of the icons for products that the customer is about to purchase provides assurance at this first step of checkout.

Photonica.com

This international stock photography agency uses the Web to provide customers with an easy way to access thousands of images in its collection. Once a customer has found a photograph that they want to purchase, they can call the nearest representative to complete the transaction. This is common approach to selling products that have complicated pricing models, such a photographs, which can change price based on the circulation of the publication, dimensions of the image used, and the rights of use.

HOME PAGE

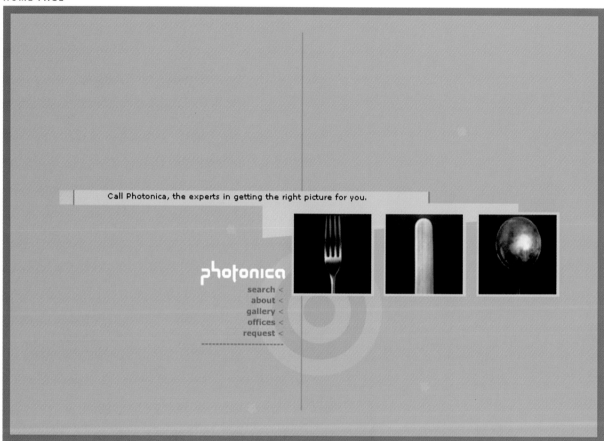

Start simple

Photonica's home page is a model of simplicity. It is as much an advertisement of the agency's style as it is an entrance to the site. Establishing tone and style is important, since Photonica doesn't have a long-standing brand like its competitors, Corbis and Tony Stone. This splash page presents the main functions of the site, along with three photos that are randomly chosen from their collection for each customer visit.

COLOR PALETTE

Background
Neutral grays allow photos and control elements to have visual prominence.

Attention
Green and orange are used for most buttons and to highlight information.

TECHNOLOGY

Front-end
- DHTML
- CSS
- JavaScript
- Frames
- Flash
- PHP

KEYWORDS

enter keywords

☑ Narrower Terms ☐ Broader Terms ☐ Related Terms
☑ Synonyms ☐ singular/plural

and/or select from the following options below

PHOTOGRAPHERS NAME   Select photographer ◆

CATEGORY   Select category ◆

ORIENTATION   Select orientation ◆

CATALOG   select catalog ◆ | Page [   ] Location [   ]

or IMAGE ID   [   ] Color ☐ Monochrome ☐

SEARCH

FIND IMAGES | RESET

Searching through thousands of photographs is a challenge, even if customers know roughly what they want. Photonica's organizational schemes allow customers to use a number of exact and ambiguous methods for exploration. The Image ID is for photographs that appear in their print catalogs, which you can also order on this site.

Repeat action
After customers have performed their first search, a quick search box appears in the core navigation of every page. This shortcut provides users an easy alternative to the more complex first search box.

Navigation
The site's navigation is consistent on every page, with a white highlight to indicate the customer's active page.

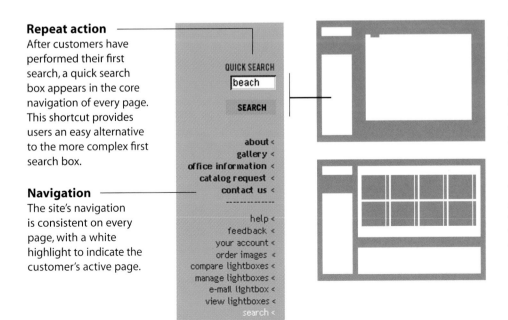

QUICK SEARCH
beach
SEARCH

about <
gallery <
office information <
catalog request <
contact us <
----
help <
feedback <
your account <
order images <
compare lightboxes <
manage lightboxes <
e-mail lightbox <
view lightboxes <
search <

Template design
Photonica must rely heavily on templates to drive design, because the site is basically a search engine that provides dynamic results from a database. The top template is static, used for presenting messages or functions to the user, such as the advanced search box in the top image. The bottom template is used for browsing and presentation of images.

Photonica.com—*continued*

Interface feedback

To assist users through a unique and potentially unfamiliar interface, Photonica provides contextual feedback to users as they explore the site. When mousing over the + next to any image, the search bar at the top of the Web page turns orange and instructs the customer how to add the image to a lightbox. The bar also gives a little information about the image.

SEARCH RESULTS

Break it up

In this set of search results, more than nine hundred images match a keyword search for "beach" photos. In a perfect example of chunking, the search results are broken into easy-to-digest units of eight images. Photonica uses a contact sheet metaphor to present results in an orderly fashion. They also offer the metaphorical lightbox—a place to store images while continuing to browse.

How to buy

Scrolling text boxes, also called tickers, are often misused on the Web as gee-whiz graphic junk. Photonica uses this small space to notify customers of how to contact a sales rep in order to buy an image. Clicking on this box takes the customer to a complete set of buying instructions.

Design for content

The grid space dedicated to the photo is built to accommodate all shapes of images, yet maintain a large enough size to see the photo clearly. The grid also helps the rest of the page maintain a consistent shape. To see a larger version of the photo, a customer simply clicks on the image. This is handy for designers that might want to test-drive the image in a layout.

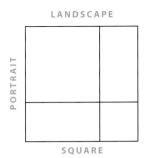

Useful relationships

If a customer finds a particular style of photo that they like, they can click on the photographer's name to see all the other photos in the database that he or she created. Or customers can find images that have been similarly classified, by clicking on any of the image's keywords.

PRODUCT PAGE

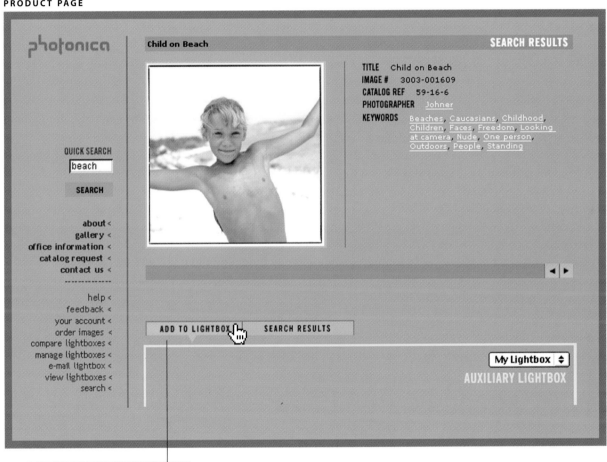

Lightbox

When a customer adds an image to the lightbox, the page is quickly refreshed and the image is shown in the lightbox. At any point, the customer can remove the image by clicking the minus button below the thumbnail. This shortcut prevents the customer from always having to go the lightbox page to remove items.

Easy to browse

Instead of forcing customers to return to the search page, they can use the orange forward and backward buttons to continue browsing search results.

217

Photonica.com—*continued*

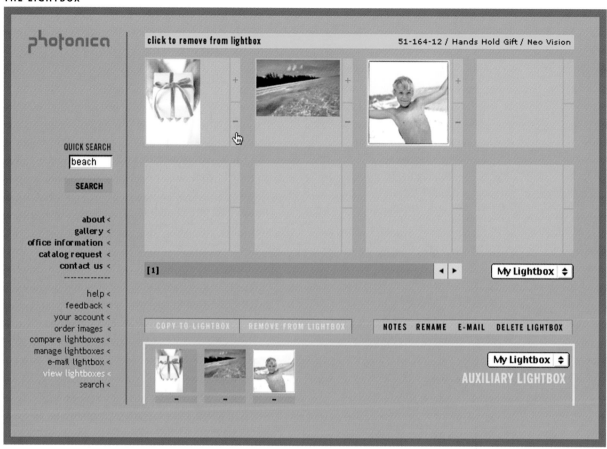

Consistency
What customers learn on one part of
the site they can apply to others. The
lightbox, for example, works exactly
like search results. Photonica uses
a small color change (from orange
buttons to green ones) to help
customers differentiate the lightbox
experience from search.

Directing action
Language is a powerful design tool.
Photonica opts for the most succinct
and direct terms when pointing
customers to an action. Instead of
techno-centric terms like "submit,"
or clever terms like "loupe," they use
specific terms: delete, select, rename.
This practice prevents ambiguity.

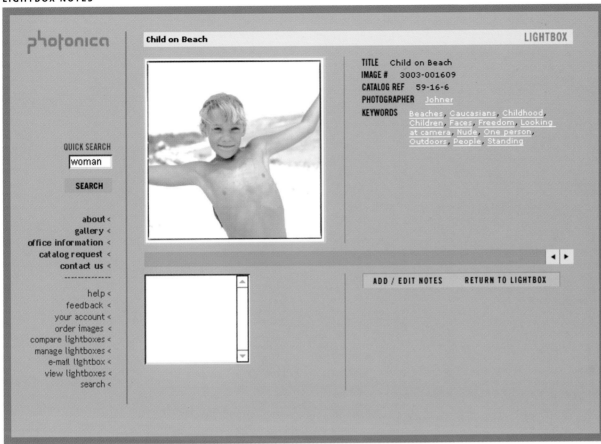

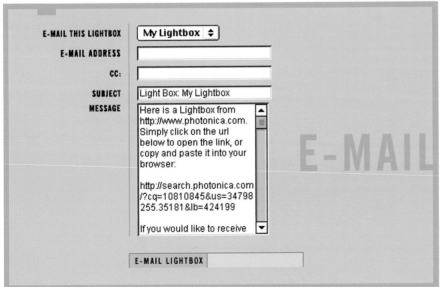

Personalization

The lightbox is an excellent example of relevant personalization, but the customization doesn't end with image storage. Customers can also add comments to photos, then e-mail a collaborator, client, or coworker the lightbox of images. This feature shows Photonica's understanding of their customers' process. Designers often need others to sign off on an image for purchasing approval.

Audion

The Internet enabled software programmers to easily start small digital storefronts on the Web and bypass the costly distribution and manufacturing process. Panic is a two-person outfit in Portland that makes Macintosh software programs, including Audion, a popular Audio CD and MP3 player.

COMPANY HOME PAGE

Known metaphors

Panic only develops software for the Macintosh, so they know their audience will be familiar with the Mac interface. Their home page uses elements from the Mac operating system's windows, icons, and utilities to define the style of the Web site. For example, when a customer clicks on "What's New?" a yellow Mac-style sticky-note pops up on the page with the information. Panic uses this pop-up style of presentation frequently throughout their site.

COLOR PALETTE

Accent over neutrals

Panic's home page uses accent purple over a neutral olive. The Audion section follows a similar palette using blue-gray neutrals for the page background and other non-navigational elements, then relies on complementary colors to draw attention to information and navigation.

TECHNOLOGY

Front-end
- DHTML
- CSS
- JavaScript

 ABOUT DOWNLOAD FACES BUY SUPPORT FUN

NEWS

SEP 27

CD burning? Maximizer and echo effects? Scads of 10.1 improvements? FREE UPGRADE? Yes, it's **Audion 2.6!**

SEP 27

We're ready for Mac OS X 10.1, with great 10.1 specific features like faster resizing, and a dock menu. If you're a Mac OS X user, grab the brand new **Audion 2.6 for X!**

JUL 10

Audion 2.5, a major upgrade, is **up**. Best of all, the upgrade is free for all Audion 2 owners.

JUL 10

Audion 2.5 for **Mac OS X, too!**

JUL 10

A new batch of faces are **now available!**

 AUDION 2
PLAY, ENCODE, AND PERFORM WITH STYLE.

Hi! I'm a single tool that bravely handles all your audio playing needs -- I'm easy to use, but with a ton of advanced features just waiting to be discovered. I can play your Audio CDs, your MP3s, and your streaming network audio, and now, I can encode, edit, mix, sort and manage, visualize and hypnotize. Best of all, I've got that Panic design - light, simple, and powerful. It's nice to meet you! **Ready to graduate from iTunes? Then go on, download me!**

How does Audion stack up to the competition? <u>See for yourself!</u>

X How does Audion fit with Mac OS X? Incredibly! <u>Read the Mac OS X Commandments!</u>

WHAT'S NEW IN 2?
CLICK ON THE 🔍 ICON TO LEARN MORE ABOUT A FEATURE

🔍 **Dock Integration**
(2.6) Do everything in the dock!

🔍 **Handy Toolbars**
(2.5) Easier access to cool features.

🔍 **Mac OS X Perfect!**
(2.5) Loads of treats, Mac OS X only! Look!

🔍 **CD Burning**
(2.6) Burn audio in one quick click!

🔍 **Portable Device Support**
(2.5) Transfer to your RIO or Nomad!

• **Easy CD Playback**
(2.5) Just pop in a disc, and hit play!

Personality

Panic's clean, intricate style of Web design mimics the attributes of their software—simple and powerful. Click on any magnifying glass icon, and a customer gets a pop-up window with a short text explanation of the feature, along with screenshots and movies for those who want to see the feature in action.

🔲 **FEATURE DETAIL**

One-Click CD Burning

Drag some MP3 tracks into a playlist, click the Burn button, and in a few minutes you'll have your very own custom Audio CD courtesy of Roxio Toast and Audion 2.6!

Requires Roxio Toast 5.0.2 or higher.

144K   12K

Panic considerately points out what to expect—the download size and file type are displayed with each rich media experience.

221

Audion—*continued*

PERSONALIZATION

Enable obsession

Building community around a product breeds loyalty. Audion uses "skins" technology to encourage users to redesign their program's interface and to then share their designs with others. This page is Audion's repository for all the faces created by the Audion community. When a customers gets tired of their current interface skin, they can come to this page to download a new one. Click on the magnifying glass and the skin appears as a pop-up floating on the page.

Know your audience

The introduction of a new Macintosh operating system, OS X, created some challenges for software makers as well as customers. Early adoption brings inevitable speed bumps. To help assuage concerns, Audion's makers created a set of commandments to emphasize their programming prowess and control in this new Macintosh environment.

Lighten up

These Ten (X) Commandments are brimming with attitude, conviction, and passion. But the page also feels personable. This copy doesn't read like a marketing VP is trying to convince you that Audion will slice, dice, and puree your MP3s. Even when discussing technical details, Audion is saying in between the lines, "We love music and we love good software. Let's jam."

MAC OS X COMMANDMENTS
DON'T ACCEPT ANYTHING LESS FROM YOUR MAC OS X APPLICATIONS!

 Work The Dock

Ever flexible, the dock is a great place for applications to provide shortcuts and status. With Audion 2.5, we provide an Audion dockling so you can keep Audion hidden and control it from the dock. Even better - the track and time is displayed live in the dock!

> Quit Audion
> Bring Audion to the Front
>
> Encode Playlist
>
> Play/Pause
> Previous Track
> Next Track
> Stop
> Eject

 Conquer Quartz

Transparency? Shadows? Reflections? Highlights? Thanks to Quartz, it's all possible, natively. Audion uses Quartz for each of the over 600 Audion faces.

 Understand long filenames.

Wow. It's about time, isn't it? You can now have filenames like this one - lengthy and descriptive.

Your Mac OS X application should be able to read and write long filenames, just like Audion 2.5.

XTC / You And The Clouds Will Still Be Beautiful.mp3

 Pretty icons.

Accept no substitutions. Scalable, high-color, emotive and, for us, Iconfactory-fresh!

Audion—*continued*

Easy, secure

The purchase process for Audion takes four steps and fits on one scrolling Web page. Messages along the way reinforce the site's sensitivity to security and privacy. Personal expressions like "give us your life story" and "you will become our best friend" help to build trust.

Feedback

When the customer clicks "process my order," a JavaScript checks to make sure that all the data has been entered. If something is missing, a pop-up box presents a feedback message, without removing all the information you typed in.

If the data is correct, the script presents a Mac-friendly confirmation box that builds trust that the order was received.

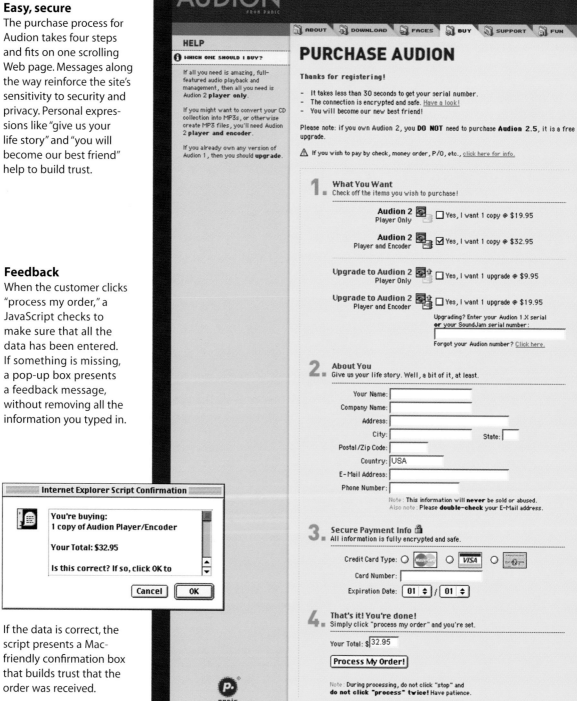

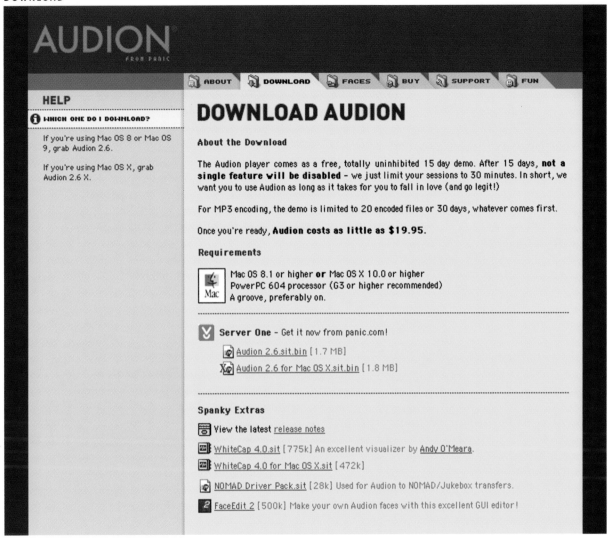

Contextual help

One of nicest elements of Audion's Web design is the instructional help boxes placed in the upper-left hand corner of every page. On the download page, the instructions help customers decide which version is appropriate for them. On the face page, this space becomes a search box. The consistent placement trains the customer to look in the upper left whenever they need help.

Herman Miller RED

Innovation and style are hallmarks of this seventy-five-year-old brand of office furniture. (In 1968, HM revolutionized the American workplace when it developed the notion of cubicles.) The Herman Miller RED line was created to give small, fast-moving businesses "simple, quick, and affordable" options. Their business model for this line is to sell easy-to-assemble, modular furniture over the Internet, that can be delivered and put to work in about a week.

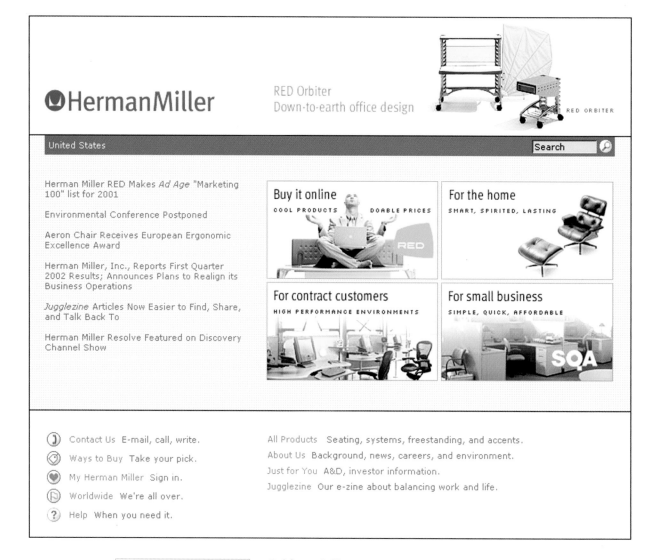

Guide and direct

The corporate Herman Miller Web site seeks to maintain their well-known high quality in customer service, as well as market their products to a variety of customers—executive, small business, and home. But their e-commerce area targets a younger, hipper audience than their traditional sales channels. As a result, the look of the commerce area is designed to be more appropriate to their target.

Brand attitude

The home shopping page establishes the core grid of the visual experience along with a few product teasers to get a customer started. Like much of this site, this page is designed for scan-and-click navigation. The page features only two prices, five product images and a "what's new" box—a stark contrast to Amazon, where every millimeter of space is crammed with products or links to categories of other products. Sites with fewer than five hundred products can use this posterlike approach because they don't have to showcase inventory breadth and depth up front.

FIXED WIDTH

VARIABLE DEPTH

COLOR PALETTE

Active, hip

There is tremendous color energy on this site, enough to overpower the visual experience. But HM manages to make it work because it relies primarily on one shade of color balanced with pockets of white space. The signature blue is used to define grid structure and labels. Blue's complement, orange, is used to signal key buttons on each page. This contrast allows the customer to quickly locate control elements.

TECHNOLOGY

Front-end
• JHTML
• DHTML
• CSS
• JavaScript
• XML

Herman Miller RED—*continued*

RED GRASSHOPPER

If you're called Grasshopper, you'd better have great legs. RED Grasshopper desks do. Their U-shaped design with elliptical ribbing makes them amazingly strong and surprisingly lightweight. And thanks to all the other RED Grasshopper products, there's no need to get jumpy about storage or privacy needs. Choose a 1-, 2-, 3-, or 4-high shelf unit and decide now or later whether you want doors on any of them. Screens come in translucent or tackable versions. They all converge in what we call "soft docking" – nuzzling nicely without precise connections – so you can move them around, mix and match them, and they always look good and work well.

Graphical browsing

Customers can read short copy blocks on the Herman Miller site if they want, but it's not necessary. All products are treated as icons. There are no model numbers, descriptions, or prices on many pages. Just point-and-click on the icons, and they will lead you through the purchasing process. The extraordinarily small icons that appear in the left-hand navigation area are surprisingly easy to recognize, and more useful than generics like "shelf" or stylistic terms like "Grasshopper Storage Unit." This approach works because the number, type and category of products are limited. If a designer tried to mimic the idea on a major retail site (like Macy's or Buy.com), the icons would become concentration navigation.

BROWSE ICON

NAVIGATION ICON

Minimal text

The type on the Herman Miller site is quite small, but it's not a problem because there are so many visual targets to hit. In fact, if the type were much larger, the text might overwhelm the images. If customers want to read more, they can click the Details link above the image.

Add to cart

There is no dominant shopping cart icon on this site, because Herman Miller does not need one. When a customer clicks on Add to Cart the page is quickly refreshed with a feedback message and a Go to Checkout button is added to the page.

As the customer continues through the site, the Go to Checkout button persists on every page.

Dig deeper

When customers are making a purchase of more than $1,000, they may need information beyond a brief description to make a proper purchase decision. With each product, HM offers links to detail pages, the story behind the design and a larger version of the photo. The customer can easily compare the features of one chair with others.

Useful relationships

Furniture is often featured as a collection. HM always serves up a few related products as well as linking to a page that displays the entire collection. They also provide easy links to related category pages.

PRODUCT COMPARISON

This comparison list goes much deeper, but notice that Herman Miller organizes the page so that the most likely aspects of comparison—price, dimension, assembly—are pushed to the top.

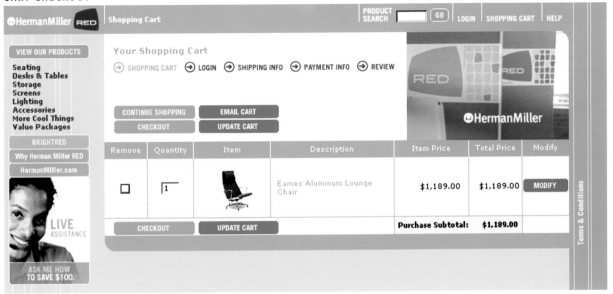

Short, easy steps

Product icons follow customers into the shopping cart environment, providing the customer with visual reassurance that they are buying exactly what they chose. The shopping cart presents customers with an explicit set of five steps that they will need to complete. Privacy and security reminders, as well as a link to live assistance reinforce the stellar customer service that defines the Herman Miller brand.

Rackspace.com

Founded in 1999, Rackspace Managed Hosting is one of largest managed hosting companies in the world, with more than 2,000 customers in fifty different countries. The site's design reflects three key principles of success in the crowded field of hosting: fanatical customer service, trust and authority.

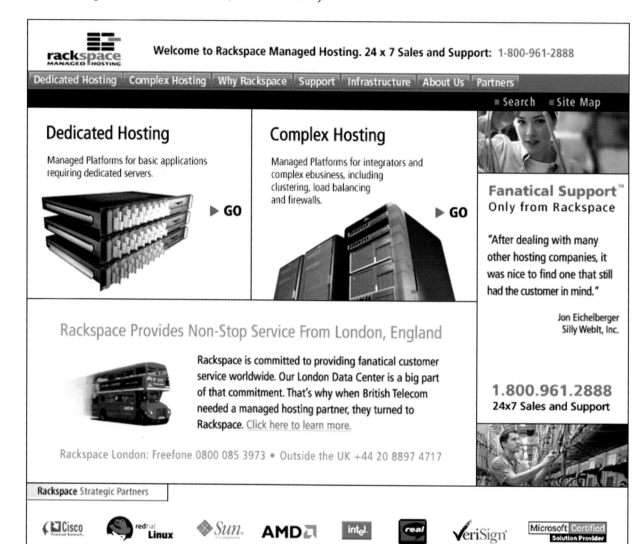

Build confidence

When selling any service, you are selling the invisible. The sale is closed on brand confidence. Home page photos of Rackspace employees put a human face on the amorphous service of Web hosting. An extremely rigid and consistent grid pervades Rackspace, reinforcing the message: "We have everything in our place. You can trust us." Logos of top technical partners bolster Rackspace's service legitimacy.

COLOR PALETTE

Accent over neutrals

Red, black, and white define the brand, while neutrals accent service elements and the order process.

TECHNOLOGY

Front-end

• DHTML
• CSS
• JavaScript
• PHP
• Flash

Known metaphors

Most customers are familiar with pull-down menus in their operating system. Rackspace shows its programming savvy (again, a service confidence builder) with a slick DHTML replication of this navigation tool.

Why Rackspace	Support
Rackspace Advantages	
Why Managed Hosting?	
Case Studies	
Customer Testimonials	

PRODUCT PAGE

Dedicated Hosting | Complex Hosting | Why Rackspace | Support | Infrastructure | About Us | Partners

:::: *dedicated hosting*   ▪ Search   ▪ Site Map

1-800-961-2888
Call Us Now! 24 x 7 Sales

E-mail Sales

Call Me Back

— Dedicated Hosting —

▼ **Dedicated Hosting**

Linux

Sun

FreeBSD

Windows NT

Windows 2000

▶ **Additional Services & Products**

▶ **One-Hour Servers**

▶ **Custom Build a Server**

▶ **What is a Dedicated Server?**

▶ **Help me choose an OS**

▶ **Sales FAQ**

Add-on Products & Services

▶ Monitoring

▶ Network

▶ Software

▶ Security

▶ Database

▶ Backup

▶ Network Attached Storage

Want to succeed on the Internet?

You have to be dedicated.

Rackspace makes it easy to get up and running on your own dedicated server. You'll get root access on a server built specifically for you. Just click on an OS below to start configuring.

Once you submit your order, we'll have it built and on-line in 24 hours, guaranteed! And we back up your servers with our *award winning fanatical customer support*, 24 hours a day, seven days a week. Plus, you have the flexibility of month to month contracts and upgrades as you need them!

Products   Services

For Dedicated Servers

click here

Get A Server

① Choose an Operating System...

Linux   Sun Solaris   FreeBSD   Windows NT   Windows 2000

◉   ○   ○   ○   ○

② Then choose one of these two options:

View Our Recommended Servers   **Custom Build Your Server**

Get The Facts

○ Help me choose an operating system

1-800-961-2888
Call Us Now! 24 x 7 Sales

Yes. We want to talk to you.

Most Web sites assume that you'll get all your answers online. They bury their phone numbers and consign your complaints to e-mail oblivion. Take Rackspace's lead and make sure your site clearly displays a mailing address and a phone number — one that connects with a real person.

Rackspace.com—*continued*

Have personality

Three-dimensional icons, buttons, and illustrations are the cornerstone of Rackspace's visual personality. They are meticulous, elegant, and clean. Along with consistent replication of key brand colors and typography, Rackspace's visual style strengthens the hallmarks of their business. The text that details products and services is specific and free of marketese.

 Monitoring and Reporting
Analyze your server and site performance with Appliant Monitoring and WebTrends.

Context is the key

The labels on Rackspace's buttons were designed with potential customer tasks in mind. The text is direct and action-oriented. Notice that the dedicated hosting solution does not offer a Contact Sales button. Because this is a pre-packaged service offering with few optional extras, Rackspace would rather have the customer complete the purchase themselves. With more complex offerings, it's better to have the customer call a sales person.

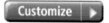

COMPLEX HOSTING SERVICE

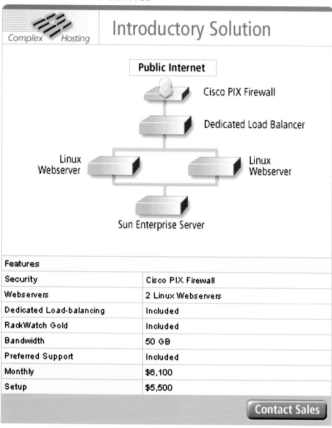

Features	
Security	Cisco PIX Firewall
Webservers	2 Linux Webservers
Dedicated Load-balancing	Included
RackWatch Gold	Included
Bandwidth	50 GB
Preferred Support	Included
Monthly	$6,100
Setup	$5,500

Contact Sales

DEDICATED HOSTING SERVICE

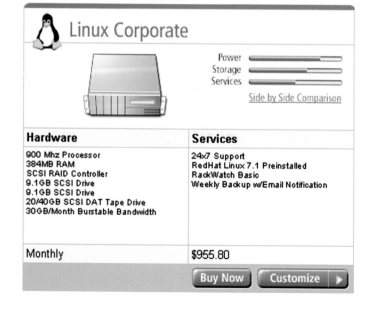

Linux Corporate

Power
Storage
Services

Side by Side Comparison

Hardware	Services
900 Mhz Processor 384MB RAM SCSI RAID Controller 9.1GB SCSI Drive 9.1GB SCSI Drive 20/40GB SCSI DAT Tape Drive 30GB/Month Burstable Bandwidth	24x7 Support RedHat Linux 7.1 Preinstalled RackWatch Basic Weekly Backup w/Email Notification
Monthly	$955.80

Buy Now   Customize

Live and in person

Rackspace understands that not all customers are comfortable with buying online. This intro page to placing an order offers three options for completing the deal, including an immediate online chat with a Rackspace sales rep.

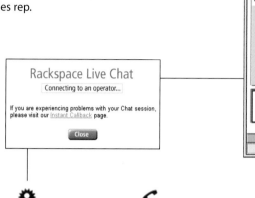

| Chat with Sales Live | Instant Callback | E-mail Sales | Frequently Asked Questions |

How To Place Your Order

Your Session Number is 19236238

You have 1 server in your shopping cart .

🔍 Take A Look   ⊕ Add A New Server

Total Monthly Fee	$ 285.80
Total Setup Fee	$ 270.80
Contract Term	Monthly

VAT at the prevailing rate will be charged where appropriate.

Choose from any one of these options:

A Place your order online.

B Contact our sales team regarding this order (and any questions you may have).

C E-mail the details of this order to yourself and others.

D Save your session and return later.

Appendix
COMMERCE DESIGN—
beyond the browser

Technology changes, but people do not. The quickening pace of technical development has made it harder to predict what technologies will be created and how quickly consumers will adopt them. There are just too many unforeseeable influences that can affect how people decide to use new technologies.

The classic example is e-mail. E-mail was a feature added almost as an afterthought by the early fathers of the Internet. Without fanfare, it was quickly used in ways unintended and unimagined by its creators. Today, e-mail is the most popular and important use of the Internet.[1]

It's clear that we can't predict the future. But we can prepare for the eventuality that the browser will not be the only way customers will access your commerce site. Research shows that mobile Internet-enabled devices are poised to outpace personal computers as the preferred way to get information online.

These new devices will have much smaller displays and be varied in design to fit specific lifestyles and customer goals.

Their effortless portability will allow the customer to shop anywhere and anytime.[2] However, their very variety and customization create headaches. For example, the compatibility problems faced with PC browsers will be nothing compared to the challenges of providing desirable commerce experiences on everything from cell phones to PDAs.

For a company to succeed, its designers will have to focus on the new tasks and goals each device makes possible. The new digital shopping experiences will be shaped by the type of device, its bandwidth capacity, and its form factor (physical size and shape). In Fig. A.1, we explain how to break down the characteristics of a device.

Adjusting for the type of device is only the beginning. The personal computer has a clearly defined context. People sit down at a computer, wait for it to start up, connect to the Internet, and launch the browser. Because of the effort required, people only go online when they want to do something.

With other Internet-enabled devices, the context changes with differences in location, connectivity, and interest (See Fig. A.2). These variables provide marketing opportunities. A video store might send a rental offer via cell phone, knowing that the customer is driving by a local branch.

Fortunately, the principles of good information, interaction, and presentation design will help you design for good commerce on any device. "For years we've said the customer is king, but never has that maxim been as true as it is today," says Elaine Rubin, president of ekrubin Inc. and chairman of Shop.org. "Customers are in control, and the mantra of 'shop any time, anywhere' is rewriting the rules."[3]

FIGURE A.1: CONSIDER THE DEVICE

New appliances require examination of attributes that will affect usability and the customer's tasks and motivations. When designing a commerce site for a device other than a personal computer, consider these characteristics:

Form factor: What is the size and shape of the device? Is the display small or large? Does it have a keyboard, keypad, or stylus?

Modality: Can the user interact with the device through touch (keyboard, stylus, touch screen), sound, or sight?

Connectivity: How is the device connected to the Internet? How fast is that connection? Is it always on and reliable or intermittent?

Performance: How much processing power, memory, and battery life does the device have?

Display: What is the screen size, resolution, and color capability?

FIGURE A.2: CUSTOMER CONTEXT

Creating a commerce experience for mobile devices requires a detailed analysis of other factors that affect customer behavior. Consider customer context while designing.

Location: Where is the customer — outside, in a car, in a store, in a hotel?

Interest: How valuable is the commerce information to the customer? Is she comparison shopping or impulse buying?

Device: What is the customer's device and why did she choose it?

Demographic: Customer demographics can help tailor content offerings.

Familiarity: How well do customers know and understand this shopping experience?

Emotional state: Will the customer be accessing information under a high-stress environment or a relaxed situation?

Anytime, Anywhere, Any Device

Silicon Valley marketing guru Regis McKenna has advised companies to "prepare for the eventuality of anything" in a digital world.[4]

Faced with an array of immature platforms and technologies, many companies are focusing on how to repurpose and deliver Web assets instead of having to re-create the content for each new device.

This strategy is made possible by technologies that separate content from design, such as XML and XSL. The content exists in a relational database but has no presentation code tied to it. The designer can create a new set of presentation templates that will display the data in a form that is appropriate to each device.

To explain this concept, a tech team may show you a diagram that looks something like Fig. A.3. It would be nice if repurposing assets were as simple as creating a new template. But it's much more complicated than that.

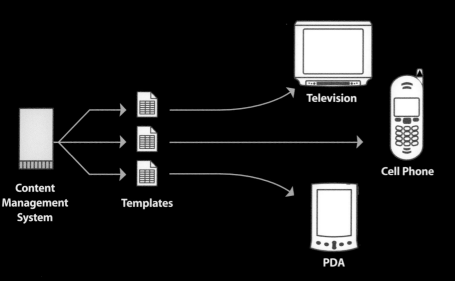

Content Management System

Templates

Television

Cell Phone

PDA

FIGURE A.3: REPURPOSING CONTENT

Highly detailed and well-structured content can be published to the Web using design templates. With a new set of templates, it's possible to publish this one set of content to many other devices.

When you are asked to design templates for a new device, you'll need to start at the beginning of the design process. Review the business goals for transacting with customers in light of the uses of this new device. New target profiles may need to be created, because it's unlikely that they are identical to the Web site customers.

Conduct a thorough review of the content inventory that was created for the Web site. Some new content will likely need to be created. At the very least, some content will need to be edited for it to be appropriately displayed on the new device. You will need to create new information and interaction design models based on the new profiles and the device limitations. It is only after you have completed this process that your design can succeed in meeting customer's goals and expectations.

There are truly a mind-boggling variety of Internet-enabled devices being developed— everything from vending machines and refrigerators to cars and wrist watches. In this chapter, we review the nearest-term design challenges that you are likely to face (See Fig. A.4).

MyFlix.com

| DVD | Video | Players | Forums | About | Help |

MY COLLECTION | BEST SELLERS | NEW RELEASES | BARGAIN DEALS | USED SALE | DVD FORUMS

SEARCH

All Products

GO

Advanced | Tips

MY CART 🛒

Qty	Item	Price
1	X-Men	$11.45
Shipping		$5
Total:		$16.45

CHECKOUT

BROWSE GENRE

Action/Adventure
Comedy
Disney
Documentary
Drama
Family/Kids
Foreign/Art
Horror/Suspense
Music/Musicals
▸ Sci-Fi/Fantasy
DVD Players
DVD Forums

▸ DVD > Sci-Fi/Fantasy > Popular

DVD
PRODUCT PHOTO

The Matrix (1999)
List Price: $25
Our Price: $15
You Save: $10 (40%)
Availability: 24 in stock
Rank: ★★★★★

Trailer: RealVideo 56K | 300K | Help

Other Available Formats:
VHS, VHS widescreen, VHS subtitled in
Spanish, Theatrical

Movie Details
Rated: R for violence and language
Starring: Keanu Reeves, Laurence
Fishburne, Carrie-Anne Moss
Director: Andy & Larry Wachowski
Read More

DVD Details
• Region 1 encoding (US and Canada only)
• Color, closed-captioned, Dolby, anamorphic widescreen
• Commentary by Carrie-Anne Moss, Zach Staenberg and John Gaeta
• Isolated musical score with comentary by composer Don Davis
• Behind-the-scenes documentary "HBO First Look: Making the Matrix"
• Hidden special effects documentaries
• Follow the white rabbit to nine behind-the-scenes featurettes
• Production notes, theatrical trailer(s)
Read More

ADD TO CART

QTY 1

MAIL A FRIEND

myfriend@yahoo.co

RELATED

• Limited Edition
  Collector's DVD
• Original Score
• Music from the
  Matrix

© MyFlix.com | Company Info | Partners | Contact Us | Store Locator | Privacy Policy

Original Web page

Designers will soon face the inevitable challenge of providing many versions of their sites to multitudes of different information devices. To create usable interfaces, you will have to understand the unique display, connectivity, and usability issues of each device. Here are some presentation considerations for adapting our hypothetical site, MyFlix.com, on different devices:

MyFlix:DVD:Sci
The Matrix '99
$15 Save 40%
4 Stars
R: Keanu Reeves, Lau
BACK   BUY

**WAP
(Web-enabled phone)**
When designing HDML or WML sites, keep necessary keystrokes to a minimum, since typing on a nine-keypad is difficult for customers, and will increase their chance of making errors.

PDA
PDAs usually have screens only 200 pixels wide and offer limited or no color capability. Design a less dense page and keep menu options limited to facilitate simple navigation.

From: MyFlix.com

Subject: $10 Off "The Matrix"

Dear MyFlix Film Fan,

Being a Sci-Fi fan we thought you should know "The Matrix" is on sale for $15 (Reg. $25).

Copies are going fast. If you would like us to hold one for you simply reply to this message or visit www.myflix.com.

MyFlix.com Staff

Handhelds
Popular wireless handhelds usually can only handle text messaging or e-mail that's free of HTML content.

Interactive Television
Televisions have a lower resolution and blurry displays compared to computer monitors. Do not try to cram a lot of data on to the page. Use flexible tables to accommodate different browser widths.

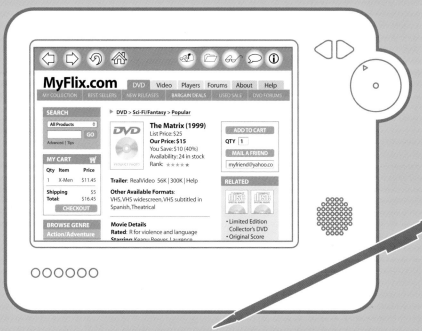

Tablets
Tablets are flat-panel displays with touch sensitivity. Most have similar resolutions to customers' normal computer monitors. The primary input mode is the stylus, so keep buttons large for easy selecting.

E-mail

From a presentation perspective, delivering a commerce experience to e-mail clients is similar to delivering a browser-based design. E-mail presentation is no more than an HTML Web page delivered to a customer's e-mail basket.

But the commerce content and its purpose in this experience is wholly different from that of the browser. Usually, a customer has asked to receive an e-mail notification about special deals, inventory availability, and new product offerings that might meet their interests. This is called permission-based e-mail. It can be extremely successful for something so inexpensive to create.

A survey from DoubleClick, an Internet advertising company, revealed that more than 82 percent of all Web users had made a purchase online as a result of an advertisement they received through e-mail. The study also found that 37 percent of shoppers made an immediate purchase in response to an e-mail.[5]

Unlike the browse and explore invitation of a normal Web page, a good commerce e-mail is a call-to-action. In Fig. A.5, we show a typical commerce-based e-mail.

FIGURE A.5: DIRECT MAIL

E-mail should not be designed like a commerce site's Web pages. An e-mail is a quick, targeted message with specific content. Much like a printed advertisement, the design should focus on the sale of the products.

MYFLIX.COM

<u>Unsubscribe</u>

—> *DVD DISCOUNT DEALS NEWSLETTER*

IN THIS ISSUE

Closeouts: *The Matrix*, *Rush Hour* and *Event Horizon*, now only $10!

Also: 40% off on this week's new releases: *The Phantom Menace*, *Cape Fear*

PRODUCT PHOTO

PURCHASE

The Matrix for only $10!

Availability: 59 in stock
Ships: Within 24 hours

Rated: R for violence and language
Starring: Keanu Reeves, Laurence Fishburne, Carrie-Anne Moss
Director: Andy & Larry Wachowski

MyFlix user rating: **4.7/5 stars** (from 1073 votes)

Customer reviews

Dan L. of Auburn, AL: "This movie has exceptional special effects, beautiful cinematography, an excellent soundtrack, well-crafted dialogue and respectable acting."

PRODUCT PHOTO

PURCHASE

Rush Hour closeout special: $10!

Availability: 105 in stock
Ships: Within 24 hours

Rated: PG-13 for violence and language
Starring: Jackie Chan, Chris Tucker, Julia Hsu
Director: Brett Ratner

MyFlix user rating: **3.9/5 stars** (from 2121 votes)

Customer reviews

Michele of Utica, MI: "This is a hilarious action-comedy that has great comedic performances, funny lines, and good music. It's a movie that action and comedy fans should see."

Be flexible

E-mail templates should be designed with a grid that can flex. Because e-mail clients can be configured by the user to virtually any width, you will want your e-mail pages to flex to fit the available viewing space.

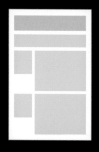

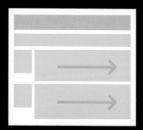

When designing e-mail pages, follow these guidelines:

- **Do not duplicate a page from the site.** A Web site's global and local navigation are inappropriate in the e-mail environment. Stick to simple layouts that include a small logo, a product image and the text of the offer. In Fig. A.5, we show an example of an acceptable layout for e-mail newsletters.

- **Use templates.** Customers frequently sign up for e-mail that arrives at regular weekly or monthly intervals. Using templates to generate e-mail will keep the structure and presentation of the content consistent and predictable. If the e-mails are different each time, the customer will not be able to apply knowledge gained from a previous interaction.

- **Offer HTML and text versions.** Some customers' e-mail clients do not have the ability to view HTML e-mail messages. Provide customers with the option to receive text-only versions. Remember, some customers may be receiving these messages on cell phones or PDAs.

- **Keep it light.** Customers don't want their e-mail basket to hit its limit because of hefty HTML pages. Nor do customers like to wait for e-mail messages to download. As always, the faster, the better.

- **Keep text brief and concise.** Customers scan e-mail messages just like they scan Web pages. They do not like to read large blocks of text. Provide links to learn more on the Web site.

- **Special offers win.** Customers prefer to receive e-mail about exclusive deals, discounts, or offers targeted to their areas of buying interest.

- **Use the subject field.** The title of the e-mail that appears in the e-mail client is called the subject. Make the subject explicit to the e-mail's content, rather than a generic label. For example, use "MyFlix Special: $50 off on orders above $200" instead of "MyFlix Weekly Discount Newsletter." Always include the company name in the subject so that it can easily be identified in a list of other e-mails.

- **Give customers an easy out.** Make sure there is an clear indication of how the customer can get off the mailing list.

Kim MacPherson's *Permission-Based E-mail Marketing That Works* and Stevan Roberts' *Internet Direct Mail: The Complete Guide to Successful E-Mail Marketing Campaigns* are great resources for case histories, etiquette, and best practices for the writing and design of e-mail.

Cell Phones and Pagers

Major telecommunication companies worldwide have invested billions of dollars in new network technologies and handsets to give the customer the ability to access the Web using their cell phone. Despite this significant investment, designing a great shopping experience for a phone is, and will remain, a challenge.

Most Web-enabled phones use WAP (Wireless Application Protocol). WAP is an a communication standard that allows mobile devices to connect to the Internet and exchange content in the form of WML (Wireless Markup Language) or HDML (Handheld Device Markup Language). WML and HDML are markup languages that resemble simple HTML.

Manufacturers may continue to create phones with greater capabilities, larger screens, and better means for input. But delighting customers will require a shift in thinking for designers — away from graphic embellishments and towards concise and sparse presentation.

FIGURE A.6: WAP IS NOT THE WEB

Your WAP phone site should be very different than your HTML site. While HTML looks similar to HDML and WML, designers should not create a smaller text replica of a Web site. Since typing on a phone's keypad is a major usability problem, provide customers with select lists. Keep information brief and choose a strict navigation hierarchy to make it easy for customers to find specific information.

Designers creating for WAP sites should examine a customer's tasks, usage environment, and device characteristics of their target phone before site development. Here is how MyFlix.com might look on a cell phone:

Home page
Phone screens can only display a few lines of text. Keep number of choices to a minimum.

Browse options
Web pages can display many options. This screen offers only the most likely options.

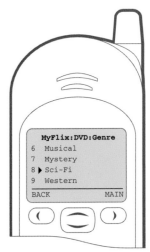

Browse by subject
Limit options to two screenfuls. Use the screen title to remind customers of their location.

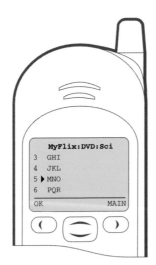

Subcategory page
Organize large amounts of data into alphabetical or numerical groupings.

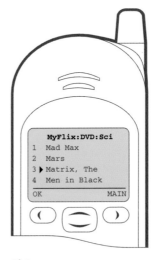

Lists
Truncate titles or names to the screen width so they don't wrap and disrupt the list structure.

Data
Abbreviate essential information as much as possible. Offer customers a More link for details.

FIGURE A.7: KEYPAD INPUT

Data entry on cell phones is limited by the nine-key alphanumeric pad. Each button is the equivalent of three or four letters. To get to the fourth letter, a user must press that button four times. Inputting data in this manner is cumbersome.

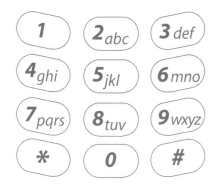

Spell "Gap"
3 clicks
G = Press 4 once
A = Press 2 once
P = Press 7 once

Spell "Cars"
11 clicks
C = Press 2 three times
A = Press 2 once
R = Press 7 three times
S = Press 7 four times

Here are few considerations in designing a mobile commerce experience:

- **Make navigation obvious.** Unlike Web sites that have dedicated space on a screen to navigation elements, Internet-enabled phones display limited amounts of text. The designer must use links to integrate navigation into the content, and make sure other navigation elements are consistent in both location and function.

Most navigation is reduced to a short word, like "back," "main," and "OK." Those labels should be placed in the same place on every page and should behave consistently. In Fig. A.6, we show how a customer might navigate though a Web site on a cell phone.

- **Provide concise and meaningful content.** Because of its tiny screen, numeric keypad and lack of a mouse, the phone doesn't make a good device for surfing the Web. Trying to force existing content onto mobile devices has resulted in confusing applications that are ill-designed for specific customer tasks.[6] With many cell phone screens little larger than a square inch, content must be optimized to make sense. Designers will have to make sure key services are located within the first few lines of text to make them immediately apparent to customers.

- **Put your company name in the title bar.** With little or no room for highly identifiable design, WAP sites become hard to tell apart. Placing your company's name in the title bar at the top of the phone screen will help the customer remember what site they're on.

- **Make your URL guessable.** Don't use www.yourstore.com/goingmobile/ use something like wap.yourstore.com or www.yourstore.com/phone. Also, the shorter the URL, the fewer customer typing errors.

- **People don't like to type on the phone.** A cartoon in the *New Yorker* showed a man pecking away at his cell phone. His wife turns to her friend and says: "He'll be the first one to write a novel on a cell phone, if he doesn't go insane first." The nine-key alphanumeric telephone pad requires a user tap a button several times to enter a character (See Fig. A.7).

- **Be quick.** Customers are willing to spend some time searching on a Web site for what they need. Mobile Internet users do not go online to browse, but to perform short, focused tasks like checking a flight departure or the weather. They need information and services immediately.

- **Test on several phones.** While WML and HDML are standardized and easy to understand, the mini-browsers on cell phones interpret and display the code differently, like browsers on personal computers.

PDAs and Handhelds

Handhelds come in many different shapes, sizes, capabilities, and quality of connectivity. Some can show HTML and act like mini-browsers. Handhelds typically have larger screens than cell phones and are already designed for easy data entry, using a stylus pen and handwriting recognition software. Some PDAs even have extensions for keyboards.

Unlike the cell phone, a customer buys a PDA for more than just voice and data communication. PDAs are personal productivity tools. Designers need to be familiar with a PDA's capabilities and how people interact with them.

Designers often have extensive experience with Web browsers but might have little or no exposure to PDAs. Before you begin a PDA site, you need to understand what makes designing for a PDA different.

Mobile devices are used in a social setting and while in transit. Designers need to account for the environment in which the customer will be accessing the commerce information. For example, the customer may be sitting in an airport or riding on a bumpy train. In this environment, the customer might have an unreliable or slow connection to the Internet. Some PDAs anticipate this situation by downloading additional data in the background. This allows the user to interact even if a signal is temporarily lost, i.e., inside a tunnel.

Along with mobility, people are usually looking for greater convenience. Therefore, designers must create Web sites that are instantly accessible and understandable. Anything that threatens immediate results, such as forcing customers to drill through unnecessary menus, will lessen the chances of a positive shopping experience.

As well, the medium is not mature. With few established standards, designers face a constantly changing array of devices and complexity. For example, Palm has some wireless PDAs with black-and-white displays, and others that show full color. When designing for handheld devices, it's important to consider:

- **Platform:** While the Palm OS is the dominant PDA platform, Windows CE has made serious inroads. Some newer PDAs even support the open-source Linux operating system. The browsers that exist on these systems vary wildly in their display abilities.

- **Screen size.** Designing a page for a Palm Pilot is like arranging your inventory in a one-room strip mall store. By comparison, a 17-inch monitor is a massive warehouse. Keep the design simple and focused on content.

- **Information organization.** Maintain a strict hierarchical information path, with fewer than nine choices at each level. A PDA and a cell phone have very similar display areas. You can offer a limited amount of scrolling on a PDA, but page length should be minimized.

- **Stylus input.** While easier to use than a cell-phone keypad, the stylus is somewhat limiting for text entry. Minimize form fields that require extensive text entry.

- **Bandwidth.** Some users can access the Internet using a speedy wireless connection while others crawl at a speed similar to that of a 14.4k modem.

- **Bitmapped graphics.** A handheld's bandwidth is usually low, so make your images as small as possible. Bitmap images display well on the lower-end handhelds, as well as being fast to download.

- **Modules.** Many handhelds, such as those made by Handspring, can extend their functionality and power through the use of add-on modules. These modules can turn the handheld into a digital camera, phone or GPS device. The use of modules might change or alter the commerce experience.

Web Pads and Tablets

These devices combine the capabilities of laptop computers, with the portability of hand-held devices. Web tablets have large color screens and significant processing power compared to handhelds. Some even include hard drives. Like handhelds, these devices depend on the stylus pen as primary method of input. Users tap on-screen keyboards or use handwriting-recognition software to enter data.

Because of their price (more than $1,000), Web pads are targeted at business and commercial applications. For example, some companies are using Web pads as portable kiosks at conventions. But tablet manufacturers are making a new foray into homes, positioning their product as an easy solution for those who don't want a full-fledged computer but still want e-mail and Web access.

Because the larger monitor and operating systems are similar to the typical personal computer, the design considerations are similar. The primary focus of differentiation between these devices and a standard computer is the stylus pen as the method of input and the mobility of the customer when using tablet.

Interactive TV

Though it's not getting as much media attention as the mobile devices, commerce over interactive television systems has tremendous possibilities. Using ITV, companies will be able to reach consumers who are unable or unwilling to buy a personal computer.

Resolution, screen real estate, and remote control input are some of the challenges facing designers of interactive television commerce experiences. Companies like Microsoft[7] and Cognetics[8] offer these guidelines for designing ITV experiences:

- **Distance to device.** Computer users are typically 2 feet or less from a monitor. With TVs, viewers usually sit 4 to 10 feet away from the screen. This means that type should be relatively large to maximize readability.

- **Typography.** Use sans-serif type for maximum readability. Most experts recommend a dark background with light color text. Anything below 24-point is not legible at typical viewing distances.

- **Colors.** Though TV is a currently a low-resolution medium, it has the capability of displaying millions of colors. Regardless, some colors and combinations (like large swatches of red and white) can appear to bleed, shift, and flicker. Some designers test colors by using a scan-converter to display their work on a TV and a computer monitor at the same time.

- **Safe image area.** Unlike a computer screen, the display boundaries of television screens vary from set to set. The "safe area" that will show on just about every TV is about 10 percent smaller than the entire viewing area. Make sure all navigation and action elements fall within the safe area.

- **Navigation.** Customers typically use their TV's remote control to run interactive TV systems, so navigation elements like pull-down menus and scrolling pages won't work on interactive TV. The best navigation is simple, and is designed for the easily accessible main buttons on the remote control.

Kiosks

Companies have been using kiosks for commerce applications longer than any of the devices mentioned in this chapter. Now that kiosks are Internet-enabled, a wide range of services can be provided on them. Today's retailers are using kiosks in three major categories:

- **Self-service transactions.** Shoppers can buy catalog merchandise, Web-only products, or goods and services. Customers can use kiosk applications to personally configure merchandise such as home entertainment centers, PCs, or blue jeans. Kodak is using kiosks to allow customers to scan, alter, and print photographs.

- **In-store product information.** Shoppers can learn about new products or complex features and compare alternatives. Customers explore digital forms of products such as music, books, movies, and video games before they buy.

- **Customer care.** Customers access personal account information such as reward points or transaction history; locate merchandise in the store; or find and print content related to products such as advice and tips.

Kiosks are designed and located with specific customer needs or goals in mind. For example, British Airways uses self-service kiosks to let passengers avoid long lines for boarding passes.

Because kiosks usually need to serve a wide range of potential customers, do not design their interfaces using interface controls like scroll bars and close boxes. These controls may not be familiar to noncomputer users.

Almost all kiosks use touch screens, along with buttons on the device, as the methods for inputting data. Remember Fitt's law when designing buttons for touch screens: The bigger the target, the easier it will be for customers to tap on it. Fingers are not stylus pens.

The Future

If all these devices become powerful delivery tools for commerce, then the ability to transact over the Internet will become mainstream and pervasive. It will follow us everywhere from the home to the car, from work to dinner and the movie theater. Buying habits will inevitably change.

To prepare for this eventuality, designers will need to assess the pertinent factors— whether it's the advantages of the device, the goals of the customer or the brand identity— and synthesize them into a rewarding commerce experience.

The most visually talented designers won't necessarily succeed in commerce design. In this new arena, success requires a multidisciplinary view of the design process—information, interaction, and presentation. By respecting this process, your design will always be a profitable instrument for the conversation between the business and the customer.

[1] Pew Internet and American Life Project Survey. (Nov–Dec, 2000). http://www.pewinternet.org/reports/chart.asp?img=6_internet_activities.jpg

[2] The Yankee Group research report presented at Mobile.Net conference projected over 1 billion wireless devices worldwide by 2003 and more than $50 billion of commerce transactions in the U.S. will be wireless. (New York, Nov. 2000.) http://www.yankeegroup.com/

[3] Reda, Susan. "The Multi-Channel CEO: What does it take to succeed?" http://www.omnitailing.com/m_omnitailing.cfm

[4] McKenna, Regis. *Real Time: Preparing for the Age of the Never Satisfied Customer.* (Harvard Business School Press, 1997)

[5] "2001 Consumer Email Study." DoubleClick Inc. http://www.doubleclick.net/

[6] Schmidt, Carsten. "Mastering Mobile Site Design." Forrester Research (Nov., 2000)

[7] "Microsoft TV Design Guidelines." http://www.microsoft.com/tv/working/content/desguide.asp

[8] Quesenbery, Whitney and Reichart, Todd. "Designing for Interactive Television." http://www.cognetics.com/presentations/whitney/itv_design.html

INDEX

A

Accessibility of site, 116
Access to Internet, method of, 29
Adobe Acrobat, 69
Adobe GoLive, 69
Adobe Illustrator, 69, 170
Adobe LiveMotion, 69
Adobe Photoshop, 69, 135
Adobe Premiere, 69
Advertising, 72, 183
Alphabetical organization, 31, 80, 83–84
Amazon.com, 45, 119, 124
    cart/checkout, 110–111, 167
    database information, 63
    home page, 152
    personalization, 111, 114
    product page, 158
Ambiguous organization, 82–86
Animation, use of, 39, 69
Apple Computer, 36–37
ASP (Active Server Page), 67–68
AUA model, wireframe, 100
Auctions, 12, 205–206, 96, 125, 169. *See also* Christie's
Audience organization, 83–86
Audion case study, 220–225

B

Back-end system, 63, 180
Bandwidth, 26, 29, 249
Barnes & Noble, 11
Barneys New York Web site, 191
BBEdit, 69
Beta tests, 184–186, 194–195
Blue Nile, 154, 162–163, 166
    home page, 94, 151
    product page, 105, 129, 159
Brand identity, 121–124
Breadcrumbs, 85, 106, 143, 210, 229
Browsers, 180–181, 183
Browsing, 108, 153
    case studies, 209, 217, 228
    WAP phones, 246
Business, Web site's role in, 8–13
Business layer, site architecture, 61
Business model, importance of, 11–12
Buttons, 102–103, 141, 156, 234
Buying. *See also* Checkout; Shopping cart
    history, 43
    how to buy information, 216
    preferences, 43

C

Caching, 64
Category page, 153–155, 211, 246
Cell phone. *See* Web-enabled phone (WAP)
CGI (Common Gateway Interface), 68
Changes to site, 183, 190–195
Checkout, 110–112, 128
    case studies, 200–201, 213, 231
    templates, 165–168

Christie's, 125–126

    auction calendar, 169
    category page, 155
    home page, 150
    product page, 160
    search page, 164
Chronological organization, 31, 83–84
Chunking, 31, 85, 106, 156, 215
Client-server architecture, 60–69
Cluster, server, 60
Code, comments added to, 192
Color, use of, 41, 131, 134–136
    brand identity, 121–122
    case studies, 198, 203, 208, 214, 220,
        227, 232
    color blind design, 136
    interactive television, 251
ColorMix.com, 135
Company information, 72
Concentration navigation, 31
Consistency, 34–35, 178
    case studies, 205, 218
    interface, 139, 143
    templates, use of, 146
Consultants, use of, 74–78, 177
Content, 70–78, 85. *See also* Product pages
    costs, 75–78
    customer tasks and, 98
    design for, 125–127, 217
        (*See also* Organization, site)
    for Internet-enabled devices, 239
    inventory list, 72–73, 239
    navigation and, 108
    product comparison, 230
    product recommendations, 43
    proofreading, 183
    sources of, 73–78
    Web-enabled phones, 247
    workflow, 74–76, 78
Content management systems (CMS),
    63–64, 146
Contextual navigation, 106–108
Continuum organization, 83–84
Control elements, 72
Conventions, use of, 119
Corel Draw/Corel Photo Paint, 69
Cost, Web site, 75–78, 176
Creative Good, 44, 110
CSS (Cascading Style Sheets), 59, 138
Customer
    choices of, 211 (*See also* Shopping cart)
    experience, 10–11, 44–45
        (*See also* Interaction design)
    goals, 50, 55, 97, 108
    information needs (*See* Content)
    Internet-enabled devices,
        context of, 236, 237
    knowledge of, 50–51, 94, 223
    movement of Web page to, 26, 28
    segmentations, 51
    task list, 96–98, 232
Customer assistance. *See* Help, customer
Customer profile, 51–55, 95
Customer service, 189

D

Databases, relational, 58, 61–63, 86–89
    case studies, 217, 230
    WAP phones, 246
Demographics, target audience, 50
Deneba's Canvas, 69
Design principles, 22–45. *See also*
    Consistency; Personality;
    Personalization; Speed
    ease of use, 30–33
    ads, avoiding, 44–45
DHTML (Dynamic Hypertext Markup
    Language), 59
Dial-up access, 29
Disabled persons, access of, 116
Dithering, color, 135
Documents, printable, 69
Download, product, 225
Download time, 24–29, 183
Dynamic pages, 26, 66–69, 162

E

Ease of use, 30–33
eBay, 12, 125
E-mail, 219, 236, 242–244
Exact site organization, 82–86
Experience models, 101–103, 207
Eziba.com, 208–213

F

Fads, avoiding, 44–45
Failure report, 187–189
FAQs, 72
Feedback, 189, 216, 224
Field study, 94, 176
Final Cut Pro, 69
Fitt's law, 141
Flash design, 44, 191
Flowchart, site. *See* Map, site
Flowerbud.com, 198–201, 127
Focus groups, 176
Fonts, 137, 251
Forms, 199, 202–204, 112–113.
    See also Checkout; Shopping cart
Forum tasks, 96

G

Gant chart, 78
Geographical organization, 31, 83–84
Geographic information, target audience, 50
Global navigation, 106–107, 153
Global tasks, 96
Goals
    customer, 50, 55, 97, 108
    project, 48–49, 95
Graphic buttons, 141
Graphic design, 44–45, 131–138, 183, 249
Grids, 131–133, 161, 227, 232

H

Handhelds, 240, 248–249
Handspring, 127, 149, 153
    cart/checkout, 165, 168
    product page, 95, 156

HDML (Handheld Device Markup Language),
    245–246
Help, customer, 72, 106, 168, 203, 205, 225
Herman Miller RED case study, 226–231
Hierarchy, site, 86–88, 204, 98, 249
High speed access, 29
Home page, 148–152, 226–227, 232, 246
HotMetal Pro, 69
HotWired Style: Principles of Building Smart
    Web Sites, 45
HTML (Hypertext Markup Language), 58–59
    e-mail, 244
    mockup, 1207
    scripting languages, 67–68
    static template, 145
    tables, 132
    text editor programs, 69
    WYSIWYG HTML editor programs, 69
Humane Interface, The, 30
Hypertext, 86–87, 89, 139

I

Icons, 206, 228
Illustration programs, 69
Image editing programs, 69
Industry standard organization schemes,
    83–84
Information architect, 20, 81, 89, 94
Information design, 46–89
    content (*See* Content)
    customer, knowledge of, 50–51, 94, 223
    organization of information (*See*
        Organization, site)
    profiled customer, design for, 51–55, 95
    project goals, 48–49, 95
    technology (*See* Technology)
Inmates Are Running the Asylum, The, 52
Interaction design, 41, 90–117
    accessibility, 116
    completing, 116
    experience models, 101–103, 207
    forms (*See* Forms)
    least effort, principle of, 92
    mental shortcuts, use of, 93
    navigation (*See* Navigation)
    personalization (*See* Personalization)
    scenarios, creation of, 94–97
    shopping cart/checkout (*See*
        Checkout; Shopping cart)
    task analysis, 96–98
    tenacity, rule of, 93–94
    testing, 183
    wireframes, 98–101, 116, 170
Interactive television, 237, 239, 241, 251
Interactivity by Design, 47
Interface, 30, 72, 222, 139–143.
    See also Feedback; Navigation
Internet access, 29
Internet Direct Mail: The Complete
    Guide to Successful E-Mail
    Marketing Campaigns, 244

J

Javascript, 68
JSP (Java Server Page), 67–68

Shayne Bowman and Chris Willis are co-founders of Hypergene, a Dallas-based media consulting and design firm. They develop, design, and produce communication and commerce projects for clients in business, media, and technology. Bowman and Willis are recognized leaders in design with more than 150 awards from Communication Arts, The American Advertising Federation, The Society of News Design, and The Society of Professional Journalists. They write and speak frequently on media strategy, creative development, and graphic design.

Series Editor Cynthia Baron is technical director in the department of visual arts at Northeastern University, and she teaches in the department and the multimedia studies program. She was a contributing editor for *Critique* magazine, has been published in several periodicals, and has authored or co-authored four books, including *Creating a Digital Portfolio* and *Windows for Mac Users*.

Acknowledgments

The authors would like to thank the following people for their assistance with this book:

- Our families—Karla, Hannah, Michele, and Gavin—for being understanding and supportive, and for showing us what it really means to shop.

- Our publisher, Winnie Prentiss, a paragon of patience.

- Our agent, Neil Salkind, and the wonderful staff at Studio B.

- Our editor, Cynthia Baron, who infused our writing with clarity and simplicity.

- Our friends and colleagues: Elle Tracy for her professional insight and enthusiasm in the project; Ellen Kampinsky for her keen wit and relentless energy; Chris Kozlowski for all the hard work on our illustrations and for being this book's target profile; John Sanford, Ron Biggs, James Gardner, and the folks at Circle.com for their real-world insight and advice; Mark Walters; Bob Dickman; and Lawrence Lee at Tomalak's Realm.